D1627618

In Time of Trouble

IN TIME
OF
TROUBLE

AN AUTOBIOGRAPHY BY
Claud Cockburn

READERS UNION
RUPERT HART-DAVIS
LONDON 1957

This RU edition was produced in 1957 for sale to its members only by Readers Union Ltd at 38 William IV Street, Charing Cross, London WC2 and at Letchworth Garden City, Hertfordshire. Full details of membership may be obtained from our London address. The book has been reset in 10 pt Georgian type and printed by the Northumberland Press Ltd, Gateshead upon Tyne. It was first published by Rupert Hart-Davis Ltd in 1956.

Contents

I WAR GAMES

IN OUR LITTLE HOUSE, THE QUESTION WAS WHETHER the war would break out first, or the revolution. This was around 1910.

That period before the World War I has since got itself catalogued as a minor Golden Age. People living then are said to have had a sense of security, been unaware of impending catastrophe, unduly complacent.

In our neighbourhood, they worried. They thought it was the Victorians who had had a sense of security and been unduly complacent.

There were war scares every year, all justified. There was the greatest surge of industrial unrest ever seen. There was a crime wave. The young were demoralised. In 1911, without any help from Television or the Cinema or the Comics, some Yorkshire schoolboys, irked by discipline, set upon an unpopular teacher and murdered him.

Naturally, alongside those who viewed with alarm, there were those who thought things would probably work out all right. Prophets of doom and Polyannas, Dr Pangloss and Calamity Jane, all lived near us in Hertfordshire in those years, and I well remember being taken to call on them all, on fine afternoons, in the open landau, for a treat.

At home, the consensus was that the war would come before the revolution.

This, as can be seen from the newspaper files, was not the most general view.

At our house, however, people thought war was not any nicer than revolution, but more natural.

It was in 1910 that my father desired me to stop playing French and English with my tin soldiers and play Germans and English instead. That was a bother, for there was a character, on a white horse, who was Napoleon – in fact, a double Napoleon; because he was dead Napoleon who fought Waterloo, and also alive, getting ready to attack the Chiltern

Hills where we lived. It was awkward changing him into an almost unheard-of Marshal von Moltke.

Guests came to lunch and talked about the coming German invasion. On Sundays, when my sister and I lunched in the dining-room instead of the nursery, we heard about it. It spoiled afternoon walks on the hills with Nanny, who until then had kept us happy learning the names of the small wild flowers growing there. I thought Uhlans with lances and flat-topped helmets might come charging over the hill any afternoon now. It was frightening, and a harassing responsibility, since Nanny and my sister had no notion of the danger. It was impossible to explain to them fully about the Uhlans, and one had to keep a keen watch all the time. Nanny was no longer a security. (An earlier Nanny had herself been frightened on our walks. She was Chinese, from the Mongolian border, and she thought there were tigers in the Chilterns.)

One night, at hay-making time, when the farm carts trundled home late, I lay awake in the dusk and trembled. Evidently they had come, and their endless gun-carriages were rolling up the lane. My sister said to go to sleep; it was all right because we had a British soldier staying in the house. This was Uncle Philip, a half-pay Major of Hussars whose hands had been partially paralysed as a result of some accident at polo.

His presence that night was a comfort. But his conversation was often alarming, particularly after he had been playing the War Game.

In the garden there was a big shed or small barn, and inside the shed was the War Game. It was played on a table a good deal bigger, as I recall, than a billiards table, and was strategically scientific. So much so, indeed, that the game was used for instructional purposes at the Staff College. Each team of players had so many guns of different calibre, so many divisions of troops, so many battleships, cruisers and other instruments of war. You threw dice, and operated your forces according to the value of the throw. Even so, the possible moves were regulated by rules of extreme realism.

The Game sometimes took three whole days to complete, and it always over-excited Uncle Philip. The time he thought he had caught the Japanese Admiral cheating he almost had a fit – not because the Japanese really was cheating, as it turned out, but because of the way he proved he was not cheating.

12

The Admiral and some other Japanese officers, on some sort of goodwill mission to Britain, had come to lunch and afterwards played the War Game. As I understand it, they captured from the British team – made up of my father, two uncles and a cousin on leave from the Indian Army – a troopship. It was a Japanese cruiser which made the capture, and, at his next move, the Admiral had this cruiser move the full number of squares which his throw of the dice would normally have allowed it. Uncle Philip accused him of stealthily breaking the rules. He should have deducted from the value of his throw the time it would have taken to transfer and accommodate the captured soldiers before sinking the troopship. He found the proper description of this cruiser in *Jane's Fighting Ships* and demonstrated that it would have taken a long time – even in calm weather – to get the prisoners settled aboard.

The Admiral said, 'But we threw the prisoners overboard.' He refused to retract his move.

Uncle Philip hurled the dice-box through the window of the shed and came storming up to the house. Even in the nursery could be heard his curdling account of the massacre on the destroyer.

'Sea full of sharks, of course. Our men absolutely helpless. Pushed over the side at the point of the bayonet. Damned cruiser forging ahead through water thickening with blood as the sharks got them.'

Even when the Japanese fought on the British side in World War I Uncle Philip warned us not to trust them.

His imagination was powerful and made holes in the walls of reality. He used to shout up at the nursery for someone to come and hold his walking-stick upright at a certain point on the lawn while he paced off some distances. These were the measurements of the gunroom of the shooting lodge he was going to build on the estate he was going to buy in Argyllshire when he had won £20,000 in the Calcutta Sweep. Sometimes he would come to the conclusion that he had made this gunroom too small – barely room to swing a cat. Angrily he would start pacing again, and often find that this time the place was too large. 'I don't want a thing the size of a barn, do I?' he would shout.

Once, some years earlier, his imagination functioned so powerfully that it pushed half the British Fleet about. That was at Queen Victoria's Diamond Jubilee in 1897, when the Fleet was drawn up for review at Spithead in the greatest

13

assembly of naval power anyone had ever seen. Uncle Philip
and my father were invited by the Admiral commanding one
of the squadrons to lunch with him on his flagship. An
attaché of the Admiral Commanding-in-Chief was also among
those present.

Half-way through lunch Uncle Philip began to develop an
idea. Here, he said, was the whole British Fleet gathered at
Spithead, without steam up, immobile. Across there, was
Cherbourg. (At that time, the war, when it came, was going
to be against the French.) Well, suppose one night – tonight,
for instance – some passionately Anglophobe commander of
a French torpedo-boat were to get the notion of dashing
across the Channel in the dark and tearing between the lines
of the great ships, loosing off torpedoes. The ships helpless,
without steam up. In twenty minutes, half of them sinking.
In an hour, Britain's power reduced to the level of Portugal's.
By dawn, the Solent strewn with the wreckage of an Empire.
Before noon, mobs crazed with triumph and wine sweeping
along the Paris boulevards, yelling for the *coup de grâce*.

He spoke of this, my uncle said, not as an idle speculation,
but because he happened he have recalled, on his way to this
lunch, that in point of fact a French officer, just mad enough
to carry out such a project, was at this moment in command
of a torpedo-boat at Cherbourg. (His voice, as he said this,
compelled a closer attention by the Admiral and the attaché
of the Commander-in-Chief.)

Certainly, he said, he had met the man himself, a Captain
Moret, a Gascon. Hot-blooded, hating the English for all the
ordinary French reasons, and for another reason, too: his
only sister – a young and beautiful girl, Uncle Philip believed
– had been seduced and brutally abandoned by an English
Lieutenant, name of Hoadley, or Hoathly, at Toulon. A
fanatic, this Moret. Had a trick of gesturing with his cigar
– like this (Uncle Philip sketched the gesture) – as he, Moret,
expatiated on his favourite theory, the theory of the under-
rated powers of the torpedo-boat as the guerilla of the
sea.

'And there,' said Uncle Philip, in a slightly eerie silence,
'he is.' He nodded ominously in the direction of Cherbourg.

On the way back to Cowes in the Admiral's launch, my
father upbraided Uncle Philip. A nice exhibition he had
made of himself – a mere Major of Hussars, lecturing a lot
of Admirals and Captains on how to run their business. Also
they had undoubtedly seen through this yarn, realised that

this Moret was a figment of Uncle Philip's imagination, invented half-way through the fish course. Then, and during the remainder of the afternoon and early evening, Uncle Philip was abashed, contrite. After dinner that evening they walked by the sea, taking a final look at the Fleet in the summer dusk. Silently my uncle pointed at the far-flung line. Every second ship in the line was getting up steam.

People told Uncle Philip that if he would employ his gift of the gab in a practical way, not spend it all in conversation, but take to writing, he would make a fortune – like Stanley Weyman or someone of that kind. It seemed a good idea, and while waiting for the Calcutta Sweep to pay off, he wrote, and published at the rate of about one a year, a number of historical romances. They included *Love in Armour, A Gendarme of the King, The Black Cuirassier,* and *A Rose of Dauphiny.* It was unfortunate from a financial point of view that he had a loving reverence for French history, which he supposed the library subscribers shared. The historical details of his stories were to him both fascinating and sacred. He refused to adjust by a hair's-breadth – in aid of suspense, romance, or pace of action – anything whatsoever, from an arquebus to a cardinal's mistress. Once you were past the title, you were on a conducted tour of a somewhat chilly and over-crowded museum.

However, he did make enough out of these books to feel justified in buying a motor car in the days when that was a daring and extravagant thing to do. He reasoned that since the Sweep would ultimately provide a motor car as a matter of course, it was foolish to spend the time not having a motor car just because the Draw was still nine months off.

He was not its possessor for long. He was superstitious. The car was of a make called Alldays. He showed it to my father. My father was against motor cars. Some people of his age were against them because they went too fast. My father disliked them because they did not go fast enough. He took the view that if people were to take the trouble to give up horses and carriages and go about in these intricate affairs instead, it was only reasonable that the machines, in return, should get them to wherever they wanted to be in almost no time – a negligible, unnoticeable time. The fact that even with one of these vaunted motor cars you still took hours and hours to get from, say, London to Edinburgh, struck him as disgusting and more or less fraudulent. Later he felt the same way about aeroplanes. He was thus not enthusiastic about Uncle Philip's motor car, and when he saw the maker's name on the bonnet, he unkindly murmured the quotation, 'All days run to the grave.'

Uncle Philip took fright and sold the car immediately at a heavy loss. Of this I was glad, not because I thought the car would run him to his grave but because I thought it would get him into a dungeon. He had a chauffeur called Basing, and I once heard somebody say, 'That man Basing drives too fast.' He had been known to exceed the speed limit of 20 miles per hour. In those days when people spoke of motor cars they spoke also of police traps. My idea of the police was simple and horrifying. I thought they would soon manacle Uncle Philip and leave him to rot in a cell. We should never see him again.

This is one of those griefs which are caused to children by the seemingly frantic irresponsibility and ignorance of adults. When I was seven, I read the opening lines of some book of elementary science which said, 'Without air we cannot live.' I crept about the house opening windows, and repeatedly re-opening them secretly after bewildered and seemingly suicidal grown-ups had closed them against the bitter autumn winds.

Real life, like curry, which he ate Anglo-Indian fashion – so hot it would have charred an Indian's stomach – was never quite sharp enough for Uncle Philip. The weary present he made endurable to his taste by a sort of incantation. He re-cited old French ballads aloud as he walked to the village, or simply shouted agreeably sonorous words. You asked him where he was going and he peered through his monocle and shouted, 'I am on my way to the headquarters of his Supreme Excellency the Field-Marshal Ghazi Ahmed Mukhta Pasha. When the past tasted a little flat, he peppered it artificially. No one was safe from his cookery. He was talking to me once about his grandfather, a worthy officer, I believe, of the Black Watch who had died peacefully but at a rather early age. Finding the story dull, Uncle Philip told me that in reality, though it had been hushed up, his grandfather had shot himself in melodramatically scandalous circumstances. I think that at the time he actually believed he was actually doing the deceased a good turn – making him more interesting than he had, in fact, managed to be. Uncle Philip was my mother's brother, and I asked her about it. She was in a dilemma. She wished to deny it as authoritatively as possible. On the other hand, she hesitated to tell a child of seven that his uncle was a monstrous liar.

As for the future, Uncle Philip seasoned it with the Calcutta Sweep and the imminence of a very interesting war. As things turned out, he never did win the Sweep, and the war was no fun either. He got himself back into the Army, despite his crippled hands, but the cold and damp undermined his health and laid him low.

The theoretical basis of Uncle Philip's belief that war was coming soon was quite simple. He thought any Government which supposed itself to have a reasonable advantage in armaments and manpower over its neighbours or rivals would go for them as soon as it was convinced that this was the case and provided the weather was suitable for the type of campaign its armies preferred. In this view he had the concurrence of my Uncle Frank, my father's elder brother, who in other respects was so different from Uncle Philip that he might have been brought up on a different planet. But he did enjoy the War Game, finding it more sensible than cards, and even made, in collaboration with Uncle Philip, some suggestions for changes in the rules which were sent to the Staff College, or whatever the strategic institution was that used the Game, and I believe adopted there.

He was a banker and a Canadian, and he took, uninhibitedly, the view that the world was a jungle, and civilisation a fine but flimsy tent which anyone would be a fool either not to enjoy or to treat as a secure residence. Compared to the rest of the family he was rich. Enormously so, I thought at the time, for there seemed to be nothing he could not afford, and I was told once that he actually had a lot more than Uncle Philip would have if he drew the winning ticket in the Sweep.

During those years, when we were moving about southern England looking, my father kept assuring me, for somewhere to settle down permanently, Uncle Frank was a frequent visitor, fleeting, but as impressive as a big firework.

His headquarters were at Montreal, but the place where he felt at home was Mexico. He spent a lot of time there, helping to organise some kind of revolution or counter-revolution – nominally in the interests of the bank, but mainly because that was the kind of work he liked. The details were never fully revealed to us. This was due partly to discretion, partly to the fact that the precise lines and objectives of the undertaking – which once had been a quite simple business

17

of violently overthrowing the Government – had become year by year increasingly complex and uncertain.

Nobody seemed to know just whose side anyone was on, which generals and politicians and rival financiers and concessionaires were good – that is to say, pro-Uncle Frank – and which bad. Not, I think, that he cared much about that. He enjoyed a colourful kind of plotting for its own sake, regardless of the monotonous aims of the fogies back in Montreal.

People would say, 'But I thought So-and-So was the man you were supporting? Wasn't he the one who was so good and was going to save the country?' And Uncle Frank would say vaguely that that had been before that business when Whatsisname shot up that bunch of Thingummies that time in Vera Cruz. There would follow a story full of sunshine and pistols and oil – very exciting and even intelligible, as far as it went, like a single battle-scene from a Shakespearian drama.

It seemed to be wonderful to have a job where that sort of thing was your business. and you were praised for your hard work doing it. The banking business attracted me a good deal – a banker, evidently, was something between Long John Silver and the Scarlet Pimpernel, and rich, too, and respected. The clerk at the local branch of the London, County, Westminster and Parr's became a figure of romance. I made up stories about his secret life.

Uncle Frank proclaimed himself a 'reactionary'. This piece of news went around among the neighbours and was applauded. They were deep-blue Conservatives, but already nervous of calling themselves, uncompromisingly, 'reactionaries'. Yet they found it comforting when someone else was unashamed to do so. My mother, active in the Women's Conservative Association and the Primrose League, did not care for the word at all. A devout and serious Christian, she was often bothered by what she read of socialists because she could not, instantly and absolutely, see where they were so wrong. To her horrified ear, they kept sounding as though they had ideas rather like Christ's.

This hesitancy of mind ashamed her. She felt it to be a kind of betrayal of Mr Bonar Law and Lord Balfour. She would steady herself by thinking about the atheistic opinions of socialists in France.

Uncle Frank was, in his way, more disturbing, as a fellow-traveller in the Conservative caravan, than the Christian-

18

looking socialists roaming the desert. He treated all politics as some kind of sordid Mexican brawl about money and land, and took for granted that anyone pretending to a different attitude was merely practising a cunning hypocrisy, deceiving simpletons for the sake of votes. To listen to talk about patriotism, the good of the community, progress and the imperial ideal, except when the words came from a platform for a practical political purpose, bored him shockingly.

He was in constant fear of having people bore him, and carried antidotes about. He was a big man, and his clothes bagged on him under the weight of financial reviews, stock-market reports and similar documents which were in some of the pockets, and fat little volumes of Homer or Herodotus which he carried in others. He must have had an idea that when he wished to abstract himself from company he became, by virtue of his wish, invisible. He would go to some local gathering and, at tea after dinner, slide a paper or book on to his knee so as to read it while people were talking to him. 'I don't think anyone noticed,' he would say afterwards.

His period of popularity among the local gentry as a visiting imperial lion from the Great Dominion did not endure. He was taken to some garden party held in the Conservative interest, and there introduced by the Vicar to a young barrister who had political ambitions and was popular for his renderings of 'Yip-I-Addy-I-Ay'. This person said to him, 'I must say, Mr Cockburn, I do admire your courage – I hear you are not afraid to call yourself a reactionary.' He then, according to my father, who was present, neighed.

Uncle Frank, who had been in a trance, looking at the back view of the village church and meditating on episodes of the Trojan War, or the current price of hogs in Chicago, or whatever it was, took a moment to focus on this remark, and the musical barrister filled the pause by stating that he himself was a bit of a reactionary, too.

Uncle Frank shouted his approval. 'You're absolutely right,' he said; 'everything since ancient Greece has been a mistake. Of course, the real trouble is Christianity, don't you agree? My idea of a real, dangerous damn fool is the Emperor Constantine. What an ass!'

My father remarked gently that the Vicar quite possibly did not agree with him. Uncle Frank, when he was talking to one person, often forgot that anyone else was present, and he now turned to the Vicar, with an apologetic bow. 'I don't,' he

19

said, 'mean to say a word against Christianity as a religion. It's fine. But it's unsuitable.'

'Unsuitable?' said the Vicar.

'To the human race,' said Uncle Frank. 'That's where Constantine was a damn fool. Another hundred years of steady persecution and they'd have had the Christians licked. They could have got right back. After all,' he said to the Vicar, 'as a God there wasn't much wrong with Zeus.'

The story went around that he had sworn at the Vicar and insulted the Church of England, but he was not there to hear it, for next morning he succumbed, once again, to what my father referred to as 'Frank's deplorable weakness for this fellow Aitken'. He went off to London to see the Canadian financier, Sir William Maxwell Aitken, afterwards Baron Beaverbrook, who had lately embarked on the English stage of his career.

They had been financial associates, and later close friends in Canada, and all his life Uncle Frank secretly thought that Max Aitken was practically the only man in England who approached things realistically. Secretly, that is, so far as our household was concerned, because my father, although he had never met the future Lord Beaverbrook, and insisted he had nothing against him personally, thought he was a portent – boding no good.

After the first war, and the rise of the newspaper proprietor to immense power, my father was more than ever convinced of this.

My uncle, when he was in England, liked to go and talk about money, and imperial politics, and – on occasion – religion and poetry with Rudyard Kipling and Bonar Law and Lord Beaverbrook at the latter's Surrey home. One day, when he was planning such a visit, my father said to him that if he went from our house to Lord Beaverbrook's, he need not bother himself to return. Thereafter, when he wanted to make such a visit, Uncle Frank pretended he was only going to London for a couple of days on business. But since he needed an intermediary who could forward urgent cables to him if necessary, he had to take me into his confidence.

'It's a pity,' he said, 'your father should feel this way about Max. Your father,' he added sadly, 'doesn't understand about Max.'

Though he found such an association shocking, my father felt sorry for Uncle Frank, considering that he should be pitied rather than censured.

20

'No doubt,' he would say in extenuation of his brother's choice of friends, 'a banker has to associate a good deal with financiers and people of that kind. Naturally. Your Uncle Frank has had a hard life, you know. You see, ever since he was a young man, he has had to deal with *money*.'

This, to his mind, melancholy fact, explained a great deal. It explained why his brother, of whom he was very fond, should have developed a view of life which seemed to my father lacking in delicacy and understanding of reality.

Each of them had been initially propelled along their widely divergent roads by the same force – namely the high principles of my grandfather, a younger son of Lord Cockburn, the great Scottish Advocate and Judge who shone so brightly in the Golden Age of Edinburgh society. The adults surrounding my grandfather's youth were gay, civilised and earnest. They would not have understood how, later, earnestness became a term of disdain, and were supposed to be incompatible with gaiety. They took life, as the saying goes, seriously. To take it any other way would have been, in them, a sign of despair.

When my grandfather was about fourteen he liked to make explosions by pouring gunpowder out of a horn into the kitchen furnace. Then his hand slipped, the whole of the gunpowder slid down the stone funnel into the furnace, and the explosion blew off his right arm. It was a horrid disaster to which relatives near and far reacted immediately and in the same way: before the week was out he received from uncles, aunts and cousins all over Scotland eleven separate presents of writing-desks, to encourage him to lose no time in learning to write with his left hand.

He learned not only to write but to drive a carriage and pair in a dashing manner. He went to India in the service of the old East India Company, lived in an oriental splendour which caused remark even in those unbridled days, became a Judge in the Administration of the new Indian Empire, and retired to Edinburgh intending to spend the remainder of his days in reasonably rich comfort. He lived, in fact, well, and was astonished at the comment of the son of some Rajah who came to visit him. The young man had seen my grandfather only with the trappings of a high British official in India. After what in Edinburgh was esteemed a rather magnificent dinner, the Indian asked permission to pose an indiscreet question. 'Sir,' he said, 'after your life in India, is it not irksome to exist in this state of indigent obscurity?'

Later, the indigence became, comparatively speaking, a fact. The cost of living rose. So did the number of relatives who for various reasons had to be supported by grandfather. Many of them were young women, more or less distant cousins whose parents had left them penniless. It might, even then, have been possible for them to support themselves by some kind of work, but they said, 'Our dear mother would not have liked it,' and that, in the circumstances of the time, was undeniably true. In the end, grandfather had to get a second house in Edinburgh to put some of them in. Seeking to ease the financial strain, he took his own immediate family to Bonn, on the Rhine, which was cheaper and warmer.

Frank, eldest male among seven children, was to go to work – in Canada, because friends said it was a fine place for a young man, particularly a Scotsman. Arrangements were made to get him, for a start, a good job in an engineering concern there. It was a new and prosperous concern and prospects were said to be fine. Just before he sailed, it was discovered that the managing director of this firm was a friend of an intimate friend of grandfather. The mutual friend had actually written to him asking him to keep a favourable eye on Uncle Frank. My grandfather was appalled. He felt at once that this necessitated a change in the carefully laid plans. As he pointed out to Uncle Frank, there was now, as a result of this deplorable turn of events, a distinct possibility that this director in Canada would feel obliged to show special consideration and favour to the lad – advance his interests by various means, give him preferential treatment. This would be morally wrong. In the circumstances, the only proper course was for Frank to write, withdrawing from the job in the engineering firm, and – on landing in Canada – simply do the best he could. That was how he happened to start working for a moribund bank at Quebec. He worked sixteen or seventeen hours a day and ate only at breakfast-time. Late at night he drank cocoa, which he tried to make more interesting and long-lasting by each night decorating the cocoa-jug with elaborately painted Greek verses and proverbs. The largest inscription he made on the jug was the Greek text of 'For the night cometh when no man can work' – *Nux gar erchetai*, etc. Years later, the jug stood prominent on the study mantelshelf in his big house in Montreal, and was referred to by the staff – bidden to treat it reverently – as 'the Nuxgar Jug'.

The period of penury and cocoa did not, in fact, last very long. Thousands of miles from Bonn, and exhilarated by the atmosphere of Canadian business, Uncle Frank soon pushed his way out of the torpid bank for which he had originally gone to work and into the Bank of Montreal which was booming and brimming with opportunity. But at Bonn, in the meantime, another crisis had occurred.

For more than a year it had been understood that my father was to enter the Indian Civil Service, an ambition which had been his since he was fifteen. Indeed, to a young man brought up on Plutarch's *Lives* and the history of Rome, the Indian Civil Service in those days seemed to offer limitless scope for the realisation of boyhood dreams – a subcontinent to be organised and governed, power to be exercised over millions of people, a game with whole kingdoms and principalities on the board.

At that time the examination for the Indian Civil Service was the most rigorous and the most highly competitive in existence – the prospects and prizes of that Service attracted hundreds of the more brilliant and the most ambitious. The age limits within which candidates were eligible were such that you could make, if necessary, three attempts in three successive years. Almost nobody expected to be among the winners at his first attempt, which was regarded chiefly as a trial run, a way of getting, so to speak, to know the course. If you did fairly well then, you could make your serious attempt next year.

My father at his first attempt failed by only two places. It was considered a spectacular achievement. His success at the second attempt seemed certain. But, perhaps made over-confident by this achievement, he was rash enough, in the course of a theological discussion with grandfather at Bonn, to disclose that under the influence of German philosophy he had become an atheist.

Grandfather was distressed, but felt that his first duty was to the Indians, whom he had so long helped to govern, and to the British Empire in India. He still had some influence at the India Office and with the Government of India. He travelled to London, saw influential and authoritative friends holding power in that branch of Government and disclosed the unpleasant situation which had arisen. It was obviously monstrous, inadmissible, that an avowed atheist should get into the Indian Civil Service, particularly as the young man concerned was evidently of exceptional ability and might

23

quickly rise to a position of power and importance. Grandfather believed strongly in the value of the Christian religion as an ideological instrument of imperial rule. An atheist in such a position might cause havoc and wreckage. He therefore desired those in authority to take whatever steps were necessary to ensure that, however brilliantly he might perform in the examination, my father should not be admitted to the Service.

He then returned to Bonn and reported his actions to my father, who knew quite enough about the working of what is nowadays called 'The Old Boy Net' to realize that as things now stood he had considerably less chance of entering the Indian Civil Service than he did of entering the Church of England and becoming a Bishop. Enough strings had been pulled in London to keep an Archangel out of Delhi if he were caught disbelieving in the Thirty-Nine Articles.

He was bitter about the way things had turned out and wished he had kept his mouth shut about atheism. But he liked and admired people who knew their own minds and had convictions upon which they really acted, and he did not quarrel with grandfather.

'After all,' he said to me long afterwards, 'a person ought to carry his beliefs to their logical conclusion. I think I should have been rather dismayed if father had done anything else. It would have seemed so feeble. Given his opinions on religion and government, it was the only sensible thing for him to do.'

'He might,' I said, 'at least have tried to convert you.'

'But you see,' said my father, 'he took for granted that everyone else's views were as unshakable as his own. And he would have thought, too, that I might be tempted to make a false pretence of conversion – which would have been bad for my moral character; and then, later, when I was Lieutenant-Governor, I might have come out in my true colours and started massacring the missionaries, or forced them to give readings from Feuerbach from their pulpits.'

It was, however, clear that life at home had reached an *impasse*, and, not wishing to take any further chances with grandfather's convictions, my father sold all his books and all except one suit of clothes and disappeared to London. When his family next heard from him, he had secretly sat for, and passed, his entrance examination for the Eastern Consular Service, which was then a kind of half-way house between the Diplomatic Service – for which you needed a lot of money –

24

and the ordinary Consular Service which dealt mainly with commercial affairs and was confined to Europe and the western hemisphere. The point about the Eastern Consular Service was that it functioned east of Singapore, and that it was possible to pass from it into regular diplomatic service in the Far East.

He went to China and never left it until he was thirty years old. From his nineteenth to his twenty-second year he was British Vice-Consul at the then awfully remote city of Chungking. It was the most isolated British agency in Asia. The city had three hundred thousand inhabitants and was the pivotal point of trade along the Yangtze between central China and the south-east. But foreign trade was officially barred. In the whole of those four years he saw only half a dozen Europeans – none of them, as he remarked with satisfaction, 'unduly obtrusive'. Since there was almost no trade, there was no tiresome routine work. His duties, in fact, were vague. He was simply an outpost. His life was full and happy, gay and studious by turns. There were at Chungking excellent professors of philosophy, poetry and calligraphy. The political intrigues in which as British agent he became involved were intricate, dangerous and delightful. Once a month he conducted a public exercise in imperialism.

At that time it was forbidden for foreigners to reside on or even visit that part of Chungking lying on the right bank of the Yangtze. Rightly, the Chinese believed that if you gave the foreigners an inch they would take an ell. Once a month my father – designing to establish precedents and break down this ban – used to send a formal notification to the Governor, who resided on the right bank, that the British Vice-Consul proposed to call on him on a certain date. The Governor, not wishing to make a formal breach of relations, always acceded. On the day fixed, my father was transported across the river, and was met on the opposite bank by the Governor's litter, with a heavy guard of soldiers. The steep streets to the Governor's residence were lined with furiously hostile crowds – their natural hatred of the intruder encouraged and stimulated when necessary by agents of the Governor. They pelted the litter with stones. Every couple of hundred yards the litter was halted while the soldiers battled with the populace.

At the Governor's residence the Governor entertained the Vice-Consul and they talked for a couple of hours. At some point during the conversation, the Vice-Consul took occasion

25

to remark with satisfaction that it was now evidently the policy of the Imperial Government to permit an Englishman to visit the right bank of the river at Chungking. At some other point the Governor would take occasion to express his satisfaction that in this single instance it had been possible for the Imperial authorities to suspend for a few hours the inviolable rule against the presence of foreigners on the right bank, and that the efficiency of the troops had sufficed to curb, on this particular day, the profound indignation of the people.

The parting ceremony was also a somewhat elaborate man-œuvre, it being necessary for the Vice-Consul to take his leave in words carrying the general sense of *au revoir*, whereas the Governor must give to his courteous parting remarks the un-mistakable nuance of an adieu. Then came the progress back to the river, with stoning, battles and occasional blood-shed.

When I was a little boy I thought it must have been a very grand feeling to be carried thus in a magnificent litter, an outpost of Empire with hostile thousands roaring for one's blood. 'Didn't you,' I asked my father, 'feel grand and trium-phant?'

'A little, sometimes,' he said. 'But then I tried, too, to remember that to those people I didn't look grand at all. I reminded myself that to them I was physically an evil-smell-ing monkey, and in character and status a vulgar barbarian thief trying to break into China. An excellent spiritual exer-cise.'

Much later, when I was sixteen or so, I bothered him with another sort of question.

'Were you always absolutely sure it was a good thing to try to extend British power in China?'

'Absolutely.'

'But you don't much like English people. You prefer Chinese.'

'Hang it, I like some English people.'

'Not many.'

'True.'

'You don't care for their attitude to life. You know they bore you to death. Secretly, everything they say seems to you platitudinous or else untrue.'

'A lot of Chinese are awfully silly, too.'

'And you spent more than half your life working to help the English dominate the Chinese.'

26

'It's nothing to do with people. It's a question of realising an idea.'

' "The Imperial Idea"?'

'I hope you're not getting that deplorable habit of picking phrases out of newspapers and using them without knowing what they mean. A good thing to do is to read two pages of the *New Oxford Dictionary* every day. You get the exact derivations of all words and their differing shades of meaning at different periods. An excellent habit.'

'You seem to be changing the subject.'

'Let's play a game of chess.'

He seemed unaware of any contradiction in his attitude. He did not care to argue about it. He did say once that talking to me about it was like trying to explain music to a deaf child. It was tedious to make clear to a person who did not grasp it immediately how one could deplore almost every material and spiritual manifestation of the Empire and still dedicate oneself to its expansion and consolidation as the highest Good.

Between leaving Bonn and retiring, he spent more than thirty years in China and Korea, and less than that number of months in England. Except for the countryside in spring-time, he did not care much for anything about England. About the personalities and forces – political, financial, commercial – which motivated and directed the imperial machine, he had, as they say, no illusions. He found them comical, subjects for savage ribaldry. Or pathetic. Or sordid. And often simply ignoble. The machine, on the other hand – that was admirable and good: a fine bit of work, satisfactory and even inspiring to tend. Perhaps his reference to music was the clue. He was listening, perhaps, to some strange symphony. The rest was as irrelevant as would be the fact that the composer took dope and the conductor lived on the immoral earnings of women.

He moved into the Far Eastern Diplomatic Service and as 'Chinese Secretary' at the Peking Legation was for a long time the principal liaison between the British Government and the foundering dynasty of the Manchus. Secretly he intrigued on behalf of an immense scheme which he thought might ensure British domination of Asia for generations. The idea impressed him – others, I suspect, had the same motives earlier and independently – while watching the special Legation Guard of Punjab Lancers sent up from India. Suppose, as a gesture of friendship and courtesy, the British Government

27

were to offer to lend certain trained Indian troops to the Imperial House as a reliable bodyguard against the subversive elements which seethed around it? He knew, from discreet soundings, that important officials in the Palace would be favourable. They would like to have troops who would be safe from contamination by revolutionaries and throne-seekers. Over a period of years, such a Guard – corresponding, he pointed out, to the Scottish Archer Guard of the French kings – would be developed from a toy to a real instrument of power. In a dozen or twenty years these Janissaries would become indispensable. As such, they would work for the Dynasty, but also, in the last analysis, control it and its policies. And the Guard, in turn, would of course ultimately be controlled by the Government of India.

At a suitable moment somewhere along the line – there could easily be 'trouble' in India – the Chinese Government would offer to 'facilitate' the recruitment of Chinese troops for 'garrison service' in India. Within a half-century or so, the trained manpower of China – under British control – would be on tap to hold India against any possibility of successful revolt, and the manpower of India – under British control – would be the decisive military force in China. 'The beauty of it is,' he would say, 'that the Chinese and the Indians really hate and despise each other even more than they hate and despise us. And of course that would be something that could be fostered – there would be very little danger of fraternisation. Occupying forces are bound to be thoroughly unpopular.'

By hindsight the scheme appears merely preposterous. In reality there was a kind of crazy feasibility about it. He worked at it for years, and in the days shortly before and after the Boxer Rising, when on terms almost of intimacy with the sinister old Empress Dowager, he used to discuss it in an abstract, allusive kind of way with her. When he felt that it was ripe enough to be presented, cautiously, to British 'official circles', he found that they did not by any means have the courage of his convictions. They professed themselves dreadfully shocked. Perhaps it was his method of presentation they found unpalatable. In dealing with British officials he sometimes left behind the wrappings of tact and double-talk he could employ so naturally and successfully with the Chinese, because the Chinese regarded double-talk as a courtesy and did not expect anyone even to pretend to believe in it. Apparently in outlining his plan to the British he forgot,

28

until it was too late, to make the indispensable statement that the aim of the whole thing was of course to uplift, spiritually and materially, both the Indian and Chinese peoples, offering them greater and greater opportunities of self-betterment, guiding their steps along the path to ultimate self-government.

Large phrases of this kind about the Empire were received by him with derision or an unpleasant silence. He said he liked to feel, when taking part in an all-night, whisky-drenched poker session at the Shanghai Club, that the long-term purpose of the gathering was to elevate the cultural standards of the Chinese. He caused offence at a public dinner at Amoy by declaring his belief that the true function of our business community in China, with its fine appreciation of the good things of life, was to bring some modicum of civilisation to the missionaries.

But talk 'justifying' the Empire on account of its 'good works' annoyed him in another way, too. It was as though someone were to find it necessary to 'justify' the symphony by proclaiming that the composer, conductor and members of the orchestra were all people of the purest moral character.

Just before the Nationalist outbreak of 1900 he went briefly to England, married and returned with my mother in time to be besieged in the Legation quarter by the Boxers. Because of the official acceptance of reports that the Legations had fallen and the besieged all been killed, he had the pleasure of reading his own obituary notice in the newspapers. He had always been in grave trouble with the finance-controllers in London on account of his heavy and ingeniously contrived over-spending of a special 'entertainment' allowance. He wrote to the Foreign Office, noting with pleasure that these difficulties were not mentioned in the obituary notices, based on official information, and were therefore evidently recognised as of a trivial nature. Dr Morrison, the famous China correspondent of *The Times*, who was also among the besieged, simply cabled the paper saying, 'Have just read obituary in *The Times*. Kindly adjust pay to suit.'

I was born at Peking, on the day the Japanese blew up the Russian flagship *Petropavolsk* at Port Arthur, and spent the first few weeks of life at Wei-hai-wei, which until a couple of years before had been the headquarters of the British-officered Chinese regiment which my father had seen as a primitive instrument of the Sino-Indian plan. People used to

29

stare northwards across the sea at night and claim they could see the flashes of great naval battles in the Port Arthur direction. My Chinese amah, who had seen the looting of Peking by the foreign troops, expected the Japanese or the Russians to land at any minute and massacre everyone. She was glad to take me to England, but there the boys shouted and threw stones at her in the street because she wore blue trousers, and she longed to return.

My father became Minister to Korea while it was still nominally independent, and then Consul-General as the Japanese progressively took over control. He thought the whole British agreement with the Japanese on the Korean issue disastrous. He was offered another ministerial post. Quite suddenly he announced he was weary of the whole business and retired, saying that at forty-nine it was high time to start leading an entirely new sort of life.

We rented four or five different houses in four years. Each of them was discovered, after a few months, to have some intolerable defect. Secretly, as he admitted to me later, my father had come to the conclusion that it would really be more satisfactory to buy a house in the hills west of Peking, but he wanted to give England every chance. According to my mother, the house in Hertfordshire lasted longer than the others only because it had this shed or barn which was so suitable for housing the War Game.

I had played Germans and English with the tin soldiers for a couple of years when I thought I, too, would like to learn to play the War Game. I was disappointed. Neither my father nor my uncles would teach it to me. They had given up playing it themselves. They said that to learn it now would be not only pointless but actually misleading because very soon now there would be a new war which would make all strategy, tactics and rules of the War Game obsolete.

II THE ROTHSCHILD SHILLINGS

THERE WERE SOME CHEKHOV PLAYS IN LONDON, AND people from this place, Tring, where we lived for a while, used to go up and see them. When they came back they said the plays were wonderful, but very odd. The people behaved queerly. One would have enjoyed the plays more if the characters had been more normal.

Tring was thirty miles out of London, and there were a little over four thousand people in it. There had been a little over four thousand people in it for the past forty years, and when we went to live there the Ministers of the Noncomformist Chapels used to pray for rain on the day of the Church of England Sunday School treat.

The house we lived in was about as normal as everything else. We rented it from a man called Craig, an austere figure who was an authority on some branch of the Scriptures. The only other thing commonly known about him was that he had once worn a tea-cosy on his head when the Queen came to tea with him and his wife at a hunting lodge they had in the north of Scotland, near Balmoral. His wife had asked him for the occasion to relax austerity and make small talk. He had not been able to make the small talk, but instead he had picked up a bright tea-cosy and put it on his head. He intended to indicate by this that he had nothing against a little frivolity and was as anxious as anyone to make the party a success.

Like almost everyone else that I can remember of the older generation at that period, this same man thought that chaos was breaking in upon the world. So far as his own house was concerned, he was determined to stop it. Everywhere, in rooms and corridors, there were little notices printed in his own hand, telling one what to do and not to do. 'When the wind blows from the north, we close the door at the east end of the passage in the north wing.' 'We leave the bath by the end opposite the taps, not by the side. Otherwise water from

31

our wet feet will flow southwards from the door and possibly into the passage.' The lavatories were almost papered with such notices. The thought of the innumerable things that could go wrong with the plumbing, or with the manner in which people performed their natural functions, threw Mr Craig almost into a frenzy. He did his best to keep everything in order.

Our nearest neighbours on one side were a retired Colonel and his family. As his major-domo the Colonel had an ex-batman whom he loved and trusted. The batman took drugs, but the Colonel refused to get rid of him. Once, in a state of ecstasy, the batman broke open the tin trunk in which the Colonel kept his old full-dress uniform and dressed himself in it. Wearing a scarlet coat with a good deal of gold braid, and a cocked hat with plumes, the batman went out into the paddock and there caught and mounted a cow. For several minutes he dashed round and round the paddock, waving the Colonel's sword and shouting. The Colonel told everyone that the man had had a touch of malaria, contracted during his service in India.

The house on the other side was owned by an Australian named Tuson who only came to Tring a few weeks in each year. Meeting my father in the street on his first visit, he told him that he was a student of Shakespeare. This alarmed my father, who was always afraid that people would take it for granted he had some kind of literary interests, and try to come and discuss such matters with him.

He strongly counselled us not to have any dealings with Mr Tuson. My mother, however, thought it would be un-neighbourly not to call. She did so, but nothing came of it, because the Tusons were never at home to callers. When he was not inside the house, presumably studying Shakespeare, Mr Tuson used to spend his time on his lawn wrestling with soldiers who he invited over from a neighbouring camp.

Small as it was, Tring had a kind of suburb – a village called Wigginton, or rather it was not called Wigginton but 'wicked Wigginton'. It was deemed wicked in 1912 because of the way it had been founded as a village in about 1820. The Government of that day had taken drastic but humane and sensible measures to clear London and the surrounding country of highwaymen and other criminals. It had desig-nated a number of areas in the Chiltern Hills to which such characters might go and settle down; if they did so by a certain date, they would, in effect, be amnestied. After that date, any of them found at large, or not resident in these tiny Siberias, would be severely dealt with.

I have lived in at least one other such place in the Chiltern Hills, and there, too, the natives were regarded as strange, wild, even dangerous – like gipsies – by neighbouring villagers. And the fact is that those descendants of the high-waymen really were a little strange and wild.

When the first cinema opened in Tring, a special block of seats was set apart at the back of the hall for the use of the people of Wigginton, so that they should not contaminate the people of Tring. The idea of a Wigginton boy going with a Tring girl was at that time – probably things are entirely otherwise now – generally horrifying. Except in periods of the most acute labour shortage, few Tring employers would hire labour from Wigginton, which was less than a mile away. When it was done, it was done with apprehension.

The people of Wigginton voted in the main Conservative, but when they came marching arm-in-arm down the hill to the cinema of an evening, I remember hearing them sing 'The Red Flag' – as a protest, I suppose, against something or other.

Tring lay in the heart of the Rothschild country with Lord Rothschild's mansion, Tring Park, in the middle of it, Mentmore away to the north, and a few miles to the west Halton, where Leopold Rothschild still had his pet monkeys, which used to perform tricks among the port glasses after dinner. A good many Tring people were, directly or indirectly, dependent or semi-dependent upon the Rothschilds, in compensation for which they displayed anti-Semitism. To show its independence, the town silver band when it went to the mansion to solicit contributions on Christmas morning sometimes used to march up the avenue playing 'Christians awake, salute the happy morn'! The Rothschilds used to lavish presents upon the working population. At Christmas time, pantechnicons rolled through the town, delivering expensive toys to all working-class children in the place.

One year it was announced that to celebrate either the King's birthday or Lord Rothschild's birthday – I forget which – there would be a special ceremony. This was to consist of the presentation of a silver shilling to every working-class child of Tring under the age of fifteen who presented himself or herself at the main door of the mansion between the hours of ten and three o'clock on that day.

Since the total population of the town was only four thousand, it was reasonable to assume that there could not be more than two thousand working-class children of eligible age. That is to say, it was reasonable if one left out of account some of the most vital factors in the situation.

At any rate, two thousand was the number of the bright new shining shillings which were arranged in neat piles on long trestle tables laid out on the gravel in front of the main door, with the Rothschild's bailiff, or other household official, seated behind the tables, and various other members of the staff there to assist him.

The way things were supposed to happen was perfectly simple. At ten o'clock the children would enter by the main gates, walk up about a half-mile of avenue to the front of the mansion, receive their shilling, move off up another avenue of about the same length, which debouched into the London road, and from that far gate return to the town and disperse quietly to their homes.

Maybe the Rothschilds had not, after all, been settled quite long enough in the English countryside.

In those days a shilling was a shilling. Some of the families of Tring were large. Others were small or contained an undue proportion of toddlers. Nobody felt that they had as many children under the age limit, and at the same time old enough to move fast, as was desirable. They had to borrow and they did. Choking down prejudice, they went even to wicked Wigginton and borrowed from there. They went over to Ivinghoe and even as far out on the Chilterns that way as Dunstable and Luton. From the other direction Aston Clinton and all the villages and hamlets of the Vale of Aylesbury supplied their quota. They came in some matter of twenty-four hours and rested up. They slept in kitchens, and some of them slept in cabbage fields at the edge of the town.

A few minutes after ten, when the gates were opened, the bailiff at the trestle table saw a horde of children moving towards him at a brisk jogtrot. At that time he was glad. He reasoned that the children were on time, that they were all coming at once, and that he would be through with the job as like as not before midday.

It was true that well before midday the piles of shillings had been reduced to very small ones, but the number of children trotting towards the tables had not apparently diminished. Those who had arranged the programme had not reckoned with the practicality of the people of Tring. For these latter it was not just a question of having as many children as possible to go for the shillings, but to have each child go round the course as often as possible too. Unseen by the Rothschild functionaries, the children, after getting their shillings, were running fast up the avenue to the London road, rushing out of the gates and down the highway towards the town. From the bar of the Red Lion and other public houses at the entrance to the town, keen parents rushed out shouting to the children and encouraging them. Some men, determined to overlook no bets, actually put down their drinks and ran for a few hundred yards as pacemakers with the children of their particular team. Some boys claimed to have gone round as many as seven laps before noon.

A few minutes after midday, cars with an armed man sitting beside each driver were sent to Aylesbury one way and Watford the other to collect more shillings from the banks. Still the endless band of children went round and round like an untidy conveyor belt. The telephones in the Big House started ringing London with pleas for more shillings. From the City two thousand more were hustled to Tring. It seemed absurd, but they wanted to be on the safe side.

This measure failed too. Just after two o'clock the Rothschilds had to admit defeat. There were no more shillings available. The founders of the credit system of Europe were reduced to offering payment in kind. It was announced that from then on until the closing time of the programme each child would receive instead of a shilling a slice of rich cake.

Servitors came out and laid the cake on the trestle table. But the announcement of the change of plan had hardly been made when the avenues of the mansion became deserted, and the bailiff was left alone behind the piled plates. One man boasted that he had taken in that day the equivalent of two and a half weeks' wages, with two bottles of whisky thrown in.

My father enjoyed visiting occasionally at the Rothschild house and talking about the Far East, until one evening after dinner a suggestion was tentatively made that he might care to accept a retaining fee as a more or less regular adviser on Far Eastern affairs. He became morose and gave up going to the house.

At first he made up a story to the effect that, since his knowledge of the Far East had been garnered in Government service, it would be improper for him to accept money from

35

a private firm which was proposing to exploit this knowledge. In this explanation of his refusal he himself scarcely pretended to believe.

The real one came out later. He would have had no objection, it appeared, to being paid as an expert on some other territory – say Latin America. But to be an expert on China was far too much like a continuation of his former work. He had left the Far East in order to start a new life; and that, he said, sitting with me under a string of Korean fish-bells hung across the window of his study and tinkling in the wind, was what he proposed to do.

To set the ball rolling he wrote a novel, a stilted, rather sombre affair, on a Stoic note, demonstrating in a general way that virtue had better be its own reward, because none will be available from other sources. It was published in the middle of 1914, and sank without a trace under the flood of World War I.

III   A HOLE IN THE FENCE

VIRTUS LAUDATA CRESCIT, OR 'VIRTUE GROWS WITH praise', was found, at the last moment, to be the motto of the school I was to go to, and if arrangement had been less far advanced I believe my father would have changed his mind and sent me somewhere else. It was symbolic, he felt, of a state of mind – a lax state. All very well to take the view that a pat on the back could occasionally make goodness better; but very improper, he opined, for a school, of all places, to turn this notion into an official motto. To do so was virtually to flaunt a conviction that people cannot be expected to be any good *unless* they are patted on the back for it.

It was one of those small pointers that suddenly indicated to him the extent of the gulf existing between his own ideas and those of the age in which his children were to grow up. Useless to point out that the motto was not modern – had, it was understood, been the family motto of the school's founder, in the mid-sixteenth century. What, might one ask,

36

was known of *his* character and achievements? But it was too late to back out now. We had already taken a house in Berkhamsted so that, at any rate to begin with, I could attend the 'Preparatory' section of the school as a day boy rather than a boarder.

However, he took it for granted that a school which prided itself on a motto like that, and had a headmaster who apparently supported the Liberal Party, would likely be incapable of teaching me the rudiments of Latin and Greek in a sufficiently thorough way. He therefore coached me himself for a couple of hours a day in term time and an hour a day in the holidays. These hours were happily astringent.

In school they seemed to want us to believe that Latin was on the whole fairly easy provided one took it slowly without undue exertion of the brain. My father told me sharply that to learn Latin correctly, and at a respectable rate of progress each week, was exceedingly hard, and that unless I exerted myself to the utmost I should fail miserably. These exhortations turned the undertaking into an agreeably challenging and arduous enterprise.

Some months after war broke out – I was then between ten and eleven – I told him proudly that I had been second out of fifteen in my Latin class for three weeks running, though most of the boys in it were older than myself. He was unimpressed. 'But why not be top?' he said. 'If you can be second, you can be first. This war is going to make things uncomfortable for any one of our sort who doesn't get to the top and stay there all the time. Don't take your pace from other people. I doubt if the people at the school realise what things are really like.'

The school – with its Preparatory, Junior and Senior sections – was one of those comprehensive institutions where you could spend all your life from the age of eight to the age of nineteen and a half; except, that is, for the years 1916-18, when you were liable to spend your eighteenth birthday packing for the journey to the training camp, and your nineteenth, if you were lucky enough to have one, in a Flanders dugout.

For about three hundred years after its foundation it seems to have fulfilled a useful educational function. Then, as a result of lawsuits and financial disputes, it went quite suddenly to pot. For years there were often only three or four pupils at a time, although the teaching staff seems to have been comfortably maintained on the funds of the original foundation. Some of these teachers lived in other parts of the country and never came near the place.

In late Victorian days prosperity returned. The middle and upper-middle classes were clamouring for more and more 'public schools' – because to have been to such a school had become a requisite for social and professional success and made you a gentleman at eighteen, whatever you might have been at eight. By the time I went to Berkhamsted the school had five hundred boys, and was poised somewhere between Stalky and Co. and the Welfare State.

The Rugby Tradition, the standards of the barrack-room, and intimations of modernism and 'progressive' education overlapped or struggled confusedly for supremacy.

The Welfare State had come gingerly through the door with the Education Act of 1902. The effect of that Act and of various subsequent Acts and Regulations was to compel a wide range of 'public' schools, secondary schools and grammar schools which got money grants from the Government to have among their pupils a minimum of twenty-five per cent. of boys who came from the elementary schools, paid nothing, and for whom the schools taking them were paid so much a head out of the public funds.

'It was an Act,' wrote Professor W. G. S. Adams, of Oxford, in the *Encyclopædia Britannica*, 'which represented the spirit of compromise. It gave a new impression in one most important group of institutions to the English genius for harmonising diverse elements within the State.' I suppose that at our school we had the diverse elements harmonised about as well as anywhere.

Since the 'free scholars' from the elementary schools came, in the main, not from the town itself but from homes in Watford and Tring and other towns of the area, they were known to us collectively as 'train boys'. It was a term of disdain, and quite often hatred, and in the derision and repugnance for the train boys expressed by the sons of parents who could afford to pay for their education, several of the teaching staff openly, or *sotto voce*, joined, for they felt that the presence about the place of so many of these uncouth fellows with working-class accents detracted from their own social position as masters at a distinguished school for the sons of gentlemen.

The train boys had got these free places by intelligence and hard work, in competition with hundreds of others in the elementary schools, and now many of them continued to push

38

ahead with their work in a harsh, ostentatious, menacing sort of way. These we either feared or patronised.

Among ourselves – though not often, as I recall, to their faces – we parodied and loudly contemned their unseemly Hertfordshire intonations and pronunciations, which, however, were satisfactory as being a badge of evident all-round lowness. The amusement and disgust that could be extracted from these accents were not, however, inexhaustible; but it was satisfactory, too, to be able to conclude, on first-hand evidence, that the standard of manners and general behaviour among the lower orders was low indeed; for thus to conclude gave an agreeable sense of superiority, and showed that everyone had the advantages he deserved.

Even quite earnest members of the staff, who in theory and on public occasions welcomed the train boys as demonstrating the breadth of our democracy, were privately uneasy lest, instead of the train boys being elevated to the moral and cultural level of the rest of us, they might drag us, and the school, disastrously down. Conferences on this disturbing subject were actually held between members of the teaching staff and senior boys.

The conclusion was that what was wrong was that the train boys did not live under the conditions that are necessary to make for *esprit de corps*.

What did these fellows do? They came from their homes, they got into their trains, and they then arrived at the school, where they received the tuition which had been paid for; after which they got back into the trains and went home. Some of them brought sandwich lunches in paper bags, and others – even lower – went to small cafés in the town to get something to eat at the lunch-time break.

The official view was that this meant that the train boys were in reality being defrauded of the full advantages of Public School education, and were not even being properly shown what those advantages might be. The rest of us were organised in Houses which intensified *esprit de corps*. Some big progressive came up with the suggestion that the way to overcome the train-boy difficulty was to organise them into a House, too, and this was what was done. At frightful inconvenience to themselves they were organised in this way and made to leave their paper bags behind and abandon the cafés where they had formerly met at lunch. Instead they were compelled to eat in a little house on a piece of marshy land between the back of the school and the canal which ran along the railway bridge, and they were forced also to organise themselves into House teams, so that a good deal of the leisure they had formerly had after their school hours was now gone. All the other Houses in the school had names. The two School Houses, for instance, were called Uppers and Lowers, and there was a House called St. John's and another called Incent's, and the day boys were called 'Bees'. There was another day-boys' House called 'Wasps' – their shirts were pink and white.

It took a little while for the authorities to find a suitable name to give the train-boys' House so as to raise it to a proper sense of equality with the others. However, they did get it named at last. It was called Adder's. Incent's was called Incent's because there had been a man called Incent who had founded the school. But none of us had ever heard of anybody called Adder who had founded Adder's House. It meant just snakes.

This English genius for harmony stayed with us all the way, and it was nearly at its best when it had to harmonise the view of life expressed by such ancient and uninhibited Levantines as Euripides with the way we ought to feel now.

The harmonisers had a powerful ally, namely Professor Gilbert Murray, whose translations of the poet Euripides were at this precise period sweeping the circulating libraries and the women's clubs, and for good reason: because they proved that, basically, and allowing a little bit here and a little bit there, the Great Classics of any age, including that savagely knife-fighting intellectual giant Euripides, felt – if you really got them talking – just about the way people felt and talked at a Don's tea-party on Boars Hill. It went down well, if you could swallow it at all.

One of our Classics masters was a man of independent mind, and he said all this sort of thing was tosh. He said it did not matter much whether you understood Euripides or not – after all, he used to say with an ugly sneer (the mere result, his enemies declared, of an early scar at the Battle of Mons), 'the man's dead and gone. The only important thing is to realise that, whether you understand him or not, at least he was saying something different from everything you have been taught to think, and if you want to know what that thing is, well, go ahead and read him.'

The orthodox view, however – acted upon, though never formulated in so many words – was that the literature and history of the past ought to be regarded rather in the light of a supply depot or ammunition dump from which is to be drawn whatever may be from time to time needed to reinforce the opinions, ambitions and policies of the present.

In other words, history becomes a kind of myth, devised today, revised tomorrow, to suit today's and tomorrow's purposes. From this viewpoint it is immaterial to speculate as to how many people in Sparta really had the virtues which are called Spartan. What Sparta is for is to teach people to keep a stiff upper lip when that fox-cub starts gnawing their stomachs. No need to wonder what the Romans were really like: the job of ancient Rome was to inspire the organisers of the British Empire.

It would be interesting to see a given period – say the Victorian age – analysed in terms of its attitude to previous periods of history. Who and what were its heroes in the past – not individuals only, but heroes in the shape of ideologies, maxims and prejudices? Or one could examine the successive editions of the *Encyclopædia Britannica*, from the first to the latest, trace through them the changing treatment of a few of the subjects dealt with in all editions, and thereby construct a mirror of the period in which each edition was published.

History, said Ernst Toller, is the propaganda of the victors, At school I began to form the opinion that history is the propaganda of the school authorities, designed for the purpose of keeping one up to the mark. 'Keenness' about things in general, and a high 'moral' – that is to say asexual – tone were what the school principally prided itself upon. Offenders against the moral tone, when detected, were expelled two by two; but there were few such, if only for the reason that there simply was not time for anything of that kind, at least not among the boarders, of whom, after a few years as a day boy, I became one.

It was taken for granted that any boys left alone and unoccupied for more than a few minutes were going to get up to vicious mischief, with the result that efforts were made to fill every interstice of every day with public and communal activities – many of them conducted, like the drill of the Italian bersaglieri, at the double. Paradoxically, Sunday was the moral danger zone, because to work would have been to break the Fourth Commandment and to play games would have been shocking to local opinion. Even two Chapel services could not be stretched right across the gap, and there were a couple of hours on Sunday afternoons when we had to be allowed to go for walks, in couples or groups.

On Mondays, Wednesdays and Saturdays in the summer we played compulsory cricket from two in the afternoon until dusk, and on the other days from noon until lunch-time, and again in the evenings from five o'clock – when school ended – until the light mercifully failed. The playing-fields were at the top of a steep hill about half a mile long, and to get from one end to the other of it on time one usually had to do it at a brisk jogtrot. During all the years I was there I made a total of only seven runs.

In winter and spring there was nothing between us and the perils of leisure except football, running and the school Cadet Corps. With most of us the Corps was unpopular, but I liked it. I had been brought up in expectation of a war, and there was a war going on during a good deal of the time I was at school. The thing seemed to make sense. It was a game with a visible point to it. It seemed realistic. You would be out one day on a field exercise, firing blank ammunition under command of a prefect who was also your platoon commander, and a few weeks or months later you would hear how he had been killed in genuine battle in France. I, too, became a cadet officer in the end, and used to enjoy explaining, in elaborately military terms, to elderly and diffident officers of the Brigade of Guards who came to inspect us, what we imagined we were up to.

All the other games seemed to me terribly like hard and, on the whole, uncongenial toil. On the other hand, the teaching was so stimulating that what was described as 'work' often seemed an entrancing game.

Regimentation of the kind we were subjected to is supposed, I believe, to destroy individuality, and conduce to the development of a conformist attitude. I have no notion whether this is a general truth or not. I can only say that, as a direct result of all this supervision and ordering about, one of the most valuable lessons my school taught me was how to break other people's rules. And at sixteen I read and profoundly appreciated Bernard Shaw's invaluable advice to 'get what you like, or you'll grow to like what you get'.

The fact, I suppose, is that, as a general rule, the more people try to fence you in, the more certain they are that the fence they have put around you is impregnable, the more certain it really is that if you can find a hole in the fence – and there always is one – you can get outside and remain there

42

in comparative safety, because in their ignorance the fencers do not believe that there was a hole and in consequence are not looking for anyone outside. Once I had realised that the only way in which to exist happily at school was to find a means of getting out through the fence of regulations, even days on the cricket field became tolerable and interesting, as one devoted them to observing the methods and behaviour of the authorities, and to noting the possible loopholes in their apparatus of discipline and restraint. In fine weather and even sometimes when it rained – although that was a little dangerous because the games might be called off altogether and there would be a new sort of roll-call – I used to get through the 'fence' three times a week, walk a stealthy mile or more, and then hitch-hike, driving long distances by lorry out into the lovely countryside. You could walk there without people peering and enquiring what you were looking at, why you were happy at this moment or unhappy at that, why you took this or the other direction. The whole system had taken me nearly a year to complete, in terms of observation and of foolproof construction of a counter-system to that of the fencers-in.

In the winter and early spring I used to avail myself of a hole I had found in the roof of one of the classrooms. It was a brand-new classroom, so that nobody supposed there was a hole in its ceiling, but there was. There was a way of getting through it so that one could lie on the timbers above the ceiling in almost complete security. There I spent hundreds of delightful hours reading chiefly Gibbon, Macaulay and the poems of Browning, and learning German. German was not included in the curriculum of the school course I took, and for some reason, perhaps perverse, I wanted to learn that language. As I had no one to tell me anything about the pronunciation the results were somewhat bizarre – that is to say, I could read and even speak quite elaborate German, but the pronunciation had no relation at all to the real pronunciation of the language, so that I was fluent but entirely unintelligible.

The only other relief from our routine was provided by the accident of our headmaster being a chess addict. When the craving for chess came on him, he had to play; in the fire of this passion rules, regulations and routine were reduced to ashes. As I was supposed to be the best chess player in the school, I was often invited to play with him, and at such times I would sit securely, and for hours on end, at one side

43

of a table by the fire in his study, listening contentedly to the imperious, but temporarily innocuous, jangle of bells summoning people to get on with something or other, and the shouts of prefects driving others along cold corridors without.

Charles Henry Greene, this headmaster, gave the impression of conducting the affairs of the school and viewing life in general with the same smouldering, sometimes explosive intensity which he brought to the chessboard. He was a man of powerful and vivid reactions. Certain events, sometimes major, sometimes quite trivial, seemed to strike his mind with the heat and force of a branding-iron, and for a long time would remain in the forefront of consciousness, to be referred to, commented, brooded upon aloud in a singularly sonorous voice, and with occasionally florid eloquence.

His history lessons to the Sixth Form were not so much history lessons as comments on a state of affairs in which history had taken a distinct turn for the worse. For the most part he treated history simply as a series of signposts to the probabilities and possibilities of the present. Most of them pointed to ruin. For Charles Greene was, in the widest as well as the party-political sense of the word, a Liberal, and in the crack-up of Liberalism he saw the mark of doom.

When he looked at the Treaty of Versailles, his slightly bulbous grey eyes rolled, shone and started from his head, and his yellow moustache bristled. It reminded him of every disaster in the history of treaty-making since the errors committed by Pericles. As he spoke of it he sank back in his chair, pulling the mortar-board farther and farther down on his forehead as though to shield his eyes from the sight of so much folly and horror. 'When I gaze,' he said, 'upon the activities of Mr Lloyd George, when I consider the political consequence of Mr Clemenceau, my mind, abdicating its intellectual function, shrinks, half-paralysed, from the very attempt to contemplate the abyss which opens, inevitable but unregarded, before us.'

Reading the news from Moscow and from the various fronts of the war of intervention, he would sink into an almost luxurious awareness of impending doom. The spirit of Bolshevism, he said, was permeating everywhere, and the most ordinary events and *contretemps* of everyday life confirmed his view.

Bored at the fact that they were mobilised months after the ending of the war, the soldiers camped outside the town

44

became drunker and drunker, and once rioted, breaking into the school itself and threatening to throw the headmaster into the canal. It was Bolshevism.

Prefects neglected their duties; a French master turned pacifist and started teaching his pupils that the whole war had been a monstrous mixture of crime and blunder in which people had been slaughtered for nothing; and a conspiracy was uncovered among the older boys to wear dark-blue serge suits to chapel on Sundays instead of the short black coats which were required by regulation.

All these were manifest indications of the bolshevistic way things were tending.

And then death-watch beetles were found at work in the timbers of the high roof of the Elizabethan Hall. It was horrifying, but in its awful way satisfactory – a climatic symbol of decay and violent collapse. 'Once again I have reports of slackness and indiscipline, everywhere I detect a falling off in keenness. The pernicious and destructive doctrines of Marx and Lenin are tapping away at the foundations and at the roof beams of civilisation like the death-watch beetle which even as I speak is carrying out up there, invisible to us but none the less menacing for that, its work of voracious disintegration.' Since he said all these things with a vivid sincerity, and these extravagances were the product of genuine and agonised beliefs, the effect was not at all grotesque, but as vividly impressive as a revivalist meeting.

He worried sometimes about my political future. He wanted me to have a political career so that I could take a hand at halting the general decline, and possibly reversing the trend. I held strong Conservative views, and he, though a Liberal, thought that on the whole that was probably a good thing – I should enter the Conservative Party and so stimulate its moral sense and moderate its crassness. At lunch in the schoolhouse, when no one could leave the table until the headmaster had stood up and said the Latin grace, our arguments on the origins of the Boer War, or the policy of Palmerston, used sometimes to be prolonged for as much as a quarter of an hour after the last crumbs of the suet and treacle pudding had been eaten. The discussion was conducted amid a rising shuffle of impatient feet and the rebellious tinkling of spoons on empty plates. Sometimes he would use his initiative of the Grace to cut short an argument which displeased him or to which perhaps he did not see an immediate rebuttal.

'Well, well, Cockburn,' he would say, getting slowly to his feet, 'I don't see how civilisation's going to be saved Benedictus Benedicat.'

Disruptive tendencies were at work even in the circle of his own family. As was the custom of many old-fashioned people at the period, the Greenes used at breakfast innocently to describe to one another anything interesting, bizarre or colourful they had had in the way of dreams during the previous night. Mr and Mrs Greene were unaware that their third son, Graham, had at about this time discovered Freud. He would leave the bacon cooling on his plate as he listened with the fascination of a secret detective. When necessary he would lure them on to provide more and more details which to them were amusing or meaningless but to him of thrilling and usually scandalous significance.

'It's amazing,' he said to me once, 'what those dreams disclose. It's startling – simply startling,' and at the thought of it gave a low whistle.

Since my father viewed the British Public School system with increasing uncertainty and distrust, I probably should have remained in the semi-detached position of a day boy to the end if the War had not ended when it did. During it my father had returned to government service in some job so hush-hush that neither then nor subsequently did I find out what, exactly, he was up to. When it was over he retired again, intending at last to pursue that new life which he had envisaged on his first retirement in 1908. But it soon turned out that he had miscalculated the rise in the cost of living – or, rather, its permanent character – and was now in a state of acute financial embarrassment.

A friend told him there was a good job going as chief of some inter-allied financial mission to look after the finances of Hungary. Perhaps he would like that? My father asked whether the circumstances of his knowing almost nothing about Hungary and absolutely nothing about finance would be a disadvantage. His friend said that was not the point. The point was that they had had a man doing this job who knew all about Hungary and a lot about finance, but he had been seen picking his teeth with a tram-ticket in the lounge of the Hungaria Hotel and was regarded as socially impossible. My father said that if such were the situation he would be prepared to take over the job.

Fortunately it turned out that the work did not, after all, consist in running the finances of Hungary, merely of help-

46

ing to sort out the financial claims upon Hungary of British, French, Italian and other Allied nationals. He bought a Hungarian grammar and a small book on money, arranged for me to become a boarder at the school, and got into the Orient Express.

IV HUNGARIAN GOULASH

BUDAPEST IN 1920 WAS A BATTLEFIELD WHERE everyone has come to a bad end, where all the heroes are dead and all the great causes are betrayed. 'Freedom from fear' was one of 'the Four Freedoms' very noticeably lacking there. It was a city where everyone was frightened – frightened of being arrested, frightened of being murdered, frightened of just being ruined.

A cicerone from the Hotel Gellért met me at the station as I arrived and when we got to the Gellért Bridge stopped to show me something. We got out of the car and what he wanted to show me was a place beside the piles on the Pest side of the bridge where he himself personally, he avowed, had seen the bodies of at least three hundred of the Reds who had fought for Bela Kun and Communism in Hungary, floating against the piles after being shot or driven at bayonet-point into the river by the officers of the counter-revolution. This hotel guide looked down into the Danube with an expression which it was impossible to define or understand. He was the Tartar type of Hungarian and his Mongolian eyes switched this way and that in excited movements which indicated perhaps that he was doing simply the right thing in showing the newly arrived son of a minor diplomat of the victorious Western powers something rather to the credit of the city. Or perhaps, I thought, some of his friends had been there dead in the river. Or he was glad because he had nearly fought with them himself and somehow had remained unimplicated. Or he was just a neutral telling the facts.

In my father's view we were very soon going to settle down in a nice house on the hills just west of Buda. This being so, it would be foolish to spend time and trouble looking for anything in the way of economical accommodation in the city. It would all be so temporary. For such a short time it was foolish to run the risk of being poisoned by inferior food or wearied by bad service, and therefore the prudent thing to do was to move into the best hotel in the town and take a fairly large number of rooms there so as not to be cramped. Also, in case anyone objected to this course as rash, it must be recalled that it would not look very well for British prestige to do anything else. We lived in that enormous suite at the Gellért approximately eighteen months, at the end of which it turned out that so far from any money being saved for the third and ultimate retirement, we were actually spending a good deal more than we had made. Facing facts, we moved upstairs to another suite on the top floor. This was cheaper, but the rooms were a good deal smaller. Observing that there was no point in being cramped, my father took a couple of extra ones and the top-floor suite in the end turned out rather more expensive than the one we had originally lived in. We were there for another eighteen months.

Sometimes we drove or walked about the hills west of Buda looking for a nice little house. There were a lot of them, but objections to all. The specific objections raised in each case were really unimportant, all of them had one defect in common – none of them stood on the hills west of Peking.

Most people one met in Budapest at that time seemed to have a quite heroic future behind them. The most oppressive bores were tolerated simply because they were aristocrats who had survived the revolution. Survival alone was taken as justifying their existence. They were rather oppressively anglophile, too – oppressively, because the England they loved was one which no one had ever seen. It was a country full of sportive dukes and obedient stableboys. The landscape was made up of green sward and immemorial elms. The English were essentially gentlemen, which meant that they gave their money away in handfuls or were prepared to be complacently looted by well-mannered adventurers. Quite the opposite, in fact, of the Jews one had to haggle with in post-war Budapest. As for the English women they were beautiful, though normally cold. But they were capable of being roused to sensual passion by skilled Hungarians.

In this England there were no serious political problems. This was partly because of there being a King, beloved of all, partly because of the numerous gentlemen, beloved of all, too. In England the lower classes had a nice nature, and one could afford to treat them kindly. A very different state of affairs from that prevailing in Hungary. Although, had it not been for the Jews and the Reds and the Czechoslovaks and the Yugoslavs and the Rumanians, and the uppitty peasants, and the bailiff at the estate out on the plains who embezzled, and that jumped-up ruffian at the bank who refused us an overdraft, Hungary would have been like England and we Hungarians would have been able to afford to be suave and generous and civilised too. Hungarian misfortunes were due to bad luck, to the machinations of alien elements, and to an excess of nobility and virtue among the true Hungarians. For hundreds of years they had too generously expended themselves in defending the eastern barriers of civilization, and the Jews and suchlike had taken advantage of them while they were not looking.

Hungary threw itself at me almost at once in the form of a man called – rather improbably – von Tános. He was young, and noble looking in a somewhat spectacularly haggard way. Some man who knew a man who knew a man, and there are more of such in Hungary than almost anywhere else, had induced him to turn up five days a week and teach me German and Hungarian. Except that he must have been some sort of liar, and was not a very good teacher, we never found out very much about him – never even found out where his mysterious German 'von' came from. His assignment started on Monday and on the first Monday he told me that he was the last scion of a poor but honest officer of the Hungarian army, who had fallen in the struggle against the eastern hordes, leaving this scion to maintain the family tradition as best he could. He explained that while awaiting some period of military service he was compelled to undertake such degrading tasks as teaching German and Hungarian to foreigners.

I sympathised with him so warmly that on Tuesday he said that in reality he was the illegitimate son of a nobleman of enormous wealth and prominence whose name, were he willing to reveal it, would distinctly impress me. By Thursday or Friday he had somehow had a huge estate out on the great Hungarian plain, and then the peasants, misled by Bolsheviks, had risen against him and his family, and his family had been shot before his eyes against the wall of the yard.

49

When we had drunk a good deal of wine for lunch and he was feeling elated, this aspect of his past was the one which most attracted him. But there were other days when gloom settled upon him, and he said that in fact he was merely a poor student, of aristocratic lineage certainly, but nevertheless condemned to live out of the rest of his life with little hope beyond the prospect of some pittance as a Government employee. In such moods he saw his fate as symbolic of the fate of Europe, at least of the intelligentsia of Europe. European civilisation was finished, the European intelligentsia were finished, and von Tános had had it too. These reflections slowly revived his spirits, since they proved that whatever happened or was going to happen was really no fault of his.

Deeply stimulated by such thoughts he would read aloud to me, at almost unintelligible pace, passages from Spengler's *Der Untergang des Abendlandes*. This book was currently a best-seller, not only in Hungary but all over Central Europe. Naturally so, because whatever Spengler thought he was trying to say, the thing that his readers chose to believe he was saying was that there was nothing to be done, that the game was pretty well up and, above all, that it was nobody's fault.

My father objected to these readings from Spengler. He read Spengler himself with interest and occasional approbation, but he thought it a demoralising doctrine for a young man. As happened to everyone in argument, particularly in really sincere arguments with people they love, he was driven far from his true position, and at the end of an hour of passionate discussion with me would find himself uttering views indistinguishable from those of his own father or of his own father's friends in the Edinburgh of the fifties or sixties.

I would accuse him of hypocrisy, but although I suppose the charge was in a sense true, it was the kind of hypocrisy which most fathers who love their children fall into sooner or later. They think this kind of reading, that kind of experience, were all very well for me, because I was tough and have proved it; but what deadly effects may they not have upon this tender and inexperienced creature? This loved one, they think, should be exposed only to the true and the beautiful, and in this frightful modern world of 1860 or 1910 or 1920 or whatever it may be, how insufferably difficult it is to find proper supplies of the true and beautiful.

It did seem to my father, surveying Central Europe in the early 1920s, that human nature had deteriorated considerably. And he thought that this deterioration was unnecessary, self-inflicted, self-willed. He startled people sometimes by saying in moments of indiscretion that in his opinion everyone was taking the Great War and its consequences a great deal too seriously. Since he rarely bothered to explain exactly what he meant by this, he gave offence. In the eyes of quite a number of younger men he was a walking embodiment of that type of cynical old man who was supposedly 'responsible' for the war and for the consequent misfortune of the younger generation.

What he really felt was that, after all, he had, so to speak, lived with this war for years before it happened; for years before it happened he had said that it was coming, that it would be terrible, that in his view we should survive.

It had happened, and if the British Empire could not precisely be said to have won the war, it had at least survived, which in his view was about all that anyone had a right to expect. Since he had never supposed that the war would do anything but incalculable harm to the fabric of civilisation, he simply could not understand the frustration and bitterness of the young men who said, 'You told us this was a war for civilisation, and now look.' To him the results appeared to be just what anyone in his senses would have expected, and he therefore was suspicious of people who seemed to be taking the war and its results as an excuse for every kind of intellectual, moral and political extravagance.

Why, he asked, should people take this war which, when all was said and done, was simply a larger, more extensive, more destructive war than the ones we had had before, as an excuse for demanding, as they so constantly did, 'a radical reappraisal of moral values', a 'reassessment of our entire attitude of life'?

Because he had never taken seriously any of the high-toned propaganda slogans of the war period, he never came near understanding the rage of those who had believed in them and now felt themselves betrayed. During the war itself he had never for a moment imagined that the battles were being waged in the interests of democracy or civilisation, or even of freedom; he found quite adequate inspiration in the conviction that we were fighting to prevent the German Empire from doing us down.

He used to exasperate democratic Americans by harping

on the degree of 'self-determination' enjoyed by, for example, the American Indians or the people of the Southern States. This being his general attitude, he found it extraordinarily difficult to comprehend or sympathise with the revulsion of feeling which at that time had taken place among vast numbers of young men in the victorious countries who, feeling that they had been led up the garden path for years in pursuit of a lot of imaginary ideals, now found expression for their disgust and disappointment in an exaggerated sympathy with the defeated. No doubt this reaction was strongest among people who, like myself, lived in Central Europe at the time, and were exposed to the well-organised lamentations of Hungarian landowners, German steel barons in the Ruhr and ulcerated international bankers who declared that the break-up of the Austro-Hungarian Empire and the establishment of the Succession States had made profitable business virtually impossible. Anyone who reads such truthful memoirs of the period as Bruce Lockhart's *Retreat from Glory* can see how strong was this feeling in, for example, the British-occupied territory on the Rhine.

But it was almost as strong in the British universities. Instead of the Kaiser and the Belgian atrocities and the Huns and the U-boats, the villains of the piece and the crimes against society had suddenly – and of course very naturally – turned into the cunning imperialist Lloyd George, the intransigent Poincaré, the Treaty of Versailles, the Treaty of Trianon and the Treaty of Neuilly, which were now seen to be revengefully strangling the new German democracy, ruining the gay Viennese and depriving the good-natured Hungarians – who, as everyone knew, had really been on our side in their hearts throughout – of reasonable living space. My mother, who liked everyone to have nice feelings, used to explain and try to excuse my rude outbursts against Western policy and Western diplomacy, and my emotional pæans on behalf of the nobility and the heroism of the former enemy, as being motivated simply by a natural and creditable sympathy for the fallen and the under-dog.

It would be nice to think that she was right, and she partly was; but there was a good deal of hate as well as love in this attitude, and no doubt if the starving Hungarian landowners had never existed, it would have been necessary to invent them as an excuse for a revolt against those 'old men' who, we said, as we lounged angrily beside the Danube, had ruined our lives. If anyone doubted their malign incompetence, he had only to read the works of economist John Maynard Keynes and see how, after dragging us into the war, they had now made the most unspeakable hash of the peace. The curious alliance between the British Liberal thinker and the most extreme of Central European Nationalists, who cheerfully would have chopped his ears off had they seen the slightest profit to themselves in so doing, was one of the grotesque ironies of the period, but it was an irony which escaped people like myself. With *The Economic Consequences of the Peace* nestling beside *Der Untergang des Abendlandes* on the bedside table, and von Tános storming daily into the sitting-room with news of atrocities committed by the uncultured Serbs in the neighbourhood of Szegedin, on territory which in the interests of humanity and justice should be wholly Hungarian, one experienced a satisfactory, even an exhilarating identification with the Nationalist Cause.

The cause – and von Tános himself – offered aspects of considerable and inescapable absurdity. But these absurdities of von Tános were themselves a kind of asset or protection, for they were the fault of the Treaty of Neuilly, and thus our fault – we were the people ultimately responsible for the fact that the man often acted half-crazy.

The only time I can remember when I was seriously exasperated by him was the occasion of the orgy which he proposed to organise. He took the view that until one had experienced an orgy with Hungarian girls, one had really seen nothing. Such an orgy was particularly essential to the education of an Englishman, because of the well-known tepidity of Englishwomen. We would get a couple of these splendid Hungarian girls, and a lot of Hungarian wine, and drive out to the banks of the Danube at the edge of the great plain. There under the wide Hungarian sky we would hold our orgy. It seemed to me a splendid idea and I looked forward to it eagerly. Every day for nearly a week von Tános lectured me on the superior qualities of the Hungarian women – their capacity for passion combined with a proper submissiveness, a proper realisation of the superiority of the Hungarian man.

Then on the eve of the day set for our expedition he appeared to tell me that he would be unable to go because his wife – whose existence I had never heard of before – had somehow heard about our plan and put her foot down. I expressed amazement and irritation. He said that that was because the materialistic English did not understand the Hungarian attitude to marriage. Also they had no notion of the splendid possessiveness and devotion of the Hungarian wife towards her husband. Only in Hungary was marriage conducted on so elevated a plane. His wife, who was of course active in the women's nationalistic movement, had all the Hungarian virtues developed in the highest degree. I learned by accident later that this wife of his was a big, very strong girl who often had excesses of what she called 'temperament' and used to knock him about. She treated her 'temperament' as something separate from herself, a force for whose actions and consequences she could not reasonably be held responsible.

Von Tános liked to detect object lessons illustrative of the correctness of his general outlook, and point them out to me. They were selected, for the most part, as proofs that there was, in a general way, a tremendous lot that was rotten in the state of the victorious Powers.

One of these object lessons took the form of a certain Colonel Mahon, who was stationed in Paris but used to visit Budapest at intervals in connection with some business of disarmament. He angered the resident British representatives on the inter-Allied Disarmament Commission because, though of lower rank than they, he would go behind their backs and hobnob with the chiefs of the other inter-Allied Missions. It was understood that he was able to do this on account of being secretly the representative of some branch of the Intelligence Service. But what made him an object lesson in the somewhat confused vision of von Tános was that he was an Irishman. As such he should have been a Nationalist. It was typical, von Tános used to say, of the corrosive influence of the British Empire and the cynical attitude adopted in the West towards the national movements, that this Irish Mahon should be wearing a Colonel's uniform, obviously high up in the apparatus of the Empire, and betraying the Irish Nationalist movement. And what this in turn showed was that the Westerners had no conception of the true meaning of Nationalism and that their entire philosophy was opposed to and destructive of it. And this, he said, would certainly lean directly to Bolshevism.

Apart from his hobnobbing with the French and Italian generals, Colonel Mahon used, on his occasional visits, to get around a good deal among the Hungarian aristocrats, such as the Esterhazys and the Andrassys and would talk to them knowledgeably about horses. He told me once that his sole desire was to retire as soon as possible to his considerable estates in Tipperary – 'limestone country, my boy, only country for raising horses'. It was only the necessity for some-body or other to deal with all this disarmament business – 'someone has to watch the blighters' – that kept him 'in harness'.

Naturally Mahon deplored the entire course of events in Ireland and the Irish Nationalist revolution. On the other hand, he was entirely in favour of the Hungarian National-ists because he thought they were throwing up what he had learned to call 'a bastion' against the Bolsheviks. If one tried to draw a map of the situation one found (a) that von Tános believed Colonel Mahon was playing into the hands of the Bolsheviks by not being a Nationalist and by working with the British Imperialists, whereas (b) Mahon thought von Tános was playing straight into the hands of the Bolsheviks by failing to realise that in Ireland it was necessary to sup-press the Nationalists, but (c) that on the other hand von Tános was doing a good job as bastion by being a Hungarian Nationalist and an anti-Bolshevik. Each of them thought that his views made almost self-evident good sense. On days when Mahon felt himself under pressure, he would suddenly commandeer an armed train and race about southern Hun-gary pursuing imaginary armament producers. Von Tános said that this proved the depths of degradation to which the man had fallen.

Mahon, who stated that he had been an officer of the Mun-ster Fusiliers or some similar regiment, arrived in Budapest one day four weeks after disbandment of that regiment, and gave an enormous commiseratory party. Huge tears dropped into the champagne and brandy as we drank to the old regi-ment, the past, and the glories of long ago. Unfortunately some other branch of the Intelligence Service than that in which Colonel Mahon purported to function had in the meantime been active, and now rather tactlessly uncovered the fact that, so far from having been an officer of the Mun-ster Fusiliers, Colonel Mahon had in reality been a solicitor attached to the Army Service Corps and was not, really, either an officer or even Irish. Far less did he have an estate in Tipperary, or any knowledge of horses.

We now had a situation fairly depressing for one and all. It was a little depressing, to begin with, for Colonel Mahon – exposed as a mere impostor. He was, however, possibly the least depressed among those present at that period. In fact he mentioned to me that he had never expected that anyone could get away with everything for ever. It was depressing for von Tános, who found his estimate of the situation awry. It was most particularly depressing for the British authorities, who for months had been backing Colonel Mahon and suggesting to everyone in Hungary that he was in fact the representative of the real policy of Britain on the disarmament question. It looked, I remember saying to my father, like rather a bad quarter of an hour for Colonel Mahon.

My father disagreed. With his long knowledge of official life he pointed out that, since Colonel Mahon had in fact been the official representative of the British authorities *vis-à-vis* the Disarmament Commission, since in fact he had been represented to foreign generals and other high officers of foreign powers as a reliable and distinguished British officer, with long experience of war and also of social and sporting life, it would clearly be utterly impossible for them now to disavow him, for it would cause a loss of face.

Failing to understand him, and alarmed by what I thought was the impending fate of Colonel Mahon, a man whom I liked, I said that one ought perhaps to try to do something for him. My father remarked that it would prove entirely unnecessary to do anything whatsoever for Colonel Mahon. Colonel Mahon, he said, would shortly be confirmed in his hitherto quite bogus rank as Colonel, and would be transferred to some similar occupation, probably a little farther to the south-east. And so in fact it came to pass: Colonel Mahon was relieved of his duties in Vienna and Budapest, but reappeared, on approximately the same scale, in several Balkan capitals. The affair was of course the occasion of further disagreement between my father and myself. For I pointed out that this was but one more proof of the appalling corruption and inefficiency of the Western powers. My father said that, on the contrary, it was but one more proof of their capacity to deal with awkward situations in a quiet and efficient manner.

As for von Tános, it proved entirely impossible to explain to him what really happened. His conclusion on the matter was, however, to him satisfactory. He opined that Colonel Mahon as an intelligence officer had somehow made things too hot for him in Hungary and that as his 'cover' had been ripped off he had been simply transferred to the Balkans in order to continue his functions there. He said that probably the man was a double agent – working both for the British and the Bolsheviki. I suggested that he was an entirely single agent working exclusively in the interests of Colonel Mahon. Von Tános said that the British were a simple-minded people who had no knowledge of the real shape of the political labyrinth. He also said that were I to live long enough in Hungary I would lose the absurd naïveté which my ideas at the present expressed.

A short time before the Mahon crisis I had sat, at Oxford, for a scholarship examination. At that time the colleges were grouped for scholarship examination purposes, so that a candidate could compete for a scholarship at five or six colleges at the same time. You could, so far as I remember, state in advance that you would accept a scholarship at only one chosen college of the group, or you could indicate that you were prepared to enter any college of that group which would pay you to do so. Friends of the family, many of them military men who had never been near Oxford, said emphatically that there were only three or four colleges which it was really possible to go up to. They named them. Other friends of the family who had been at Balliol said there was only one possible college.

I had to disregard them. I cared very little what college I went to provided that I went to it almost immediately and thus got away from school. I was sitting on the terrace of the Hotel Gellért drinking iced beer and arguing with von Tános about Colonel Mahon when a telegram was brought to me. It said, 'Are you member Church of England?' After a momentary mystification I realised that I must have won a scholarship to Keble College and that membership of the college must be confined to Church of England members, or at least that only Church of England members were eligible to hold scholarships there.

I was downcast. It seemed to me extraordinarily improbable that I was any such thing. Bitterly annoyed that one's movements should be hampered by what seemed to me an irrelevant obstacle, I took the telegram to my father and said despondently that it seemed that my first raid on the scholarship front had failed. He immediately asked me whether at any time I had secretly but formally been converted into any other faith? Had I, for example, been received into the Roman Catholic or Mohammedan Church? Since most of my ideas at that time appeared to him strange and even perverse, he would not have been surprised to hear that I had secretly become a Buddhist. When I told him 'No,' he said that in that case everything was in order. It seemed that once one has been baptised a member of the Church of England, one automatically retains membership for the rest of one's life unless one is formally received into some other faith. Profoundly relieved, I telegraphed to Keble saying, 'Yes.'

V OXFORD ACCENT

AN AUNT OF MINE ONCE SENT ME A DEAD SCORPION as a birthday present – she was travelling in the West Indies at the time. It fell out of a little box on to the breakfast table and the letter that fell out with it explained that she had chosen it because it was characteristic of the fauna of those parts and thus, in her opinion, more interesting and instructive than the kind of souvenirs ordinarily sold to tourists. She never sent me anything else and I thought that in the years that followed we had entirely lost touch.

However, an incident which occurred after I had been a couple of years at Oxford showed that this was not the case. Evidently she had been following my movements and career with keen family interest. By this time she had a little house in Hampshire, and once a year on the lawn she gave a small garden party or fête, in aid of sick, aged or homeless cats. The objective, as I understand it, was to organise lodging for the homeless, to provide medical attention for the sick, and to popularise the use of lethal chambers in extreme cases. My aunt had a couple of these lethal chambers in her own possession, and at the garden party these were displayed as a centre of interest and attraction on the table beside the tea-urn. Quite a number of people stayed away from the garden parties because they were horrified and disgusted by the name and purpose of these devices. Newcomers, suddenly confronted with them over the tea-cups, sometimes trembled and turned sick. My aunt said that the people who stayed away were obviously no good to man or beast anyway, and that for the others it was an educative experience.

My aunt, who looked rather like the well-known bust of

Julius Cæsar except that she had a lot of white hair and wore on top of it a hat in the fashion of 1911, used to march about among the guests in a military manner, carrying a mauve parasol which she did not open but used to emphasise points she was making in the interests of cats, waving it to draw inattentive people's notice to the lethal chambers, or prodding the lawn with it as she spoke of statistics and atrocities. She felt that hardly anyone was properly alive to what was going on, and sometimes in her indignation at apparent lethargy and indifference she would prod their feet with the parasol.

On the occasion I speak of a clergyman living in the neighbourhood brought to the garden party a young friend of his, a nondescript, rather solemn undergraduate who was down from Oxford for the long vacation. This young man took it into his head to chat knowingly and at length about the character and what he called the 'tone' of post-war Oxford. He said that of course the vast majority of undergraduates were sober, hard-working and well conducted, but one could hardly overlook and must certainly deplore the behaviour of certain flamboyant and thoroughly undesirable elements, who, because of their vulgar capacity for self-advertisement, were often treated as though they were typical of the Oxford of our day, and were getting the place a bad name in some quarters as a consequence. He knew of course, he said, that there were people who, no doubt deceived by meretricious display, thought that such persons as that awful man Evelyn Waugh, who etc. etc. etc., and an equally frightful fellow called Harold Acton, who used to shout his own poems through a megaphone and etc. etc. etc., and Robert Byron and Christopher Hollis and Basil Murray and a lot of others were 'brilliant' figures really carrying on – as they falsely pretended – the basic tradition of some older Oxford. One heard, said the nondescript young man, really hair-raising, almost unbelievable, stories of the goings-on at the club – called so appropriately the Hypocrites Club – which these elements seemed to have made their headquarters.

The group around the tea-urn tutted and listened with keen interest. The young man was happy to say that at length the authorities had taken action and suppressed the Hypocrites Club. Disgraceful scenes, he believed, had accompanied this suppression. The Club had given a funeral dinner at an hotel in Thame, and leading members had driven back to Oxford riotously in a glass hearse.

Delighted with the attention of his audience the young man was replying to eager questions, and repeating most of what he had already said, when the group was suddenly joined by my aunt, who had been only half listening while she demonstrated the working of the lethal chamber. The undergraduate was now astounded to receive a violent prod from the point of the parasol which my aunt, coming on him from behind, jabbed painfully into his heel above the top of his shoe. Turning he found himself confronted by a pair of wobbling pince-nez through which she glared at him as furiously as though she had detected him advocating cat torture. She always had a formidable, explosive kind of stutter, and now, in her rage, she stuttered more formidably than ever.

'I don't,' she said, 'know who you are, and I don't want to know. I do know that you are a nasty little tittle-tattler and a disgrace to your university.'

The young man stared in stupefaction, the circle of other guests expanded, drawing away from the storm centre.

'I happen to know,' said my aunt – though from what source she had this information she never revealed, even to myself – 'that a number of the people you mention are not only people of distinguished talent and ability, but are also friends of my nephew, Mr Claud Cockburn, a person whom you probably have not been privileged to meet.'

'Heard of him,' mumbled the young man miserably.

'About all you're likely to do,' sneered my aunt, giving him a slight bump on the side of the calf with the parasol. 'Furthermore,' she said, 'I should advise you to be extremely careful in what you say about the Hypocrites Club of which I imagine you know absolutely nothing, for the very good reason that if you were to attempt to become a member, you would, I should say, quite certainly be b-b-blackballed.'

The young man made a feeble attempt to recover the in-itiative by saying something to the effect that he hoped he would never sink so low as to seek membership of the Hypocrites Club. My aunt shouted him down.

'All I need to tell you,' she shouted, 'about the Hypocrites Club is that my nephew is a member of its Committee.' She paused in an attitude of expectation and the young man goggled at her. My aunt hammered the lawn with the point of the parasol in a frenzy of impatience. 'Well,' she said, 'in the light of what I have just told you, surely you do not propose to remain on this lawn?'

Utterly confused, he looked vaguely around at the other guests, seeking apparently some kind of explanation or support.

'Are you daring,' said my aunt, 'to try to remain here? Get out!' And with that she lifted the parasol and hit him quite hard with it on the side of the head.

He started to run and ran right out on to the road – with the expression, as my informant at the party told me afterwards, of one who has just realised the truth of the saying that there is nothing quite so terrifying as a mad sheep.

Naturally when I heard, some time later, of this incident I was very grateful to my aunt and took an early opportunity to go down to Hampshire and see her. The episode with the young undergraduate she took as a matter of course, but being thanked for it she found a little embarrassing.

'He was,' she said, 'obviously an ignoramus. He obviously had no understanding of the quality of Oxford. Oxford has the quality of—' Here her conversation began to meander somewhat, and she spoke vaguely of places which, in their physical aspect, had struck her by their quality. She floated verbally from some night scene in Jamaica to another night scene in Venice, and concluded at the corner of a street in Amsterdam. 'But I don't,' she said, 'of course mean simply a physical quality. I mean a total quality like' – she jabbed her finger towards a bowl which was, I believe, part of the exquisite loot of the Temple of Heaven at Peking – 'that.'

I expressed my surprise that she could be so familiar with Oxford in its physical or indeed any other of its aspects. She said that she had never been there. As though in answer to some unuttered exclamation or query on my part, she added, 'What difference does that make? The whole thing is simply an idea.'

Although awed by this statement I still was able to ask her whether she did not feel that perhaps the idea might in some respects not correspond to reality. She replied briskly that she saw no reason to suppose anything of the kind. 'For example,' she said, 'this Hypocrites Club that that little jackanapes was speaking of; I imagine that no doubt a good deal of drinking and so on goes on there, but at the same time it appears to me that probably it is a centre of civilised and literary conversation. A place of a certain quality. The sort of thing, in fact,' said my aunt, 'that there is far too little of nowadays.'

I longed for her dreams of that centre of intelligence and wit to be entirely true, and for her to go on dreaming it, and as I spoke to her about it, it really seemed to me that perhaps a portion of her dream really was true; and the people I had known in that noisy, alcohol-soaked rat-warren by the river seemed to take on larger proportions, perhaps to have been in reality the kind of people that my aunt thought they were. I realised, and not for the first time, that every story can be told two ways.

Our conversation wandered across the face of Oxford. My aunt, quoting some long-forgotten commentator, said that in her opinion if the Parliament at Westminster were to be described as the mother of parliaments, then the Oxford Union Debating Society could be called the nursery of the mother. I was trapped into describing how brilliant and witty were the debates at the Oxford Union, whereupon my aunt asked me for some examples of witticisms and intelligent remarks there made. I said, 'Well, only the other day a speaker there said that there was a danger that the smaller nations of Europe would become the domes of silence upon which rested the grand piano on whose keys was being played that melancholy *Marche Militaire* which formed so unfortunately large an item in the programme of the concert of Europe.'

Even as I quoted it the phrase struck me as shockingly laboured and feeble – shockingly, in fact, everything that the critics of Oxford said was typically Oxonian. My aunt, however, merely murmured, 'Delightful,' and then after a pause, 'although I personally should say a trifle mannered.'

Characteristically, since she knew Latin but no Greek, my aunt expressed particular interest in my Greek studies and begged me to expatiate upon them. In the same manner she, who in the way of philosophy had been brought up on Locke and Hume and nothing else, was almost humbly anxious to know what had gone in the philosophical line since then. I told her truthfully that my own philosophy tutor was a man who appeared to take the view that philosophy was something like alcohol – amusing and possibly stimulating if taken in moderation, but no use as a sustaining food. Of any philosophical idea less than two hundred years old he would say, 'I think you'll find that it's pretty well been exploded.' Once, straight back from Budapest with a volume of philosophy which had just appeared there, and which he could not possibly have read, I hurried to him saying that I thought this was something really worthy of all our attention. He kept the book for a few hours and on returning it to me remarked, 'I rather gather that the man is likely pretty soon to be exploded.'

'That,' said my aunt, truthfully, 'is very Oxford.'

At this piece of complacency – so Anglo-English, so un-Scottish as it seemed to me – I rather forgot myself and began to complain of the Oxfordish character of Oxford. I said that the whole thing went on far too long – my own course of 'Greats' took four years – and this was, in my opinion, I said, simply another device of the kind so prevalent in England to keep people from growing up until they were practically middle-aged. 'And please,' I begged of my aunt, 'do not say that one is, after all, absorbing atmosphere.'

I could see that in fact this was precisely what she had been intending to say, for she replied, too quickly, that it had not occurred to her to say any such thing.

In my aunt's tiny drawing-room, which smelt of tea and warm hay, I was overcome by the nostalgia which at that time I felt more and more strongly for Central Europe, and in consequence spoke wildly and harshly. In the crudest fashion I sought to depict the contrast between what I considered to be 'the realities' of Hungary and Austria and the 'artificiality' of Oxford. I did it badly, partly because I did not in the fullest sense of the term know what I was talking about.

There was some truth in it all the same. Despite everything, despite even the casualty lists of the war years, it would have been just possible at Oxford to imagine that the First World War had not taken place – or at least that it had been merely a big, ugly, necessary episode, in the sense envisaged by my father. Above all it was a fact that for most of us the Bolshevik Revolution remained a nearly irrelevant event. People who regarded it with horror, and those who looked upon it with at least a tepid enthusiasm, were unconsciously at one in viewing it with a more or less comfortable detachment, rather in the mood of people going to see a novel play or a technically revolutionary film. I took the same attitude myself. I told my aunt violently that Oxford was a place where everyone was complacently waiting the moment when any new idea would be 'exploded', whereas in Budapest it was only the old and the traditional which people expected at any moment to blow up. I thought I was speaking rather eloquently on the political and social situation, but my aunt said suddenly, 'It's all a question, you know, of the light.'

'The light?'

'Yes,' she said. 'It's a matter of the way in which the nerves of any given person's eyes react to different qualities of light. All the rest – politics, people and so on – are relatively unimportant. It is one's reaction to a particular quality of light which makes one happy or unhappy in a place.'

I had told her that the valley of the Danube was the first area in which I had ever felt immediately and completely at home, not after months or even days of living there, but immediately – within an hour. And this was true at the time, although since then I have twice experienced this same sense of being immediately at home in an entirely strange place – once in New York and once in Oklahoma City.

My aunt said there was nothing unusual in my feeling about the Danube valley, it was simply that the quality of the light in that particular area happened to be the one which I found simultaneously most stimulating and soothing to the nerves. In the same way, the light quality of the Thames valley was evidently unsuited to me.

I believe now that there really is something in this theory, although at the time it appeared to me bizarre. My aunt seemed to be treating as mere secondary trivialities the factors in the situation which I regarded as most important. After discoursing for a short time on this theory of light, she remarked casually, 'And of course having enough money is so important too. I don't suppose you have enough.'

I said that nobody had. She said, 'I should very much like to give or at least lend you some. It is a pity that the cats take all the spare money I have.'

I said that naturally I entirely understood, and I did, although it did seem rather a pity that there was not enough for all of us. For by this time my debts were relatively enormous – enormous, that is, in relation to any prospect there seemed to be of ever meeting them. They seemed to rise uncontrollably like flood water, without any reference to my efforts to increase my income. For a while I edited the Oxford University weekly paper the *Isis*, I wrote a weekly column during term time for one of the Oxford City papers, and occasionally I sold articles or a short story elsewhere. None of it seemed to make any difference, and the situation was the more harassing because, having for more than two years done almost no work of any kind which could be considered useful for the purposes of my final examinations, I now found myself compelled to get up at 6.30 to start reading, to read intensively most of the day and to dose myself with caffeine tablets so as to keep awake and working until two or three in the morning. I had never been able to attend lectures because they, like public speeches, drove me to a frenzy of boredom and impatience. I never could understand why the lecturers could not spend the time writing down what they had to say and distributing it in convenient pamphlet form. But, although not having attended lectures was supposed to be disastrous, and was naturally regarded with great disfavour by one's tutor, I did not myself find it much of a handicap, particularly as most of the lectures which I had missed a year or so before had by now dropped into print somewhere. All the same, the amount of reading to be done was prodigious and the repeated irruption of duns distracting.

Also at about this time my father had finally retired for the last time. The Financial Commission had completed its work, and in any case it became more and more apparent that the whole conception of the job in Budapest being an economy, a means of actually saving money, was an utter illusion. In these circumstances it was natural that my family should begin to hint, although in the simplest and most tactful possible way, that perhaps I really ought to be starting to think what I was going to do for a living when I came down from Oxford.

Driven by extreme distaste for committing myself at this stage to any particular career, a thought which gave me a kind of claustrophobia as though one were entering a tunnel, I sought almost frantically for possible means of evading such a commitment, and at length discovered the existence of a Travelling Fellowship offered by Queen's College to anyone who had secured first- or second-class honours in the final examinations. Apparently there was a rich man called Laming who had come to the conclusion that British representatives abroad, diplomatic and otherwise, were below par, and he had endowed this Fellowship so that people intending to enter the Foreign Service, or to function more or less permanently abroad in some other capacity, should be enabled, after coming down from Oxford, to reside for two years in any country or countries of their choice on an annual income of £250. And although in most countries of modern Europe this sum would hardly keep a person in cigarettes, at that time there were a number of places where a student without financial obligations to anyone but himself could live in comfort and freedom on that amount.

I immediately decided that his was the answer to my problem. My father was understandably downcast at the news. I would come down from Oxford at midsummer, and the examination for the Fellowship did not take place until the spring of the following year. It meant that months would go by without my attempting to find a job, and supposing at the end of that period I did not get the Fellowship after all? If I did not want to go into the Foreign Office, why should I not accept the job of private secretary to Mr Marquis of Liverpool – now Lord Woolton? In a moment of financial despair I had, in fact, appeared with several score other applicants to be interviewed by Mr Marquis. I was chosen. For an hour or two I was elated. Then claustrophobia overcame me, and I was now preparing to write to Liverpool saying I had changed my mind. My father pointed out that there were after all only Four Fellowships given each year, and they were competed for, presumably, by hundreds of the brightest people in the University. For two days the whole project of the Fellowship filled my father with gloom and foreboding. On the third day he suddenly remarked characteristically, 'I've been thinking this thing over and it seems to me that if this is what you want to do, the best thing to do is do it.'

VI VILLAGE ON THE ROCKS

THERE WAS A NOISE AS THOUGH SOMEBODY HAD emptied a bag of machinery over a dog. It was going to happen every morning, but this was the first time, and I woke, crying like a stage character just coming to after a blow, 'Where am I?'

The answer to that was that I was in a village in the Cévennes, and that this was the beginning of the first stage of the advance towards the Fellowship and all that it implied.

Since modern languages were an important feature of the Fellowship examination, it was necessary for me to improve my French. And since somewhere around ten shillings a week was all I could afford, it was necessary for me to find the cheapest place in France. This village in the mountains, strung out, gaunt and beautiful, between the rocks and the broad pebbly beaches of the Gard, with bad roads and a railway line that went nowhere else, attracted no tourists from anywhere outside the immediate area, and existed, in frozen or torrid isolation in winter or summer, hardly aware of what was happening to the cost of living outside.

Dazed by the sudden noisy awakening, I lay in bed for a moment staring out at the mountainside up to where even the scrub could grow no more and the naked rock blazed in the morning sun. There was another crash and yell outside the door. Rushing to it I saw a puny young man lying upside down on the steep stone stair, with his head sticking through the frame of a stylish-looking racing bicycle which was lying on top of him. I dragged the bicycle off him, he staggered to his feet, introduced himself. He was Lemoyne, the tax-collector's clerk.

Like most of the unmarried *fonctionnaires* of the village, he lived in this hotel. Twenty years earlier the overworked insides of a massively stone-walled silk factory in the main street had collapsed of old age during the night, and the owner, who had in the meantime turned his attention to speculation in Russian bonds, had thought it not worth while to repair them. Then a M Luzeau, a well-to-do peasant on the make, bought the place for a speculation, carpentered its insides together in a ramshackle fashion and opened the building up again as an hotel. It was named the Grand Hotel Splendide of Spain and of the Rising Sun.

Lemoyne's room was on the fifth floor above mine. Every evening he carried his bicycle up the five flights of steep and narrow stairs, and manœuvred it into his room where he placed it upside down beside the bed, carefully locking its back wheel with a chain and padlock. He had previously been stationed in the tax office of a village not far from Lille, splendid cycling country with miles of straight flat road. There his parents had presented him with this very fine racing bicycle – handlebars swooping towards the ground, narrow red tyres and all the rest of it. He went all over the Lille district like the wind. Then he was transferred to this mountainous area of the Cévennes.

His office was exactly one door away from the door of the hotel. Every morning he unlocked his bicycle and carried it – almost always with disastrous interludes – down the stairs again, mounted it, and dashed off in the opposite direction to that in which his office lay. He tore down one of the only flat streets in the village, left at the bottom up a steep incline, left again along the only other flat street, left again down a steep incline, left again into the main street, and so to the office door. There he with difficulty manhandled the bicycle into the tiny room, padlocked the wheel, worked through the morning, unlocked the machine again, and rode back right round the village to the hotel, and while he had lunch locked it again and put it within view against the wall of the dining-room. Before and after the afternoon's work the process was repeated.

I asked if it might not be more practical to leave the bicycle downstairs at night locked up somewhere. He shook an emaciated finger at me and looked at me out of the corners of his eyes. 'I don't know,' he said, 'how it may be in other parts of the world, my dear sir. I don't presume to speak of them. But you can take it from me that here in this village people have bad characters.'

He added that he was nineteen years old and begged me not to believe for a moment that he would stay for ever in this desperate hole in the mountains. 'Things at present,' he said, 'are bad, but I have reason to believe that next year they will be different.'

His attitude turned out to be symptomatic, for it really was quite a normal village. That is to say it pulsated with desires it could no longer satisfy and energies it could no longer reward. It festered with the remains of many lives that had somehow been brought to nothing much. It throbbed – sometimes it seemed to bursting-point – with passion and effort and the hope of better things.

Despite its isolation, it still lay under the heavy cloud of the war which was supposed to have ended in glorious victory nearly eight years ago. Next year, people said hopefully, things will be better, but often it seemed that they had told themselves that too often, and were resigned to a belief that the franc would continue to crash, that France's British ally would betray France once again, that the Germans would once again cheat successfully and turn out to have won the game – that history in fact had played upon France a dirty trick which ought to be exposed and frustrated; but how? In this small place there were in fact all the signs of that national schizophrenia which occurs when the national traditions in which people have been brought up fail, too markedly and abruptly, to correspond with reality.

Besides those who actually lived there, almost all the other *fonctionnaires* and 'white collar' employees in the village took their meals *en pension* at the Grand Hotel Splendide of Spain and the Rising Sun. Among them were the tax collector himself, the *Receveur d'Enregistrements*, the schoolmaster and also the engineers who were working on the railway, the manager of the local tannery and the visiting agent of an exporting business operating to Indo-China.

There were a few people also who came to spend the summer holidays in this section of the mountains because, although hot, it was cheap. These included a retired apothecary and a small business man's family from Nîmes, and two Annamite medical students from the University of Montpellier. Not among those present was the friend of a French acquaintance of mine, who had been supposed to be resident in this village and likely to help me out with my arrangements. But he had left the place for good. Everyone said he was very lucky. They also said, without having any evidence, but by way of giving the lucky one a parting kick in the behind, that there was no doubt that by this time he was engaged in the black-market currency business in Paris and helping to ruin the country for his own profit.

By this time the elder Luzeau was a very old carcass of a man, with fierce smoky eyes, who looked you up and down as though he thought he had better make haste to swindle you before you could swindle him. He sat for most of the time in the kitchen, shelling beans. Luzeau junior, a man of about thirty, ran the hotel and speculated on the side in every commodity and transaction which might yield a profit. He was what the Irish call 'a desperate chancer'. He bounded about acrobatically, all muscle and spring right up to his tough black hair which quivered on top of his head like an electrified bundle of wires. To the impudence of this man there was absolutely no limit. It was sublime. Declaring 'we are all friends here', he refused to give any of the guests keys for their bedrooms, and in consequence was able to steal freely from all of them. Once he invited three of the guests to have a drink with him in the café up the road, and, when they came, there was young Luzeau wearing a quite unmistakable silk shirt stolen from one of them and gripping awkwardly between ill-fitting false teeth a carved pipe which was the property of the second. Stupefied by this audacity, the two victims supposed that at least the man had now reached the ultimate peak of imaginable insolence, until a mumbled drooling cry from the third revealed that the dentures now shining in Luzeau's mouth were in fact a set which had disappeared from the wash table of the third guest during the night and were now being actually flashed in his face.

Accused point-blank, young Luzeau would work himself into a passion of moral indignation, denouncing evil speakers and slanderers. He made no pretence of supposing that any-one believed him innocent, but he knew that they knew that they had to live in the village to carry on their jobs, and that there was nowhere except the hotel where one could lodge or eat. If there had been, young Luzeau and his father together would certainly have rapidly made things too hot for anyone offering lodging or nourishment to refugees from the Splendide. Sometimes old Luzeau was called in to cow the guests and deal with signs of mutiny.

At dinner on my first night in this hotel, where I certainly did hope to learn French, the *pensionnaires* were all gathered at a long communal table, the low room being lit in the early dark of the south by three smoking oil lamps. The electricity had failed. The *Receveur d'Enregistrements*, a gay young man called Barrot, who had been brought up by the Jesuits and had already done his military service in North Africa, informed me that this failure was due to no fault in the electric wiring but to a fault in some contract signed by the municipality for the village electricity supply, a fault which enabled the local contractor to cut it off on the ground of alleged failure whenever he wished and charge the village all the same. People, he said, had somewhat bad characters.

But the loud protests of the *pensionnaires* with which the dining-room was now buzzing were not against this familiar failure of the electric light, but against the fact that mutton had been served as the main dish for the fifth day in succession. People, even the grey apothecary, were banging their plates with their forks, in a genteel manner, and shouting, 'Why all this sheep, sheep, sheep? Why not a bit of pork for a change?' As the noise became overpowering, there could be heard coming from the kitchen the flap-flap of old Luzeau's flimsy slippers on the tiled floor. He came in

70

trailing sparks from a badly made cigarette, holding in one hand a candle and in the other a bottle.

He glared at everyone, and the apothecary, who was 'chairman' of the long table for the week, got tremulously but furiously to his feet and made a speech. It was irrelevant to the question of whether we had mutton for dinner or not, but highly relevant to the state of mind of everyone in that village in that summer of 1926. He related the food situation at the Hôtel Splendide in this village to the European situation in general. One had been attacked, half-massacred, and was now in process of being swindled. It was dubious whether Germans, for example, would be forced to eat sheep five times a week. Looking even farther afield, he said that subversive influences were at work everywhere. He begged us to take a look at the state of the currency, the condition of the Stock Market, above all the condition of French investment in Indo-China. Everywhere, he said, these influences were active. He made no allegations but personally he had his suspicions.

At that he glared prolongedly at the two Annamite students who sat at the foot of the table holding hands. The speech made a powerful effect upon the guests, which was a little damped by the fact that in the middle of it old Luzeau disappeared, slap-slapping his slippers into the kitchen. By those in a position to peer down the half-smoke-filled passage, he could be seen sitting there with his bottle and his candle evidently waiting until the speech should be over. The moment the apothecary had reseated himself, old Luzeau came slapping up the passage again, holding the candle and the bottle, and began slowly to circle the table with the candle held immediately behind the bottle so as to illuminate its contents like a magic lantern. This bottle he thrust solemnly in the face of each of the *pensionnaires* in turn. Inside it could be seen a long worm, some inches of it standing upright, and the rest of it lying, coil upon coil, on the bottom of the bottle. Not only was it very, very long but rather thick too.

'You see that worm?' Luzeau kept saying over and over again to each of the guests in his husky, angry voice. 'You see that worm? Well, in 1918 that worm was taken out of me – me that am talking to you. In 1918 we had pork here in August and I ate it and what happened? Later, that worm grew inside me and had to be taken out, and I had it preserved in a bottle just as you see it. That's why

71

there is no pork, and never will be here in the Hôtel Splendide.'

The company was naturally overawed by this exhibition, and for a long minute or two after old Luzeau had gone off to the kitchen again with the bottle and candle there was an appalled silence and the subdued diners went to work on the mutton. The apothecary shook with futile rage but remained silent until much later in the meal, when we had all drunk a good deal of the startlingly thick and rough local *vin ordinaire*. He then began again to make a fiercely argument-ative speech. He said that if pork had been tainted to that extent in the summer of 1918, that had been due entirely to the war, to the gross mismanagement of everything, to the weakening of proper government. It was common knowledge, he said, that plagues of the most sinister character were carried during the war across the battlefields from the east. This pig disease might, for instance, very well have come from Russia, from the Polish borders, where it was well known that corpses were piled up in monumental masses, and that, owing to the uncivilised character of the people, pigs were allowed to root around among them.

He begged us to reflect that we were already in the year 1926 and it was scandalous to suppose that any such danger should exist now. If it did, this must be considered a by-product of the situation in which France had been notably let down by her allies – here he turned a sarcastic glance upon myself – and was the victim of a series of conspiracies on the part of the Germans, and also on the part of sub-versive influences which etc. etc. etc. He turned his glare once again upon the Annamite students, who maintained an air of calm – unless the fact that they were still tightly holding hands was a sign of agitation, a need for demon-strative solidarity.

As matters turned out, this episode proved to be something of a turning-point in the existence in this village of that sad old apothecary. Sad, naturally, for here he was with the money for his declining years invested in Indo-Chinese securities, here were these Annamites right in our midst and doubtless connected with subversive elements, here in fact was his world going to hell in a handcart, with nothing to eat but hard mutton, and on top of that he had to be insulted by a man like old Luzeau.

Every morning after breakfast, which consisted of a bowl of milky coffee upon which the flies sat nearly as thick as locusts, the apothecary could be seen walking in the gravelled garden of the hotel, in the shadow of the mountains which hid the early sun, his fingers twitching behind his back and his lips twitching in heaven knows what calculations and imprecations. On the other side of the gravel walked the Annamites in ostentatious enjoyment of the cool of the morning, and of the blueness of this side of the mountain below the peak already blazing in the sun, and the rising buzz of the insects.

Most of his fellow guests believed in that loquacious old apothecary. He was ridiculous, of course; but how, except on the supposition of malign forces at work in the world, could one account for everything that went wrong? How else, for example, account for the terrible and overpowering fact that, despite the ending of the war, despite the sacrifices and the victory, things refused to 'return to normal'? Lemoyne, the tax-collector's clerk, after sweating four times a day round the quadrangle of the village streets on his racing bicycle, sneered at the apothecary because he was a *rentier*, but he was suspicious of the Annamite students, too – they might be the kind of people who came over here and were respons- ible for the shortage of jobs. He disclosed to me that the apothecary had bribed the postmistress to allow him to examine the correspondence reaching the Annamites – that is to slip out of their covers the newspapers which occasionally reached them from Brussels. He was looking for subversive literature. And what, asked Lemoyne, did this prove? It proved that everyone had bad characters – the apothecary be- cause he was a dirty old man living on income from capital, and thus in a position to bribe public officials; the postmistress because she was susceptible to such bribes; and the Annamites because they were living in France and yet receiving what one could hardly doubt must be subversive literature from a foreign capital. This demonstration of the general vileness of people's characters Lemoyne found soothing. At least it explained why one was temporarily stuck here in this moun- tainous area with a racing bicycle and no flat roads to whizz along.

Barrot the *Receveur* also despised the apothecary, but on the ground that, although visibly impotent, he had made a ridi- culous attempt to seduce the daughter of the local Protestant pastor in a hedge behind the lumpy field which was called the tennis court. Sometimes, coming right down to it, he would opine that probably what he – Barrot – really had against

c*   73

Asiatics was that he felt that in some mysterious way they had a better time than Europeans – more women, for example. I asked him whether he really believed this widespread European theory that everyone else has a better time with sex than the Europeans or the other whites. He replied that it didn't, in point of fact, seem probable, but that, just in case, the thing for us to do was to go out and even up the score. This evening-up of the score took up a good deal of our time, and in the end led deviously to my becoming, for a short time, a French Government official.

It happened that one week Barrot fell madly in love with a girl who lived in the department of the Lozère, and he wanted to close his office for a few days in order to visit her. He rather often fell in love with girls in neighbouring departments, and in consequence his office was often shut for days at a time. So far as the business of the office was concerned, this would scarcely have mattered, but unfortunately at this time Barrot had become a pawn in a complicated political intrigue. He was a Royalist, and when drunk on the *vin du pays* used to roll through the streets singing, *'Les rois ont fait la France, Mais à la France il faut un roi,'* which gave great offence to the majority of the village people. Also, as I have said, he was a Roman Catholic and this village was – like the greater part of the Cévennes – a stronghold of French Protestantism, and the majority of those who were not Protestants were violently anti-clerical. Just what the background and ultimate objective of the intrigue were I never found out. Certain it was, however, that it involved giving the Catholics and the Royalists a black eye by exposing Barrot as a ne'er-do-well who, in order to pursue women like a satyr over the length and breadth of France, was in the habit of closing his office and leaving the industrious citizenry of the village – whose taxes, be it noted, paid the salary of this licentious scallywag – to stand in long queues in the blazing sun in order to obtain the official services which they had a right to expect from this particular office.

Having come to the conclusion that to close the office once again would probably be fatal, Barrot suddenly brightened up and suggested that the whole matter would be solved if I were to take on the job and keep the place open. I implored him to entertain no such idea. The political uproar, I said, would be worse than ever. Already the English were held generally responsible for the fall of the franc, the rise of Germany and the bad state of affairs obtaining everywhere. He brooded

74

briefly and then said, 'But I thought you were a Scotsman?'

I replied that this was indeed the case, but that, however important the difference might appear to me, it was unlikely to be taken into account by the villagers. All they would see would be an Englishman mingling in local politics and actually moving into a vital part of the local administrative service. Barrot, crazed evidently with love for the girl in the Lozère, said, 'Not at all, they all think that if you are English at all you are a damned odd sort of Englishman.'

It was a nice office with a wide verandah standing on piles above the river bed, covered with vine and shaded by trees. All the same, I never did quite get the hang of that job, although I was there for much longer than I had expected, partly because the girl in the Lozère apparently turned out even more wonderful than anticipated and Barrot, who had sworn to return within four days, could not bear to tear himself away. To begin with, most of the work seemed to consist in handing out *papier timbré* – paper, that is, which had to be used for the registration of transactions requiring to be set down on officially taxed paper. Three or four such people used to turn up each day and I kept the office open for a couple of hours for their benefit.

Then, however, something happened which caused me to realise that probably Barrot had had other motives for absenting himself, in addition to the pursuit of the girl in the Lozère. It appeared that in the neighbouring village of St. André some people had recently opened a tiny hotel and had hung a sign advertising it from an upper window. By night this sign was illuminated by an electric torch fixed by the window of one of the ground-floor rooms, shining upon the sign but itself inside the room. For reasons which I never discovered, the question of the rate at which this sign should be taxed came within the scope of Barrot's department. At least when I tried to refer the whole matter to the tax-collector's office, the tax-collector furiously disclaimed responsibility.

The grievous nub of the matter was that in France an outside electric sign is taxed at a higher rate than an inside sign, and the question was whether this was outside or inside. What in fact was to be done about a sign whose effects certainly were exterior, but whose source equally certainly was internal? Having heard that the French legal system was extraordinarily precise on all points, I assumed that by leafing through Barrot's law books I should presently find a precedent. There was none, or rather there were scores, all contradictory.

My position was delicate, for I knew that were I to tax the sign at the higher rate everyone in the village of St. André, and a good many people in our own village too, would of course declare that to be proof that I had been heavily bribed by Luzeau *père et fils* to occasion a potential rival financial embarrassment. On the other hand, if I chose the lower rate, life with the Luzeaux would become almost intolerable, for they would believe, and tell everyone else, that I had been seduced by offers of extraordinarily preferential rates from the hotel in St. André and was preparing at any moment to move over there. In the end I thought the best thing to do was to play it all very slowly and carefully. So every afternoon for a week, sometimes accompanied by two gendarmes, I used to cycle over in a rather solemn procession to St. André and take elaborate measurements—for example the precise size of the sign and the length of the distance between the centre of the sign and the electric torch below.

Mercifully, just before I had to make a final decision, Barrot returned. He did not hesitate for a moment to tax the sign at the higher rate. For public consumption he said that it was a matter of French logic to realise that what is important is the effect rather than the cause. He drew an alarming picture of whole streets and blocks of buildings displaying enormous exterior signs, all of them illuminated from inside windows by advertisers cunning enough to take advantage of this loophole in the law and defraud the State of taxes properly due to it. To me he said that the hotel at St. André was a rotten little hole and the food terrible: even worse than at the Splendide. Also it was too far away for him to get over to take his meals there, and it would thus be crazy to offend the Luzeaux.

Probably there would have been a nasty political row about the whole matter of my tenancy of his office, had it not been that at this moment the Annamite crisis flared up in a fashion which distracted attention from everything else.

The aged apothecary was used to taking his coffee after lunch and dinner at the café in the tiny central square of the village, where there were set out a score or so of tin-topped tables under the plane trees. The Annamites too used to go there after lunch and dinner and sit at another table playing chess. Their presence affected the apothecary like a kind of persecution, and he would sit there talking furiously into the air about the state of the world, the fall in Indo-Chinese bonds and the pervasiveness of subversive influences.

He was one day overheard by a certain Count de Rastazac, who looked like a caricature of a ruined aristocrat; and this was reasonable, because ruined aristocrat was exactly what he was. He was tall, gaunt and olive-coloured, and although by this time about forty-five years of age, wore, with a kind of disreputable grace, suits which had been made for him in Savile Row before the war. He was a man of great impatience and used often to summon the waiter in the café by smashing his glass against the rim of the iron-topped table. He happened to do this the first time I met him, and seeming to think that some explanation was in order, he turned to me, tilted his battered, 1913-style, straw hat farther to the side of his head, and said, 'You know, I assume, that my grandfather was a second cousin of your Duke of Somerset?'

At one time he had had a lot of land and country houses in various parts of the country, and a quite large house in a good quarter of Paris. These he had gambled away, and he now lived with his beautiful seventeen-year-old daughter in a broken-roofed farmhouse, reeking of brandy, three miles from the village. He too was ready and eager to believe that some very unpleasant influences must have been at work in the world to produce this state of affairs. The wild conversation of the apothecary excited him. Why, he demanded, smashing a glass as he shouted for more drink, had the police not been informed? The apothecary stated that he had been to the police and had actually shown them copies of the newspaper which he had abstracted from the post office, but they had declared that this paper was perfectly legal and that, in default of some other evidence of subversive activity by the Annamites, nothing could be done.

Rastazac, who frequently engaged in various kinds of criminal or semi-criminal activities, which included the concealment at his farm of stolen motor cars and other goods, had his own reasons for hating the police. Nothing appeared to him more natural than that there should be an alliance between them and the subversive elements. He drank a good deal of brandy, cursing and declaiming, then suddenly dashed across the terrace towards the table where the Annamites were absorbed in their chess game. He knocked over their table with his knee and went on to beat the two little men with his fists. When they resisted he kicked them. The apothecary, horrified that his words should have such immediate effect in action, hurried nervously across the terrace and urged Rastazac to desist. Rastazac turned upon him snarling and declared that he did not choose to be taught his business by some dirty shopkeeper, and give him a kick on the knee which sent the old man sprawling to the ground.

It was at this point that I and my attendant gendarmes returned from our final inspection of the hotel at St. André. The gendarmes rushed at Rastazac who, fighting drunk, and delighted to find so many sectors of the enemy forces all within reach, first lashed out at them, and then, before they could get a firm hold on him, drew a pistol from his hip pocket and started firing wildly. He was overpowered and arrested, but, with a kind of tolerance which I observed quite often in those parts, was merely beaten up, kept a night in the cells and released without any charge being made against him. Naturally this course of events was explained in the village on the ground that no doubt he had given the police valuable information on the subject of the criminal gangs with which he so often worked.

The Annamite students continued to walk about the village hand in hand and to play chess under the trees on the café terrace, but the whole episode caused the apothecary to lose face. After all, people said, he had been the cause of an unseemly disturbance. He had made charges which, however true they might be, he had been unable to substantiate. Furthermore, he had got himself involved in a brawl – had actually been struck to the ground; a really ludicrous situation for a man of his age. Public opinion turned against him and he lost all authority, even when it was again his turn to be chairman of the long table at the hotel *pension*. People interrupted him and shouted him down in the middle of the pronouncements he was fond of making on various subjects. Angered, he decided to cut short his holiday and return to Nîmes.

Even the departure of this unhappy old man was marred by farce. Only one train visited this village daily, arriving in the mid-morning and leaving again in the late afternoon. The arrival and the departure were both affairs of importance and all the *pensionnaires* of the hotel, together with many others of the inhabitants, used to go down to the station to watch new arrivals and see off those departing.

The apothecary got into the last coach of the train and the sight of the crowd assembled outside it – several of whose members cheered and made encouraging remarks now that he was actually going – caused a revival of his self-confidence and prompted him to make a speech from the window. He

78

THE TWENTIETH BIRTHDAY NUMBER OF
READERS NEWS

September 1957 · 20th Year · Volume 20 · No. 4 · (Whole Number 239)

Winter Afternoon: a water-colour by John Nash. [Reduced from 'Modern English Painters']

ART AND LIFE

About our First 'Extra' on Modern Art: MODERN
ENGLISH PAINTERS *by Sir John Rothenstein*

ART is long and life is short—and, as life goes on, art perhaps
naturally seems longer and life even shorter. We assume that
the average RU member is acquainted with the urgent necessity
of art for a civilized existence, for, along with reading and
reflection and music, it marks one of the few consistent differences
between man and monkey. But it is a sad fact, even with those so
enlightened, that the advantages are all with dead artists. Instead
of turning our eyes to the painters among us who have a special
view of our world, we prefer those men and women long dead
who were the despised and neglected of yesteryear. So easily do
we accept the art of the past, even of the recent past, that it
seems that no struggle even occurred: that Constable did not have
to exclaim: 'Surely there is room for a natural painter!' and that
the Impressionists did not have to organize a *Salon des Refusées*.

That this attitude is by no means desperate in this country is the result, to a large extent, of the activities of Sir John Rothenstein and the wonderful things he has done in his Tate Gallery. He has indeed made modern art something of a fashion, and he has seen deserted galleries crowded to capacity with crowds which would not have disgraced a famous football ground a few miles away. Those of us who live in London find our situation much ameliorated by Sir John's activities. And he has done more than organize shows of art. He has written books, and perhaps most important of all are two volumes called *Modern English Painters*, which we are offering to RU members in one large volume as our November Extra.

Now here is a book—a rare book—written by a man who is able to accept as a matter of routine that modern artists are significant. His father, Sir William, was an artist, and young John was brought up in daily conference with men earning their living as artists. For him, modern art is not something to get used to but something that he ate with his breakfast toast. He is thus able to write a book, and has done so, which is about art but is also an immensely readable biographical study. Peculiarly free from the gobbledygook and flaccid enthusiasm which passes for art criticism in our more intellectual journals, it is 'the work of a man who passionately cares for his subject, for whom the painters and paintings he describes are vitally alive.'

We print below a note addressed by Sir John to RU members. It has, of course, the humbleness of high authority, but RU members will not be misled on that account.   J. B.

A Message from
SIR JOHN ROTHENSTEIN

IT gives me pleasure to know that my two volumes, *Modern English Painters—Sickert to Smith* and *Lewis to Moore*, are to be published in a single volume by Readers Union.

It is my conviction that English painting of the present day has been seriously undervalued, not only abroad but even at home, and I long hoped that somebody would write an account of what our painters had achieved during the present century. As nobody made such an attempt, I eventually decided to try my own hand. It has always seemed to me that the part played by 'movements' and coteries was given a far more prominent place in most histories of art than it deserved, and I accordingly based my own account not upon such ephemeral movements or deceptive groupings but upon individual artists. Believing that there is little about a man's personality or the circumstances of his life that may not be relevant to the understanding of his work, I made

The physical qualities of our book are substantial—600 large pages in one volume and containing a full 64 pages of plates. It is a book for life, and has been produced accordingly. Available elsewhere in two volumes at 65s, RU members may buy this plump and seemly volume at 27s 6d. Remember, however, that MODERN ENGLISH PAINTERS is an extra book: that is to say that if you require it you must, unless you have already ordered it, even if you have a Standing Order for additionals, order it specially. Please write to Letchworth immediately, asking for a copy and naming your supplier, or to your overseas agent. If you do this promptly, the book will arrive with your November choice.

my studies biographical as well as critical. The extreme meagreness of the published information about most of my subjects made me welcome the opportunity of assembling a quantity of information—much of it of great interest and importance—which had never been published. In this I was helped by the circumstance that, through family and official connections, I had the privilege of knowing most of my subjects personally. A first survey of a subject about which relatively little has been written, that is to say when the writer has not, except here and there, been able to rely upon the researches of predecessors, must necessarily be superseded. The present volume, however, based so largely upon first-hand information, may be of assistance to later writers, and may even survive as providing a series of contemporary portraits—and in certain instances the only contemporary portraits—of a succession of the finest English painters of the age.

RU's volume appears at a moment when there are many signs that British art is becoming the focus of lively and widespread interest abroad, particularly in the United States.

THIS MONTH'S CHOICE IS
In Time of Trouble
by Claud Cockburn [*Hart-Davis 21s; RU 5s 6d*]

THIS MONTH'S ADDITIONAL (Optional) IS
The Outsider
by Colin Wilson [*Gollancz 21s; RU 8s 6d*]

THIS MONTH'S SPECIAL (Optional) IS
The Oxford Atlas
[*Oxford University Press 50s; RU 30s*]
Have you ordered this superb Standard? Act promptly; few remain.

THE TRIBE AND THE MASS

An article by Sir Harold Nicolson on

JOURNEY DOWN A RAINBOW

by Jacquetta Hawkes & J. B. Priestley, our October Choice

IN *Journey Down a Rainbow* Jacquetta Hawkes and J. B. Priestley describe a voyage undertaken together to the United States. In the vast station vault of Kansas City they parted company. She went west to study life among the Pueblo Indians: he went south to explore the mass civilizations of Dallas and Houston. The collaboration of two such gifted writers would render any book impressive. The contrasts which, in the form of an interchange of diaries and letters, they draw between prehistoric and modern patterns of living are memorable and alarming.

Jacquetta Hawkes has a natural love for empty landscapes, ancient sites, and simple conditions. For her it was an excitement to discover communities who were actually living the sort of existence which hitherto she had been able to deduce only from shards and artifacts. She left the scrap-heaps and the advertisement hoardings which disfigure the cities and roads of America for the lovely silence of Arizona and the quiet adobe villages in which the Indians live. She felt that the long tradition of these wise but utterly powerless people constituted a reproof to our lost innocence and our fading imagination.

'I believe,' she writes, 'it to be not only a happier life, but one more worthy of our kind.' Surely it was preferable for men and women to 'live humbly as badgers' rather than to surrender their souls to the hard hurry of machines? Clearly we cannot now return to inhabiting mud huts beside the stream; but 'can we not, like the Pueblos, make some conscious refusals?' Can we not learn from them that individuality, mind, and the imaginative qualities are bound to perish unless we cultivate 'peace, privacy, and some loveliness?' Her protest and her warning are as gentle as a marimba thrumming a threnody in the dusk.

The voice of J. B. Priestley, answering her from Dallas or Houston, is not gentle in the least: it is one long yell of fury at the degradation of human values. True it is that, as most visiting Englishmen, he starts his book with a few ritual gestures of apology. He expresses the hope that nothing he has written will cause his American hosts to regret their kindness: he assures them that he has 'a deepening affection' for all that is best in the American Idea, he assures them that they deserve a better civilization than the one they have created. Having gone through

4

these propitiatory formulas, he rolls up his shirt-sleeves, grasps his cricket bat, and with true West Riding vigour starts laying about him right and left.

I quite see that the circumstances were not favourable. Mr Priestley is a sensitive man who believes deeply in the value of the individual and in the pursuit of beauty and happiness. He is readily bored, loathes humbug, and is subject to afternoon fits of loneliness. The Shamrock Hotel at Houston, with all its splendour, aroused moods in him when he longed to fling himself on his bed and have a quiet cry. I am not surprised that his letters to Jacquetta Hawkes should manifest distaste: the sales resistance that he developed was acute and vociferous.

The age of the common man, he felt, seemed liable to produce only 'a dumb drilled mob.' The energy and enthusiasm which the Americans devote to egalitarianism is in danger of creating stupidity and vulgarity:

'There was a time when stupid people had to make some effort to understand and enjoy what was in print. But now every foolish or dangerous prejudice, every moronic symptom, every gaping idiocy is carefully catered for, endlessly flattered.'

To him cultural democracy has about it 'something vindictive.' The good, the valuable, are being buried 'under a mountain of rubbish.' 'Nothing,' he writes, 'can keep its true proportions, everything loses its real character.'

The restlessness of the Americans has rendered them 'the tuneless gipsies of the machine age.' They do not begin to understand how to keep quiet or to remain still: 'they are probably not afraid of anything except silence.' The only things he seems to have appreciated in the epic of America were their unselfconsciousness when dancing in fancy dress and the way they fried shrimps.

[continued on page 8

NEXT MONTH'S CHOICE IS
Journey Down a Rainbow
by Jacquetta Hawkes and J. B. Priestley
[*Heinemann & Cresset 18s; RU 5s 6d*]
NEXT MONTH'S ADDITIONAL (Optional) IS
Old Fourlegs: The Story of the Coelacanth
by J. L. B. Smith [*Longmans 21s; RU 10s*]
Copies remain. Order now.
NEXT MONTH'S EXTRA (Optional) IS
Under Milk Wood
by Dylan Thomas [*Dent 9s 6d; RU 5s 6d*]
Copies remain. Order now.
To be published on Saturday, October 5

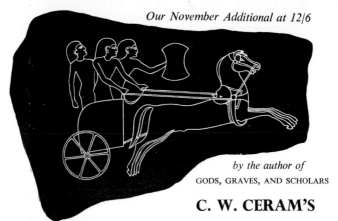

by the author of
GODS, GRAVES, AND SCHOLARS

C. W. CERAM'S

NARROW PASS, Black Mountain
The Discovery of the Hittite Empire

OLDER members of RU will remember that the choice for June 1954 was C. W. Ceram's *Gods, Graves, and Scholars*, which soon went out of print and became one of the most sought-after RU titles. In addition to this success, we received so many appreciative letters that when we heard that a new book by Ceram was to be published we naturally read it at the first opportunity, and having read it we made immediate efforts to obtain it for our members.

Narrow Pass, Black Mountain is complementary to the earlier book, since it can be regarded as a long and important chapter which was missing from it. Here is the story of the discovery of the Hittite Empire —which vanished 3,000 years ago and was *unknown* to the Greeks and Romans. It was thought that the Hittites were little more than one of the small peoples of Canaan and in large part legendary. But we now know that there was an empire that dominated the Near East, at one time conquering Babylon.

In his exciting and readable style, Mr Ceram traces the story from the first sensational reports of A. H. Sayce in the 1870's, which led to the new science of Hittitology, to the present-day investigations of Professor Bossert, whose expeditions the author accompanied.

Professor Albright, reviewing the book in the *New York Herald Tribune*, said: 'Ceram paints an unforgettable picture of this remarkable civilization. His book will enjoy an unusual success, as did *Gods Graves, and Scholars*,' whilst *The Times* wrote: 'He has made a fascinating story out of romantic material.'

Originally published by Gollancz and Sidgwick & Jackson at 25s, it is in RU at 12s 6d. Standing Orders apply and a big demand is expected. If you do not have a Standing Order and would like a copy, please order from Letchworth, naming your supplier, or, if overseas, from your usual supplier.

'The Magazine
of the Fifties'

WHY is *ENCOUNTER*, edited by Stephen Spender and Irving Kristol, by far the most widely read and eagerly discussed of the monthlies? A Cambridge student gave perhaps the best answer to this question when he wrote in the *New Statesman*: '*ENCOUNTER* is the one periodical that truly expresses the Fifties. It has articles about foreign events and trends, is markedly international in outlook, and is well aware of the new forces in society to-day.'

This tribute emphasizes, of course, only one of *ENCOUNTER*'s many virtues—its alertness to political and social trends. Those whose main interest is literature, art, or philosophy will find *ENCOUNTER* equally rewarding. What else would you expect with contributors as stimulating as Malcolm Muggeridge, Edmund Wilson, W. H. Auden, A. J. P. Taylor, Aldous Huxley, Angus Wilson, Cyril Connolly, Kingsley Amis, Arthur Koestler, and H. R. Trevor-Roper?

And don't forget that because *ENCOUNTER* is edited with such a lively sense of continuity, you'll enjoy it far more if you read it regularly.

To **ENCOUNTER, 25 Haymarket, London, S.W.1**

I enclose 36*s* for a year's subscription.

NAME. . . . .
(*Block letters throughout, please*)

ADDRESS . . . .

RU

continued from page 5]

Mr Priestley is not angry merely; he is seriously alarmed. He fears that the disease may prove infectious. He fears that the alternations in the American soul between hopefulness and despondency, between ecstasy and despair, may lead to a really perilous state of hysteria, such as 'could soon stampede crowds into lunatic action.' He fears that the giant of the modern world may not after all remain a benevolent giant, but that his rage at not being accorded the love for which he longs may render him suicidal, dragging all us little satellites into the abyss. I am not surprised that Mr Priestley, feeling as he does, fearing what he fears, should have longed to sit on his bed in the Shamrock and have a cry.

The type of mass civilization depicted is admittedly a most terrible type, and one which may well scale the ancient parapets of Europe and render us sick over here. Too blind a faith in the self-evidence of equality (which is but a deliberate form of belief) may certainly lead to a decline in human values and to disrespect for all eminence, whether cultural or ethical. I agree with Mr Priestley that there is a section of American opinion which tends to decry scholarship, taste, learning, knowledge, and even truth, as things that are fit only for the egg-heads and the highbrows. But I do not agree that this dry-rot will permanently destroy the healthy majority.

I know a few Americans who will read this book and agree with its analysis and its warnings; but they are the Americans who have escaped from their own noise to Arizona or the Berkshire hills. The citizens of Houston do not read books. This is a pity, since this joint work contains much that is wise and fine.

(Reprinted by kind permission of the *Observer*)

TO ALL MEMBERS
—A Reminder

YOU CAN GET THREE PAST CHOICES OR A BOOK TO THE VALUE OF 15s FREE IF YOU INTRODUCE A NEW MEMBER TO RU

Details July *Readers News* or from RU, London

READERS NEWS
is the magazine of Readers Union, and is distributed only to members
Editor : Oliver Caldecott
Selection Committee : John Baker, E. F. Bozman, F. J. M. Dent, A. J. Hoppé, A. E. Pigott, W. G. Taylor
Editorial, Production, Sales, address : 38 William IV St, London, W.C.2
Accounts and Distribution, address : Letchworth Garden City, Hertfordshire
Membership in Great Britain may be made through any bookshop or a prospectus |may be obtained from RU, London
EXCLUSIVE AGENTS OVERSEAS
Australia : Robertson & Mullens Ltd 107-113 Elizabeth Street, Melbourne
New Zealand : Paul's Book Arcade Ltd P.O. Box 928, Hamilton
Holland : Jacs G. Robbers Sint Annenstraat 3, Amsterdam—C
Inquiries and orders in these territories should be so addressed. Others, overseas, please apply direct to Readers Union Ltd, London, England.

was, he said, leaving us, but let everyone remember what he had so often said and remain permanently on the alert. Only thus could France be saved from the perils which encircled her.

It was quite a long speech, in the course of which he repeated almost everything that he had ever said, and before it ended the locomotive puffed off, dragging the rest of the train after it, but leaving the apothecary's coach stationary, because somebody had forgotten to couple it to the coach ahead. Everyone dashed along the line yelling at the driver, who finally brought his machine to a halt. But he said it would be too much trouble and take too much time to manœuvre the whole train backwards so as to get the last coach coupled to it, and to bundle out with his baggage and trot along the line to join the waiting train. His valedictory speech was entirely spoiled.

Although the sun still blazed and the grasshoppers whirred all day on the mountainside, the approach of the melancholy southern winter could already be felt in spirit. 'Now it will soon be winter' was the phrase everyone used to explain everything that happened – the way a person felt, an outburst of bad temper, a cloud over the sun. The agent of the exporting business was prepared to pay someone's third-class fare to accompany him to Vienna provided that the person concerned could speak some German and liked drinking wine. He was to be in Vienna for three days and needed a congenial guide who spoke German. I gladly seized the opportunity.

Just before we left, Barrot told me that according to reports in the village my travelling companion was not a *bona fide* agent of the exporting company at all but some kind of smuggler, or even a spy who had come to the village to lie low. Before we finally left everyone warned me against him, but I supposed that this was only a final instance of the firm local belief in the badness of everyone's character.

However, before we had completed our journey, travelling via Marseilles and Venice, he was arrested on the Austrian frontier and it was with difficulty that I escaped arrest myself. With great courtesy the agent, spy or smuggler or whatever else he may have been, exerted himself to make it clear to the authorities on the frontier that our connection was purely accidental, or at least had nothing to do with his real business.

In Vienna, where I had intended to polish my German to Fellowship standard, I soon became so poor that I could not

79

afford the type of instruction I wanted. I moved for a couple of weeks to Luxembourg, where life at that time was cheaper than almost anywhere else in Europe and where one had the advantage of being able to converse alternately in German or French. In London for the final six weeks or so before the Fellowship examination, someone lent me a flat in Blooms-bury. But, although I was used to being poor, I was also used to centrally heated rooms or at least – as during those dank Oxford winters – to a small room with a huge fire. The rooms of this Bloomsbury apartment so kindly lent to me were large and I could not afford fuel, so that when I was tired of read-ing in bed – a thing I in any case detest – I used to buy a penny ticket on the underground and take my books down to the platform of the Warren Street tube which was com-paratively warm and fairly well lighted. There was a little bench conveniently placed under a row of lights, and pretty soon my presence there became so familiar, and the reason for it so well understood, that the kindly station staff actually unscrewed one of the bulbs and replaced it for my benefit with a bulb of more than regulation power.

I forget how many people competed for the Travelling Fellowship that year – I think a couple of hundred, or perhaps more. They looked to me horribly intelligent and some of them I gathered had spent a good part of the past month at expensive coaching establishments in Tours or Hanover. More alarming, however, was the fact that so many of them seemed so well dressed, so well groomed. The reason this was alarming was connected with the purposes of the Fellowship as defined by its Founder. It was quite understood that the sort of per-son he wanted to benefit by his Foundation ought to be not only an efficient scholar, not only have, if possible, the 'right' sort of accent, but also be the type to make a good impression at, for example, a diplomatic luncheon party. In order to examine the qualifications of candidates from this point of view, each in turn had a brief but vitally important personal interview with the Provost and dons of Queen's College.

An attempt was made to give this interview something of the character of an informal social occasion. One was ex-pected to sit at ease in a comfortable chair and was offered sherry.

When I sit at ease I like to cross the calf of one leg over the knee of the other, but unfortunately in the course of my wanderings my shoe leather had worn through utterly, and where the soles of my shoes should have been only my socks were visible. Indeed, having had to walk some distance from my rooms in the college to the place where the interview took place, I could not be sure that my exhausted socks had not given way too, leaving the bare flesh showing. In any case, either socks or flesh would create an abominable impression, so that throughout the conversation I had to sit rigidly in an entirely unnatural position trying to remember, while chatting in an easy manner, to keep my feet flat on the carpet. Also I am in the habit of gesticulating a good deal when I talk; but since the cuffs of my shirt were almost spectacularly frayed and had to be kept out of sight, this habit too had to be abandoned for the duration of the interview, and I sat hunched like some semi-petrified gargoyle, my hands gripping my wrists so as neither to display the frayed cuffs nor even to suggest to the minds of the examiners that the cuffs could not be shown.

Candidates had been required to fill up a form showing where they had been during the period between the end of the last summer term at Oxford and the date of the examination. Simply to keep the record straight I had put down that I had spent a couple of weeks in Luxembourg. After some more or less light-hearted conversation and casual questioning, the Provost suddenly remarked that he observed I had spent some time in the Grand Duchy of Luxembourg. I said I had been there for a bare fortnight.

'And what,' he asked, 'did you gather of conditions there?'

I got off a rather sapient piece about the operations of the International Steel Cartel, which had its headquarters there, together with some observations upon the possible effects of a recent Luxembourg decision to hitch the Luxembourg currency to the belga rather than to the franc. Meaty stuff, I secretly opined, after only a fortnight in the country. The Provost tapped the table impatiently, and his expression was that of a man who does not relish having his time wasted by chit-chat about trivialities.

'Yes, yes, yes,' he said, 'very interesting, no doubt, but what I would really like to know is what you gathered about the varying systems of land tenure in the north and south parts of the Grand Duchy?'

All this was harassing enough, but still more disconcerting was the fact that my Oxford creditors had chosen this moment to make an attack in force. Whether this was an unhappy accident, or whether they had somehow learned that I was sitting for this Fellowship examination and considered it a suitable moment to turn on the heat, I have no idea. For whatever reason, they became suddenly implacable and menacing. (In fairness I should say that there were some noble exceptions.) Several of them threatened legal action, and it was grimly evident that although a man with bare feet and frayed cuffs might possibly still clutch at the Fellowship, one who had just been served with several writs could not.

I interviewed the fiercest of the creditors and begged them to hold their hand until after the results of the examination had been announced. They refused. Maddened by their short-sighted folly, which threatened not only my career but the prospect of their ever getting paid at all, I decided that only a bold policy could save the situation. The result of the examination was scheduled to be announced a couple of weeks or so after the written part, which lasted several days, was concluded. I gave them all post-dated cheques for sums adequate to satisfy them temporarily, dated for the day the results were due to be announced. Personally I had no doubt that I should win one of the Fellowships, and of course in that case the bank would be quite happy to advance the money. But I could see that the creditors probably would not be entirely satisfied with this security, and I did not mention to them the fact that the cheques would be payable only as and when I was successful in the Fellowship examination.

Although as the written examination proceeded I became more and more confident, I was undoubtedly aware of a sense of tension and excitement which probably was not shared by candidates in more comfortable circumstances. The examination ended and a week or so passed, and then something happened which made me feel that fate was deliberately hitting out at me.

My father had told me long ago that if one wished to be lucky one should always believe in luck – that people who cursed their luck suffered for it. I did my best to carry out this policy now, but it was difficult because what had happened was that one of the examining dons had caught a cold, or contracted some other minor ailment, and the announcement was made in a notice to the candidates that declaration of the results would be postponed by a week beyond the scheduled date.

It was only after a half-hour of despair that a possible solution occurred to me. I wrote a letter to one of the principal examining dons – a charming man who had already showed me great kindness – saying that I had just heard that a relative of mine, who had helped me greatly throughout my academic life and took a passionate interest in my career, was dangerously ill. In fact it was doubtful whether this relative could survive for more than a few days. Surely, it would be tragic if, on account of this accidental change of schedule, my relative should pass away without knowing whether I had succeeded or not – particularly tragic if I had succeeded and this news came too late to cheer the last hours.

The good-hearted don wrote to me immediately – I had of course taken the precaution of going to London before sending him my letter so that his reply, if any, would be in writing – saying that he could not in any way officially anticipate the result, but that, speaking as an individual, and purely on the basis of his own personal estimate, he would say that I would not be deceiving my relative if I indicated that I had obtained the Fellowship. With this letter I dashed back to Oxford, interviewed the bank manager, who fortunately was aware of the position of the don in question on the examining board, and asked him whether on the strength of it he would meet the cheques which were now due to be presented within a matter of three or four days. He agreed.

Naturally I had to sign documents which in fact meant that in the course of the next couple of years something like half the whole of the Fellowship payments would have to be handed over to the bank.

The prospect did not much bother me. It seemed to me that these were rivers that could be crossed when we came to them.

Also those early years in Budapest during the inflation time, when the value of money in your pocket could be halved between breakfast and lunch, and halved again before dinner, had made it hard for me to focus at all steadily on any financial problems, or to treat such problems otherwise than as entirely fluid and impalpable.

Hesitantly I decided that it would be proper to go and say good-bye to my college tutor. Hesitantly, because he was a man who shunned humans even when they were absolutely calm. Excited ones affected him like asphyxia. I tried to remain absolutely calm.

Naturally he was always glad to see the last of anyone, but he dreaded the potentially emotional business of the actual 'good-bye'. Wearing a russet-coloured suit, he lay as though camouflaged on a russet-coloured sofa. I saw him groping for some seemly valediction. He looked despairingly at the ceiling and then along the bookshelves all round the room, all full of works by philosophers who either had been, or were just about to be, exploded. 'Hitherto,' he said at last, 'your life has been neatly criss-crossed by school terms and holidays, university terms and vacations. Now you are going down from Oxford and you have – well one may say that you have a straight run to the grave.'

I mentioned that to start off the run I vaguely planned to connect myself with *The Times* newspaper. My tutor thought it a fate considerably worse than death. Did I realise I would probably have to speak to comparative strangers, and write about events as though they were important? But being very properly uninterested in my future he made no other attempt to dissuade me.

At the outset, before I had heard of the existence of the Travelling Fellowship, a job with *The Times* had been a mainly negative ambition, formed to avoid the Foreign Office which had been so long and so highly recommended that I could think of it only in the words of the songster as 'a wonderful opportunity for somebody – somebody else'.

To the advocates of a Foreign Office career the notion of 'going in for journalism' was pitiably degrading. 'And mark you,' as a friend of my father told me sternly, 'split what hairs you will, mince words as you may, in the last analysis *The Times* is nothing more or less than *sheer journalism.*'

It seemed certain that journalists had the choice of being absolutely servile (as reported by another very old friend of the family who had the latest information from Germany under Bismarck), or corrupt (the conviction of another who had personally known Caillaux), or intolerably vulgar (the view of a fourth who had always said Lord Northcliffe should have been hanged).

I discovered very soon that these hesitations and *hauteurs* were paralleled at Printing House Square. Applications for employment poured in, sometimes producing a kind of *folie de grandeur.*

Brilliant and sound I grant you. But brilliant and sound enough for The Times? *This one mentions his triple First, his double Blue and his uncle the Bishop. Estimable, but the dear good chap does only speak four languages. Is one justified in giving him a trial when some nearly perfect aspirant may already be on his way from Winchester to Balliol? Is, indeed, anyone, anywhere, truly worthy of* The Times?

This was the awfully solemn thought which at that time sometimes oppressed Printing House Square, and if held long enough, could have led to a total depopulation of *The Times* offices everywhere. For even correspondents of the London *Times* sometimes perish or lose all sense of values and seek other employment. I had myself already met one who had resigned – for a reason which, though uncommon, seemed sufficient. He had formed the opinion that his appointment as a part-time correspondent had been a Parthian act of malicious sabotage by a retiring foreign editor with a grudge against the paper. 'My having the job,' he said with candour, 'was intended simply to discredit *The Times* in the eyes of the world.' His resignation was a touching gesture of loyalty to the paper's best interests.

In these circumstances I had been warned, back in the previous summer, that to fill up one of the regular application forms for a job with *The Times* would be worse than useless. To begin with it would reveal the fact that one was actually in need of a job, a state of affairs which could be regarded as ignoble. However, before entering the Fellowship examination, it had been necessary to state in an application form what exactly one proposed to do after the two years' period of the Fellowship – in what capacity was one going to take advantage of the benefits received from the Fellowship and fulfil the wishes of the Founder.

Most people said that they were aiming for the Diplomatic Service; a few whose fathers or uncles controlled businesses operating abroad indicated they would be ambassadors of commerce. I had been warned, indirectly, that merely to say that one had an idea of being a journalist, a foreign correspondent of some kind, would be absolutely fatal. There were bound to be several among the examiners who would instinctively feel that the fewer British journalists there were running about the world the better. Also they would take the view that any man of birth and education who deliberately announced his intention of becoming a journalist probably was beyond salvation, even by the exceptional facilities afforded by the Travelling Fellowship. 'But *The Times*', I said. 'Surely if I say I am going to be a correspondent of *The Times?* Think,' I said, 'of Russell! Think of Dr Morrison! Think of Wickham Steed!'

My adviser agreed that *The Times* would possibly pass muster, 'Although,' he said dubiously, 'it *is* journalism, you know.'

Thus, unknown to *The Times*, I was forced to commit myself to becoming at some future date one of its correspondents.

The residential conditions attaching to the Fellowship were elastic – you could spend the whole two years in one town or country, or you could keep moving about. The only absolute condition was that you must be in a town with a university. I wanted to get back to Central Europe, and just after the results were announced I met a man who said he was a good friend of *The Times* correspondent in Berlin and would give me a letter of introduction to him. Up to the last moment I had been wavering somewhat between Berlin and Vienna, but this decided me. I bought, on that wonderfully long Oxford credit, some suits which more than adequately expressed the gaiety and even flamboyance of my mood. To compensate for the distress experienced at the interview, I had four pairs of shoes very expensively made for me and had a lot of silk shirts made for me too. When all these garments had finally been constructed, I took off for Berlin.

When I got there it emerged that the man to whom I had the letter of introduction had been transferred – had not been in Berlin for nearly two years. But by that time I was there, and the smell of Central Europe had a new tang to it.

VII   THE TOADS WAITED

TOADS USED TO COME OUT OF SWAMPY GROUND IN the Tiergarten and sit looking out of the backs of their heads at the packed buses, the racing taxis and the limousines and the huge German touring cars, roaring eastwards and westwards on the Charlottenburger Chaussee, which strikes unswervingly across the green heart of Berlin.

The toads, motionless except for the slow blink of their eyelids, were the only immobile creatures in sight, and gave an impression of cynical watchfulness. Their performance was corny but impressive; by hindsight even more impressive than it seemed at the time.

The sight of these squat, old-looking observers, gazing backward at everything that happened, sharpened the sense of impermanence, of foolish vulnerability in the face of inimical and indifferent forces of destruction, which could always be felt so strongly in Berlin. In Berlin you felt that the deluge was always just around the corner. There is a book or short story (well known but I have forgotten who wrote it), about a city which establishes itself in the sandy desert, defeats the desert, and just when things seem safest is – at first almost imperceptibly – attacked by the desert, defeated by it and finally engulfed. Similarly in Berlin you could without difficulty believe in a day when the toads and perhaps worms and snails would, after so long awaiting their opportunity, note that the human defences had collapsed, and take over.

I have known scores of people who have lived in Berlin most of their lives and always had this sensation about their city. It could be oppressive or stimulating according to one's mood or temperament. What caused it I do not know. It cannot have been, as some people have suggested, the relative newness of Berlin compared to, say, Vienna or Paris, for great areas of Paris and Vienna are no less modern than most of Berlin, and in any case neither Chicago nor Kansas City produces this sensation. Perhaps my aunt was right and it is a trick of the light playing on the nerves of the retina. I think it is a character in Jean Giraudoux's *Siegfried et le Limousin* who remarks that there is more mystery and terror in a single pine tree in the streets of Berlin at midday than in an entire French forest at midnight.

A German whose life was full of energy and trouble once told me the story of a slightly tipsy man who was plodding along the Charlottenburger Chaussee. He had come all the way from the Imperial Palace at the far end of Unter den Linden, and another mile or so of the Charlottenburger Chaussee, and he was on his way along the dead straight Kaiserdamm and Bismarckstrasse, to the far-distant Reichskanzlerplatz. He stopped somebody to ask whether he was going right for the Reichskanzlerplatz. The man said, 'Yes, yes, you can't miss it. Straight on, it's an absolutely straight road the whole way.' The tipsy man, who had been asking his way every few minutes since he started out down Unter den Linden, groaned and said, 'Well, so many people have told me that, I only hope it's true.' My German friend told me this story with emotion. It appeared to him to have some general application to life.

At first in Berlin I lived on the Bismarckstrasse, because I was romantic and somebody had pointed out to me that there one was living on a sector of a highway which ran direct from Amsterdam to Moscow. A little later, on account of a love affair – or rather two love affairs, the first of which was frivolous and the second serious – I moved to an apartment on the Kurfuerstendamm, and early on a spring morning of 1946 I looked out of a window and saw a view, or rather a caricature of a view, which had greeted me for months in the spring nearly twenty years before. In this latter spring, when the sunshine was thick with dust blowing off the rubble and ruins of Berlin, I was at the Hotel am Zoo on the Kurfuerstendamm where British journalists were quartered and taken care of with the melancholy, subfusc efficiency of the army. This hotel, or 'press camp' as it was called, was only two street numbers away from the house where I had lived in 1927.

The apartment, on the second floor, had been noble and enormous, so that at first you hardly noticed that it contained mountains of furniture covered up in dust-sheets. The owners had taken the time to cover up their furniture and then suddenly gone off – fleeing, it was said, from something or other. Just what this something was nobody seemed to know. Some people said they were involved in a bank swindle, others that they were harassed in the ordinary way by creditors, others again that they had taken it into their heads that revolution was likely to break out at any moment, and were in flight from the wrath to come. The concierge evidently felt that she was offering an entirely adequate explanation when she said simply that no doubt the strain of life in Berlin had proved too much for them.

Probably none of these theories was true – each simply expressed the subjective feeling different people had about the kind of thing that could cause anyone to get out of Berlin in a hurry. Whatever the reason may have been, they were prepared to let their flat for a song to anyone who would keep it occupied and prevent burglars taking away the furniture, so that one could live there very cheaply and conduct one's life commodiously without being interfered with or spied upon by a landlady.

A little way down the avenue on the farther side there had been a smart, rather self-consciously 'modern', bookshop where I had spent a good deal of time. From my window it seemed that in 1946 the bookshop was still there, but when I walked across to it there was nothing but a façade with holes where the shop windows had been, and piles of rubble behind. I made some desultory enquiries but nobody knew what had become of the proprietor. I had never liked him but I had liked to be with him because he seemed to combine so many of the characteristics of the Berliner – including the fact that he had been born in Breslau. He identified himself strenuously, emphatically, self-consciously with the city and at the slightest stimulus – a question or the mildest criticism – he would rattle off a string of those clichés which the Berliners always had ready to describe what they liked to believe were the characteristics and qualities of a Weltstadt. It seemed to be an act of protective self-enlargement, as though 'we Berliners' became desirably bigger, smarter, more cynical, more ruthless, faster moving, more gloriously 'modern' by repeatedly reciting like some incantation the hugeness, harshness, and above all the roaring 'tempo' of the city seen as a living entity. This bookseller was ashamed of nothing, because the only qualities he would have been ashamed of would have been slowness in thought or action, gentleness, or sentimentality, and since he lived in Berlin he could not believe that any of these weaknesses could be his. He did not simply hustle, he insisted that you should take note of the tempo he was hustling at, and if possible exclaim over it incredulously, a tribute which often seemed necessary to maintain his self-confidence. Someone – perhaps it was Giraudoux again – said that when a Frenchman buys a motor car, he thinks of it as a means of transport, but a German, particularly a Berliner, does not see the car as just a car, because he is intoxicated with the thought that under that bonnet is symbolically pulsating the spirit of the twentieth century. This bookseller had had the shop on the Kurfuerstendamm for a number of years and always had kept it punctiliously 'up to date,' changing his stock with every change in the intellectual fashion. This of course could have been the ordinary routine of good business, but the curious fact was that although he had seen one intellectual dogma after another pass from veneration to derision in a couple of years – become in fact 'exploded' – his belief in the absolute validity of each fashionable thought or idea seemed to be complete. He had believed in Spengler, he had believed in Keyserling, but they, by the time I met him, were long since outmoded, and at that time his shelves were brash

89

with volumes which seemed almost to stink of optimism. The Wall Street Stock Market had begun its long climb towards the heights of 1929, the American banks were pouring their money into Germany, German steel mills and shipbuilding yards were working to capacity, and German business in general, freed of debt by the inflation just ended, was booming in a way that only a few years before would have seemed a maniac's dream of prosperity and power. Looking round that bookshop you felt that you were being briskly informed that every conceivable problem, political, financial, commercial, moral or spiritual, had been solved or was in process of being competently solved by experts, and that if there were any problems still not being dealt with, that was because they were unimportant and not worth bothering about. If the tempo could be kept up the time was not far distant when everyone would know just how to get the best out of everything from sex to sewage. There were innumerable works on rationalisation of industry – which was going to solve all industrial problems, particularly in the Ruhr. And a particularly agreeable aspect of the situation was that all this prosperity and progress was seen as the proof that poor old Karl Marx had been barking up the wrong tree. Admittedly there had been a nasty moment, lasting in fact from the start of the Russian Revolution until the suppression of the Spartacist Revolt in Germany and even after, when it had looked uncommonly as though Marx had been right; and people like the bookseller had lived in anguished indecision as to how long it might be safe to wait before jumping on the Communist bandwaggon.

Now rationalisation and America together had changed all that. Every two or three months it seemed there was a new book by a German Liberal or by a Socialist who had been to the United States and returned with the information that 'der Americanismus' or 'der Fordismus' had made nonsense of all previously held economic theories, and that wages would go on getting higher and higher and consumer demand greater and greater and profits larger and larger in a virtuous circle for ever. They had exciting and at the same time comforting titles such as *The Land of Limitless Possibilities* and *Ford answers Marx*. Even the pessimists in Berlin were, if one may say so, optimistic. The time was soon after the Arkos Raid, Anglo-Russian relations were worse than they had been for years, and people wrote books to prove that very soon there would be an Anglo-Russian war. Though few people explicitly said so, and fewer still had any clear picture of the character of such a conflict, Berliners like my bookseller thought instinctively that this would be a good thing because Britain would first render a great service by smashing up the Kremlin, and then fall exhausted by the effort, leaving Germany master of the situation and comfortably dominant as she would have been had she secured in the first World War that victory of which she had been so unfairly and mysteriously deprived.

The bookseller, whose name was Herr Uhlmann, rejoiced in stories purporting to illuminate the rushing, bustling, businesslike character of the Berliner always ready and proud, it seemed, to sacrifice good manners to efficiency. Thus an Austrian, because ridiculously soft, goes up to the window of the station booking-office and is left standing there for ten minutes because he is too polite to shout at the clerk inside. At length the Austrian raps gently on the counter with a coin and says, 'Doesn't one get any service here?' The clerk leaps up and roars back at him, 'You aren't served here, man, you're dealt with.' It made Herr Uhlmann feel good, evidently, to be a citizen of a town where the railway clerks behaved like that.

Once I told him how on the previous day I had been visited at the flat by a policeman who cross-questioned me about my friends or acquaintances in countries other than Germany, and showed particular interest in the question of what kind of correspondence I had with them – did they write to me often, and so on. I was indignant at this questioning, but also nervous because I thought it indicated that they took me for a spy and might upset all my plans by expelling me from Germany. Herr Uhlmann listened to my account and was visibly pleased. The episode, he thought, was typical of the intrusive efficiency of the Berlin police. I went on to tell him how the policeman had finally asked me to accompany him to the police station to interview his superior officer. There seemed to be nothing else to do and I went with him in a high degree of alarm and exasperation, expecting to be violently interrogated by some brutish Prussian officer-type.

When I got there the superior officer was a Prussian all right, but in appearance and manner resembled rather a small farmer of the north German plain than a city police officer. He had long yellow moustaches and gentle blue eyes, and when the policeman had reported to him on our conversation he said apologetically that he was very sorry to have bothered me, but the fact was that he had a small nephew who was a keen stamp collector and was at the moment in the tuberculosis ward of a sanatorium. He, the officer, had promised to do everything in his power to add to the boy's collection of foreign stamps, and had taken the liberty of asking for my co-operation.

Herr Uhlmann was disgusted by the story, which indicated that there were gentle and kindly people in Berlin – even in the Berlin police force. It made him so uneasy that a couple of days later he referred to my experience and said that he thought I must have made it up, or else I had misunderstood what the officer was saying.

He was happy to think that Berlin was not only faster moving than any other city but 'wickeder' too. His own sexual tastes were normal, though – except when drunk – he made a point of treating his various women with a maximum of off-handed bad manners and harshness which he described as 'realism' and 'unsentimentality', but he took a genuine civic pride in the countless cafés and cabarets in the neighbourhood which were frequented exclusively by homosexuals, male or female, and the little dance halls where all the male dancing partners were dressed as girls. When a new one opened he would take me to see it. 'I bet you wouldn't see a thing like that anywhere but in Berlin,' he would say with satisfaction. 'What a bunch of perverts, eh?'

With all his cocksureness, his almost mystical faith in 'modernism', he combined the characteristic German belief in some kind of cosmic doom impending, a Götterdämmerung and a universal smash-up. He never defined precisely what he thought was going to happen, but the idea attracted him and gave him satisfaction – a death urge of a more than normal strength. And then this urge, this hypnotic attraction of spectacular and universal disaster, had been played upon once too often by Dr Goebbels, and there was this heap of rubble covering, no doubt, innumerable copies of *Mein Kampf* and whatever similar literature had constituted Herr Uhlmann's last stock-in-trade.

VIII   UNTER DEN LINDEN

AFTER DISCOVERING ON THE FIRST DAY I WAS IN Berlin that the man whose presence there had been the whole reason for my coming to this capital was no longer present, I got the name and telephone number of his successor as *The Times* correspondent and the next morning rang him up – at 8.30 a.m. so as to create a good first impression of alertness, not one of those slouching Oxford decadents.

This might have been disastrous, because the correspondent had only just reached bed after one of those tiring journalistic evenings in the Berlin of those days, which used to start about 6 in the afternoon and rarely ended until 6 or 7 in the morning. However, Mr Norman Ebbutt was a man of warm-hearted goodness and this he displayed immediately, pretending that it was time for him to get up and behaving in general as though I really were an old friend and had come with a letter of introduction to him. He even pretended to believe that I might actually be of use to him in *The Times* office in Unter den Linden. With extraordinary tact he somehow managed to suggest that I might be doing him positively a favour by coming and 'helping'. He must have known that he, of course, would have to spend hours teaching me to do things he could have done himself in a tenth of the time.

It was true that he was alone and grievously overworked, because at that period a mild manpower crisis, starting in remote parts of the world, but developing by a kind of chain reaction, was afflicting the foreign organisation of the paper. Two correspondents had acted vexatiously and had to be transferred to other posts.

In those days it was nearly impossible to be sacked by *The Times*. You just got a less important and less interesting job at about the same pay. This civilised policy worked excellently and removed the root cause of many journalistic crises. This cause is fear of the sack. It is a fear more potent and menacing in journalism – at least in foreign correspondents' journalism – than in most professions, because in so many cases the foreign correspondent has through no particular will of his own been suddenly whisked on to a standard of living obligatorily high on account of the paper's prestige, and has often inadvertently convinced some girl that this is the standard of living to which she may confidently become accustomed, and then found himself involved in a fearful rat-race of competition, pursued – at least in his nightmares – by other young men who want to live on that standard too and will put him off it unless he quickly and repeatedly does something that will impress the London office. As the London office frequently does not know what is really impressive about the events in the country to which its correspondent is accredited, and is thinking only about what it imagines will impress Birmingham or Newcastle to-morrow morning, the correspondent is tempted into vicious journalistic ways.

One of the two unfortunates of *The Times* who had to be transferred had developed 'views' on something or other – and in *The Times* language 'viewy' was a dreadfully damaging epithet. Another had embarrassed the British Legation in a capital city in Latin America, where he was a part-time correspondent. He had turned up with a girl to whom everyone was quite prepared to believe him married. But he was painfully high-principled, and he publicly disabused them of this idea. For valid reasons he was not, and could not be, legally married to her. He wanted to make that perfectly clear. On the other hand he must insist that she be invited with him to all official functions as though she were indeed his wife. Otherwise he would feel obliged to boycott such functions and make scenes.

The Legation in the foreign capital wrote to the Foreign Office, and the Foreign Office wrote to *The Times* asking them to reason with their man. Could he not, *pro forma*, and to avoid affront to stuffy foreign diplomats, courtiers and ecclesiastics, pretend he was married to the girl? Or at least cease to deny it? Or else leave her at home?

The Times wrote to the part-time correspondent, so reasoning. Much later one of the foreign editorial staff who had been in charge of the delicate negotiations told me the outcome. 'He simply wrote that she was his wife in the eyes of God. Surely,' he said, sighing, 'he couldn't have expected *The Times* to see eye to eye with God, could he?'

These disturbances occurred at a moment when whoever

was acting as St. Peter at the gates of Printing House Square was in a mood of such haughtiness that if the Archangel Gabriel had slipped out for a moment he would have found considerable difficulty in gaining readmittance. As a result the pipe-line had run rather dry. Also the paper was at that moment going through one of those terrible periods which all papers pass through every few years, when the idea gets about that everyone is spending far too much money, and that the best interests of the organisation will be served by cutting down expenses all round. This produces a situation in which a horrible type of man whose speciality it is to find how other people could live more cheaply and do the same amount of work nevertheless, gets temporarily into a position of power and influence, so that for a while none can say him nay. If this goes on long enough, in the end the paper suddenly misses a big and important story, the economy expert is demoted with contumely, and people go round telling one another to 'think big'.

People slow in the uptake, who are still trying to economise, are demoted too, on the ground that they evidently are not thinking big enough. Obviously it is very important for a journalist to know which phase his newspaper happens to be in at a given moment. On the other hand, in case of doubt it is always reasonable to assume that the safest thing to do is to be rather expensive. The proprietors or the shareholders are unlikely to have any very expert knowledge as to the difference between good journalism and bad, and therefore their only criterion of the value they may be getting for money is the amount of money they are actually spending. For people who think of things in terms of money, it is extraordinarily hard to believe that a man who is costing XX pounds a year is not a better journalist than some poor wretch who has pared the cost of his services down to X pounds. This was a point which Norman Ebbutt never fully grasped.

Although personally a man of the greatest generosity, he was, as regards business, of economical mind. He even had some sort of conscience about *The Times's* money, as though it were part of his business to look after their profits for them. He was daily offended by the fact that the office floor Unter den Linden was covered by absurdly expensive carpets, and that there were almost equally expensive and entirely unnecessary curtains on the windows. There was nothing much he could do about the carpets, but at the time I arrived the curtain situation had come to a head. The situation was that the curtains needed either cleaning or mending – I forget which – and this, whichever it was, was going to be a long job. Somebody – the secretary I suppose – foreseeing this, had gone out and ordered new curtains to take their place while they were away. Ebbutt was outraged and intended to cancel the order. Although I had known him for only a few days, he had already been immensely kind to me, and I esteemed and liked him very much. I felt sure he was making a mistake.

The original carpet and curtains had been put in by his predecessor, who had been there during the inflation period and had, I believe, lived in a suite at the Adlon Hotel almost next door. Nobody but millionaires could, of course, afford to live in the Adlon Hotel nowadays, and Ebbutt had been right to take a flat in the middle suburbs, but I felt that to leave the windows without curtains – a fact which would certainly be reported by some grapevine to the London office – would be a dangerous move. What would happen if, while we were curtainless, the economy wave suddenly broke and subsided? Word would immediately go round that Ebbutt was by no means on a par as a correspondent with his costly predecessor, and he would be accused of failing to understand what was due to the prestige of *The Times* in a foreign capital. Rather pathetically, he said that he thought *The Times* would probably appreciate his gesture of economy. I said that what was appreciated on the 3rd of May might be regarded with disdain and disfavour on the 20th and that the thing to do was to swagger and keep on swaggering until the economy blitz was over.

Ebbutt refused to be convinced and cancelled the curtains. Months later I heard a man on the business side of *The Times* describing how he had taken his wife on a jaunt to Berlin and they had gone into *The Times* office and he had been disagreeably surprised, indeed humiliated, to see that the place had no curtains. It had proved to him, he said, that Ebbutt had no *savoir faire*. This was in a sense true, and to me, at least, he endeared himself immediately by his obvious incapacity to credit the fact that it could conceivably be necessary to spend more than a few minutes a day in the mean and absurd little intrigues and manœuvres which, it must be admitted, play so large a rôle in the lives of many.

He was intelligent and courageous, and he needed to be, for

he was a man of goodwill. He even believed that one day he would go to the British Embassy in the Wilhelmstrasse and find out what the policy of the British Foreign Office was, and perhaps that would turn out to be intelligent and courageous too.

Politically he was, I suppose, what could be described as a Left Wing Liberal, which meant, at any rate in his case, that he hoped for the best in everyone. He used to take me to drink beer with Herr Stresemann, who was Foreign Minister, and in whom at that time Liberals believed. Personally I found that Stresemann was entertaining provided that you did not believe in him. He was one of those Germans who had, at a fairly early date, discovered that the way to get away with being a good German was to pretend to be a good European. He had a wonderful act in which he pretended to be not only fat, which he was, but good-hearted and a little muzzy with beer into the bargain. In reality he was as quick and sharp as a buzz-saw, and if being a sharp, fast-moving buzz-saw was not enough, he would hit you from behind with a hammer. We used to sit in the late spring in the garden of the Foreign Office drinking beer and playing a kind of diplomatic chess game which would have been risible if it had not been serious.

I think it was Stresemann, sitting under a fruit tree, talking about European unity, who first sowed in my mind the doubt as to whether my warm-hearted enthusiasm on behalf of the victims of the World War, my romantic belief in the Nationalist movements of Central Europe (Nationalist even when they were disguised as the resurgence of Central European democracy), and my conviction that the Treaty of Versailles had been a disastrous diplomatic crime, really covered all the facts.

I do not mean to imply that I cleverly saw what the old boy was really up to. I simply had an impression; an impression, that is to say, that if this was the kind of old boy I had been feeling sorry for and enthusiastic about all this time, I probably had been making a mistake. I think, although here I may be doing Ebbutt an injustice, that Ebbutt, just because he longed so much for European unity, for people to be reasonable and blissful, believed a shade more in Stresemann than he should have. If that were so, he certainly erred in the company of several million other people of goodwill. Stresemann's eulogies of peace, in the then militarily vulnerable condition of Germany, came back to my mind years later when I was talking to the British Military Attaché at the Washington Embassy who had just returned from a visit to Cuba where he had inspected the Cuban army. He said, 'I have taken a very careful look at the Cuban army, and my tour of inspection has convinced me that, for the moment at any rate, the adherence of Cuba to the Kellogg Pact outlawing war as an instrument of national policy is absolutely sincere.'

Some years after the war, Stresemann is reported to have said that the attitude of the victors to the 'new German democracy' was 'our tragedy and your crime'. It was the kind of remark he was good at making, and I recall that at the time I first heard it in the late 1920s I thought it a poignantly apt summary of the situation. Later I had doubts, and later still worse doubts. I use the word 'doubts' advisedly because it suggests the kind of thing that is reputed to have happened to Victorian clergymen when they started suddenly to wonder about the Book of Genesis or something of the kind.

The analogy is by no means extensive or exact, but it expresses something of what I mean. Liberalism, the righteousness of the defeated, the wickedness of the Treaty of Versailles, had been our political bible, and now one sat with Stresemann, and one thought 'was this the face that launched all our little political ships?' Naturally I am not referring to Stresemann's physical face as such—although that, too, was a map worth studying. Nor am I trying to attempt an estimate of Stresemann's personal rôle in that period between the wars which prepared World War II. If one chooses to speak in moral terms, he was no more 'guilty' than any other minister of government on either side of the Rhine or of the English Channel. But as a symbol, a sympton, he was remarkable. Viewed from afar—from Budapest or Oxford—he had often seemed the very embodiment of everything we thought we were in favour of. If Liberal patriots like Stresemann, we thought, could only be given a free hand and a fair deal by the bitter old men of the West, then these fine men, all of them good Europeans, would lead Germany, and in the end all the defeated lands of Central Europe, into a new democratic peaceful European community.

For obvious psychological reasons to which I have already referred, a lot of young men of my generation had a compulsive urge to love and cherish the peoples defeated by our fathers. On countless journeys between Oxford and Budapest

I had taken time off in Germany, in the Rhineland, in Heidelberg, in Bavaria, seeing very few people but intoxicated by the loveliness of those lands, and when I did see people, seeing them through the haze of that kind of political mysticism which I had built up around them. And now, here one was at the heart and centre of the whole dream. There was Stresemann. There was Mr Uhlmann. There were the half-dozen young men I knew in the German Foreign Office. There was a banker I knew at Wannsee who used to ask me out for week-ends to meet other bankers and occasionally outriders of the Krupp or Thyssen families from the Ruhr. One confronted them with a slight sense of shock.

My principal friend from the Foreign Office was a man a couple of years older than myself whose name – pronounced on all suitable occasions in full – was Wolfgang Gans Edler Herr von Putlitz. Perhaps his very appearance should have given one some warning of the sensational character of his subsequent international career. He was a very big man with a face like a hooded eagle, his fine grey eyes gleaming occasionally as he spoke of history, of the future and the past. As for the future, he had the 'catastrophic' German view of it. His friendly yet somehow commiserating smile and the sideways gleam of his eyes told you that he wished you well, that he loved your childish optimism, and that he was sorry that all this was going to be utterly disappointed.

Although he never obtruded such considerations upon one, he was in fact at that time often brooding on the question whether it had or had not been a good thing that the Hohenzollerns had defeated the Putlitzes at some remote battle on the North German plain in the Middle Ages. It seems that the Putlitz forces, otherwise well equipped, had failed to think at all about the possible use of gunpowder, whereas the Hohenzollerns, rather unfairly, Herr Putlitz always thought, had got guns with gunpowder and cannon balls. Naturally the Hohenzollerns had won, and – at least, according to von Putlitz – the battle was in fact the beginning of that chain reaction which had ended with the Hohenzollerns becoming the German Emperors. The potential consequences one way and another of this incident haunted him. Would it or would it not have been a good thing for the Putlitz family to have occupied the Imperial throne? Would they have acted differently from the Hohenzollerns? At that time I think he believed that they would, although he never actually said so; and in that case, of course, Germany would either have won the war or at least come out of it with a fairly advantageous peace, and he, Wolfgang, would have been Crown Prince.

One evening, pondering on these matters, we went to a little bar on the Tauentzientstrasse where he called the barman George and the barman called him Peter. 'You see,' he said, 'he calls me Peter. He is a friend of mine, I am a friend of his. In all these little bars around here they all call me Peter. But nobody knows who I really am.'

Annoyed by what, at that time, I thought an absurd pomposity, I asked him rather sharply whether he supposed that anybody really cared who he really was. He became melancholy and withdrawn, but the next day invited me to lunch and afterwards took me for a walk into northern Berlin where ultimately we found ourselves standing at the end of a long, rather squalid street in which the south wind was stirring the dust and driving it against the façades of apartment houses which had been ultra-modern three years before and were already beginning to peel.

'So what?' I said. 'Why are we here?'

'This,' he said, 'is the Putlitzstrasse.'

Filled with awareness of the melancholy of life and history, I returned to *The Times* office to continue my daily task of reading all the German newspapers published morning and evening. I think that at that time there were forty of them, or perhaps it was thirty – at any rate a great number. *The Times*, hearing through the grapevine that I had moved in, in some mysterious fashion, upon the Berlin office, had written to Ebbutt to say that they had no objection to people sitting there and learning the business, but they insisted that such people should be absolutely prohibited from writing anything for the paper. Ebbutt, so nervous about financial matters, was on this point audacious. He said,

'Of course you will write for the paper, and we will get as many pieces of yours in as we can, although naturally it will be necessary to pretend that I have sent them.'

'But supposing,' I said, 'they are no good?'

'In that case,' he said, 'we shall not send them.'

'But supposing,' I said, 'they find out that I have written them?'

'It will do a lot of good,' said Ebbutt.

We had four rooms, two of them guiltily carpeted with that expensive piece of material across which Ebbutt used to tread with the air of a Prime Minister who has found people bringing concubines into the Cabinet office. The other two rooms were occupied respectively by the secretary and the telephonist. The secretary, who had thought at one moment that she was liable to be washed out to sea altogether in the economy wave, was happy to do whatever anybody told her. The telephonist was a tough London character of astounding efficiency, and always ready to rush in and to help in some emergency. An emergency is something that occurs in any properly running newspaper office every night. He liked Berlin, but told me once that he did feel very strongly that the Germans ought to be more aware of the fact that they had, after all, lost the war. I asked him how this awareness if it existed could best be expressed. He said that just for a start they could stop trying to get twenty per cent more for a two-room furnished flat than the place was worth.

Naturally the reading of all these German newspapers did nothing to allay my 'doubts', but I liked straightforward journalistic occasions, such as the arrival of Chamberlain and Levine who flew the Atlantic shortly after Lindberg had done so. After the riot at Le Bourget, the German police determined to put on a demonstration of how this kind of thing should really be managed. The result was that half the journalists trying to report events at Templehof that night were manhandled or beaten up, with the strong approval of Herr Uhlmann who, when I visited him the next day with a blackened eye and a sore jaw, said that, after all, order is order. Despite these distractions I could not but feel that the Idea I had come to worship had moved over into some other temple.

Putlitz of course considered my attitude incomprehensible. Why should one expect anything good or inspiring from a state run by moneylenders and jumped-up grocers? The only hope was that the true professionals, military men and trained diplomats with their proper aristocratic background, might be able by their skill and devotion to prevent the whole thing running off the rails, or smashing straight into a revolution. He said that as for him, if he were going to think seriously at all, he preferred to think about the development of the German language and the perfection of his own literary style. We discussed these matters at length, but differences of taste and temperament prevented us becoming intimate. Putlitz, though profoundly romantic, disliked and despised women, and at this time looked with especial alarm and disfavour upon my association with a rather flamboyantly glittering young woman called, characteristically, Atlanta.

When I first met her I thought that she looked like Hollywood's idea of, say, a young Russian princess in exile whose family have lost all, running wild in a disillusioned manner because what does life hold but sensual pleasure? I was astonished to find that, except that she was neither Russian nor a princess, this first impression corresponded to the facts. Her dead father had been some kind of Hungarian count and her mother Viennese. Thinking that the war would end in a peasant revolution in Hungary, her father had disposed of all his lands and invested the proceeds in a lot of shaky industrial concerns in Austria, all of which went smash at once in 1918. With what he could pick out of the wreckage the father, returning to Budapest after the defeat of the Communist régime there, started to speculate in foreign exchange, lived for a couple of years like a millionaire, became involved in a frenzied scheme for financing a rising in the Ukraine against the Bolsheviks, and finally – threatened with criminal proceedings on account of some illegal financial operation in Budapest – fled to Bucharest, where he shot himself.

Her mother, a woman in her mid-forties, was meagrely supported by an elderly lover in Vienna. Sometimes Atlanta showed me her mother's letters, which were curious documents in that, read hastily, they seemed to be almost laughably censorious exhortations from a very strait-laced and primly conventional Edwardian mother to a daughter whom she suspected of dissolute goings-on. However, when you examined them more carefully, it transpired that what was worrying Atlanta's mother was that Atlanta's dissolute goings-on were taking up her time and energy without bringing in any money, and were for this reason reprehensible.

'Obviously,' I said, 'she wants you to get married.'

'Oh,' said Atlanta, in a tone that suggested I had accused her mother of some crazily unreasonable objective, 'she wouldn't insist on that at the moment. She knows how difficult it is to make a good marriage nowadays. But she thinks, of course, that I ought to get a rich lover.'

'In that case,' I said, 'you had better not mention me.' This warning, however, came too late.

'I write to her about everything,' she said. 'It excites me to describe such things in detail on paper. But I have told her your great-grandfather was a lord and that, although momentarily impoverished, you are assured of being in a year or so the Foreign Editor of the London *Times*.'

In outlook and behaviour she was something between a Viennese Miss of the old school, a camp-follower of hard-currency millionaires in the Budapest of the inflation time, and a naïvely eager American college girl of the gin-soaked years of prohibition. However, she could make you laugh a lot if you didn't much mind what you were laughing at, and her appearance certainly took one's mind off one's work. Another thing that did that was her determination that if there were not enough excitement going on already, she would create it. Almost better than anything she liked a really violent scene, and she could devise these out of the least promising materials. She took a passionate interest in politics and her ideas in this department were both commonplace and simple. She agreed with many others that the best thing that could happen would be a war between England and Russia, followed by vigorous counter-revolution everywhere. Since, however, people everywhere, and particularly the English, were utterly decadent and disillusioned, this would not take place, and society would soon simply smash itself up, so what was the use of worrying? The thing to do was to watch it all without illusions.

We began to bore each other rather and, in what I am sure she felt was a praiseworthy attempt to liven things up, she persuaded me to leave Berlin in the middle of the night without waiting to notify *The Times* office and go with her on a trip to Salzburg. When we got there it turned out that the object of the trip was to arrange an encounter between myself and a former lover of hers who was staying there, a young man of romantic temperament who for weeks past had assailed her with telegrams and long-distance telephone calls declaring that he could not live without her, and threatening alternately to shoot himself or to come to Berlin, find out with whom she was going about, and shoot him or them. Atlanta thought it would be 'amusing' for us to meet suddenly.

We were in his apartment before she told me just who he was. I had supposed we were simply paying a call on some old friend. From her point of view the meeting was only a partial success. After all the telephones and telegrams the young man could scarcely shrug his shoulders and offer us a drink, and after a tremendous amount of shouting and tears he did pull himself together sufficiently to rush into the bedroom and come back with a pistol which he fired erratically. He fired two shots, both of which crashed into a piano, before permitting himself to be overpowered and thrown to the ground by Atlanta.

We returned to Berlin the same day, both of us in a bad temper, I at having been dragged from my work for the purpose of being involved in this foolish scene, and Atlanta because the scene itself had been unsatisfactory – a let-down. I told Ebbutt the facts and he said that of course I must please myself, and he did not wish to interfere with my private life, but that if there were anything in the way of gunfire in *The Times* office, it would probably adversely affect my standing with the paper.

Irked by life in Berlin, Atlanta soon afterwards decided to go back to Vienna, but before doing so she took me to what she said would be a very smart and amusing party at the Kaiserhof Hotel – actually a charity soirée in aid of something or other, but Atlanta said, 'very exclusive'. I thought perhaps she was rashly trying to revive the affair which had petered out after the Salzburg episode, but she said frankly that she had no such motive; she was inviting me merely because she had not wanted to go to such a party by herself and did not want, either, to take the trouble to get involved with anyone else on the eve of her departure for Vienna. Also, she said, it was good for her prestige to be seen about with the Berlin correspondent of the London *Times*. I pointed out that I was not the Berlin Correspondent of the London *Times* – was not even in fact employed by *The Times* at all. She said, 'But I have told everybody that you are and they like that too, so it is no use your trying to deny it because nobody will want to believe you.'

After half an hour Atlanta furiously interrupted a conversation I was having with a Jewish newspaper proprietor who was anxious to inform himself about the inner policies of Printing House Square.

'Take me away,' she said, 'these people are all damned Reds.'

'Nonsense,' I said. 'They can't be.'

I looked hastily around the panorama of white shirt-fronts and bare shoulders, and spotted Signor X and Herr Y, the one a leading member of the Diplomatic Corps and the other a banker. 'Nonsense,' I repeated. 'X and Y aren't Reds.'

'I don't care,' said Atlanta. 'They all talk like Reds. And I despise intellectuals. Take me away.'

When I refused, she left by herself, presumably *en route* for Vienna, and I never saw or heard from her again. Nor, by

the time the party ended in the brilliant dawn of late spring,
did I very much care. For by this time I was already a little
in love again, and I realised that by the accident of Atlanta's
invitation to the party I had stepped across an unseen ditch –
dug perhaps partly by some invisible influence of my father
and partly probably by older, subtler influences and accidents
– to meet a Europe with which I had never made contact
before.

IX   THE NEW FACE

'ATLANTA,' SAID OUR HOSTESS, A VIENNESE BARON-
ess comfortably equipped with philanthropic interests, advanced political views, and a banker for a husband, 'thinks
everyone is a Red who expresses views she would not have
heard in that terrible house of her father's – full, let me tell
you, of speculators counting, as you would say in English,
their fortunes before they were properly hatched, and old
generals counting battles which had not even begun. Or in
her mother's flat in Vienna – and you know that that is really
a kind of cave into which the poor woman has retreated, and
when you go to call on her you hear, long before the door
opens, a kind of snarling, and it is Atlanta's mother snarling
at the modern world.'

I have forgotten what this party in the Kaiserhof Hotel
was in aid of, but in any case the people I met – the Viennese
bankers, the diplomats suspected of undue brilliance by their
Foreign Offices, the industrialists suspected of improper relations with socialist politicians, and the socialist politicians
suspected of improper relations with industrialists, the painters, film directors, publishers, writers, dancers and musicians
– would have been present whatever the object of the
Baroness's party, because they were all members of a kind
of perambulating salon which functioned sometimes in
Berlin, sometimes at the Baroness's house in Vienna, and
sometimes in a huge chalet, formerly an hotel, on the shores
of a lake in the Austrian Alps where she went for the summer.

D*

Naturally I cannot remember now just what was said or done at the party in the Kaiserhof Hotel and what was really said and done much later in Vienna that spring or in the summer by the lake. But I do remember that after a few hours of conversation at the Kaiserhof I had that sensation you get when you look with an inexperienced eye into a microscope, seeing nothing on the slide below but a confusing blur, and then someone adjusts the instrument to an effective focus.

Ever since I returned to Central Europe, the slide which earlier had been so clear had become increasingly blurred, and now it seemed that I had only been waiting for someone to make the adjustment. The Viennese essayist Polgar wrote that the Café Central in Vienna 'is not a coffee house like other coffee houses, but rather a way of looking at life'. And that could truthfully have been said about the people who at various times and places frequented the Baroness's travelling salon. Their opinions, of course, were diverse and usually passionately conflicting. Yet they had more in common with one another than any of them had with, let us say, von Tános, or Atlanta, or the Oxford Liberals, or Norman Ebbutt and the corps of foreign correspondents in Berlin.

Although people who disliked the Baroness referred to her circle of friends as a 'set', a 'circus' or even a 'menagerie', all these epithets, kindly or hostile, were wide of the mark, because in reality the salon was a fluid affair and – which was more important – was very far from unique. You could have found replicas of the same people all over Central Europe, and even in Paris. And it was precisely this fact of their being not unique, nothing special, which gave them their significance.

Probably I had met them – them or people like them, I mean – often before, but, inside some cocoon of sentimental Hungarian nationalism or Oxford Liberalism, had been impervious to the contact. This, in other words, was a noise which had been going on all the time but to which I had never been attuned. And this was true although neither at the Kaiserhof nor afterwards was there as much political conversation in the ordinary sense of the word as one could hear at any gathering of Anglo-American journalists in Berlin. But in politics, in the wider sense, these people were drenched, steeped, dyed.

They were for the most part Austrians, Hungarians, Poles or Russians, and some were Bulgarians or Rumanians. Most of them, too, were between the ages of twenty-five and forty-five. That is to say, all of them had been inescapably involved in the social upheavals and conflicts of the years after 1916 and had thus been involved at an age when they were still young enough to adjust themselves to those conditions. Also, being people of energy and intelligence, they were able to accept the facts of life as they knew it and, where others saw chaos or defeat, to see a pattern; a pattern, moreover, which people of energy and intelligence could take hold of, to perfect or change.

What all of them, despite their curious differences of view, shared and could not help sharing, however much it might irk them, was – to put it with a bluntness which would have offended many of them by its lack of subtlety – a recognition of Communism as the central dominating fact of our generation and indeed of our century. A platitude of course. To people nowadays such a recognition may seem a somewhat limited achievement, but I am speaking of the year 1927.

I dare say that before then I had often nodded 'yes' to this platitude myself, but it had not in any way affected my attitude to life – to, for example, the Treaty of Versailles, the agitations of the apothecary in the Cévennes, or the policies of either Herr Stresemann or the London *Times*. But these people had been impregnated by their experiences. They could no more ignore the facts of revolution and class conflict than they could the facts of astronomy. And the views of those who deplored these facts were as deeply coloured, and as pervasively informed by them, as were the beliefs and attitudes of those who continued to look upon them with enthusiasm.

When some direct references to current politics did occur, it was immediately borne in upon me that whereas I had been aware almost exclusively of the, so to speak, vertical divisions between peoples and policies, to my new acquaintances the horizontal divisions were more absorbing and in the end more important.

People who believe that the earth is round do not keep asserting that it is so, yet their attitude to everything is profoundly affected by that assumption. And the assumptions of these people were apparent even when the talk was farthest from politics. There were often moments in our early acquaintance when, after I had made some statement which seemed to me simple and even self-evident, I would be asked to repeat it as if it had been some astounding paradox, and

I presently found that the reason for this was that people could not believe that I had really said what I had said, because to them so many of my assertions sounded like assertions that the earth is flat.

'Perhaps,' I said to Madame T., the Viennese draughtswoman and painter, 'they think I am merely idiotic.'

'No, no,' she said, 'they expect anything of an Englishman.'

She and the brilliant Austrian biologist, Dr Wiesner, were better able than most to interpret the *milieu* to me – he because he loved novelty, and I was a novelty which he set himself to understand with the determination and mastery of a skilled linguist tackling a new language; she because, although in principle opposed to empires, to monarchies and to traditional aristocracy, she had at the same time a powerful, schizophrenic, almost mystical liking for what she imagined was 'the English way of life'. I found later, to my surprise, she had never been in England. When she finally did go there, a long time later, her experiences were for the most part distressing.

Her picture of this imaginary island, peopled by fine but unfortunately fictitious characters, was in its way as complete and to her as convincing as the picture my Hungarian acquaintances used to have of a country whose typical features were chiefly racecourses and polo grounds, and whose most characteristic human phenomena were Lord Rosebery and a stable-boy touching his cap.

The picture which Madame T formed of England resembled this one only inasmuch as it, too, was the product of an overpowering desire to believe that somewhere there must exist a land where the alarms, exasperations and sufferings of life here have no existence, where people are well conducted, sympathetic to one's views and endeavours, and in a general way more congenial than the types at present surrounding one.

As a very young woman her life had been rendered tragic by cruelty and violence, so that in her view the English must be above all kindly and moderate. As the exceptionally beautiful daughter of an upper-class Austro-Hungarian family, she had been in the early years of the war the central figure in a *cause célèbre* which filled the newspapers for days and, starting simply as a court case, became somehow symbolic – a kind of test case in which all sorts of political, social and moral conflicts were suddenly revealed and engaged.

108

In her teens, and before it had occurred to her that there was anything to do other than accept the outlook and conventions of her class and period, she was married to a man who may have been, as she later claimed to believe, a mere brute, or – more likely – was simply a commonplace individual, moving in a thick skin of convention and contemporary prejudice. However that may have been, the fact was that to her this husband began to appear the embodiment of the society in which she lived, and in consequence the observation of his deficiencies and vices led her to observe with an increasingly keen and bitter eye the deficiencies and vices of that society itself. When World War I broke out, the husband automatically became an officer in the army and made himself more horrifying to his wife than ever by welcoming the war as a splendid tonic for the nation, calculated to revive and restore the manly virtues of the Austro-Hungarian Empire and teach everyone else a sharp lesson.

In this, of course, he was only repeating what all the other men of his kind were saying, but to his wife, who had a curious prevision of what the war was really going to be like, he seemed a murderous monster, rejoicing that hundreds of thousands of people were going to be blown to pieces, frozen to death or rotted with disease.

Then she fell in love. The lover was, I think, an engineer; at any rate he had some job which was 'indispensable', so that he was not snatched into the army and also even in war-time was permitted to travel outside the country. I forget how long it was before they decided to run away together, but in 1915 their careful plans were at length complete and a new life was due to begin. They were to meet in Munich, go from there to Switzerland, and soon after that leave the horrors of old Europe behind and start a life of freedom and useful work overseas. The lover, I think, wanted to get to Switzerland first, and then notify the husband. However, she said that would be dishonourable and cowardly. On the news, the husband came to Munich and adopted what seemed a very restrained and reasonable attitude, talking of fate, the unsettling influence of the war, and indicating in general that he could do nothing but accept the situation.

At the last moment he said that he would like to have a private discussion on various points with the lover. The lover hesitated, but Madame T, feeling that it was the husband's right to have such a discussion if he wanted it, persuaded the lover to agree, and watched the two men walk off along the street together. The husband took the lover to his hotel room and there shot him through the lower part of the back – boasting afterwards that he had some medical knowledge and therefore had been able to place his shots in such a fashion as to render death as lingering and painful as possible.

It was hours before Madame T heard anything of what had happened, and when she rushed to the hospital where the dying man was lying, she was refused admittance on the ground that she was not a relative and she never saw him again.

The case, of course, aroused all the ordinary emotions and controversies which surround a *crime passionel*, and this affair was the more explosive because it came at a moment when war-weariness and 'anti-militarism' were already becoming serious in Austria, while to the 'patriotic' elements it seemed that to condemn or even censure an officer of the army for shooting the civilian lover of his wife would be an insult to the army, an attack upon it and its traditions. Also the unashamed behaviour of the young lovers, their cool plans to leave the country, appeared in the overheated and terrifying atmosphere of the time a sort of portent, a gesture of revolt. A few years later the husband would almost certainly have served a sentence for manslaughter, but in 1915 he symbolised the sanctity of the home, the rights of males and the honour of the army. Nothing, or nothing serious, happened to him.

To the young woman, a society which she had already felt oppressive became intolerable, and now there was no way of personal escape from it. She began to feel indeed, as the months went by, that even if some such avenue of personal escape were to be opened, she would not follow it, for she was sure that nothing of a personal or individual character could ever soothe the agony of her mind or liberate her from the vision of that street in Munich. Increasingly she began to concentrate her attention on the possibilities of some general liberation, the creation of some world in which two people would live at peace and free from the pressure of those evil forces of society which, as she felt, had destroyed her life.

She began to study the revolutionary pamphlets of Lenin and Zinoviev which were smuggled from Zürich into Austria. The overthrow of the Tsar and the Russian Revolution of October 1917 seemed to announce that there were no dreams that could not be made into realities, no retreats or defeats that could not be converted into advances and victories.

Still young, beautiful and passionately sincere, and possessed of furious energy and angry courage, she played, in the revolutionary youth movements of Vienna between 1917 and 1919, a considerable rôle. After the overthrow of the Communist régimes in Budapest and Munich and with the revolutionary tide ebbing in Austria too, she became involved in some quarrel, the details of which I never fully understood, with the Communist Party leaders, apparently on the ground that she considered them lacking in speed and energy, and thought that the road they planned to take towards the revolution was far too long and tortuous. In disillusion she devoted herself once again to painting, which she had for a number of years nearly abandoned.

She looked with an amused, rather sardonic eye upon the members of the Baroness's salon whose personal lives had been less tempestuous than her own. For people whom she thought pretentious or insincere she had a savage contempt. Perhaps on account of her own disappointments and disillusionments she thought that very few of them were likely to 'come to' anything much, and at the same time she retained a pathetic yet basically admirable hope and belief that out of the midst of all this jostling and conversation there would one day emerge wonderful people with wonderful ideas, and the world which seemed temporarily bogged down, stupefied, would move forward hopefully again. She knew, of course, usually in vivid and satiric detail, the life histories of most of the members of the group, so that whereas at the outset I had had only a superficial picture of this, to me, unknown aspect of Europe as it existed here and now, presently I began to see it in depth, against its historical background, and to be more sharply aware of complex and colourful interrelations of individual characters and ambitions, and the impersonal forces of destiny and history.

I began to be irked by my own ignorance of the events and particularly of the writings which had so profoundly affected these people's lives. Reluctantly, because I felt sure it would be tedious and utterly wrong-headed and mistaken, I bought in Vienna on my way to the chalet in the Austrian Alps a volume – nicely printed now and freely displayed in the bookshop – containing all those pamphlets and manifestos of Lenin and Zinoviev which eleven years before had had to be smuggled dangerously across Europe, and were now collected under the general title *Against the Stream*.

'The Stream' was of course the current of majority socialist opinion in most of the belligerent countries in favour of the prosecution of the war. In the intervals of canœing or boating on the icy, brilliantly blue waters of the Grundlsee, climbing to high places to see the shining or shadowy panorama of the Alps, chattering lazily under the fruit trees with fellow guests, or walking over the grassy hills by moonlight to drink freshly distilled plum brandy in the kitchens of upland farms, I set myself to examine in a rather desultory fashion those hysterical polemics, packed tight as shell-cases with high explosive. I found them shocking, repugnant, alien. They pricked and tickled like a hair shirt. They seemed to generate an intolerable heat. They existed in a world of notions with which I had no contact, and, exasperatingly, they dared totally and contemptuously to disregard most of the assumptions to which I had been brought up and educated, or else to treat them brusquely as dangerous delusions peddled by charlatans bent on deceiving the people.

I was bewildered, too, and shaken by a mysterious and violent quality of style, as though some intellectual masseur had got one's brain down on a slab and were twisting and pummelling it. 'As to that,' said the poet Ezra Pound, 'in the style of Lenin the space between word and action is less than in that of any other writer I know.'

Accompanied by the composer George Antheil, Pound had turned up in Vienna, and having read a fiction story of mine which he liked in the New York *Dial*, sent me – the first and only written communication I had from him – a note written apparently on lavatory paper in blue chalk saying, 'Hail. Dial story great. Can we meet? What chance you coming this city jolly month June?'

By his own writings I had been more profoundly affected – 'changed' one could almost say – than by anything else I had read during the previous few years, and I hurried to Vienna to meet him. I could afford only a couple of days there, but we spent several hours of them together. At that time Pound had the idea of establishing himself in Vienna and thereby, as he said with his characteristic mixture of arrogance and irony, turning the place into the cultural centre of Europe. As a first step he was going, if he could get suitable backing for it, to start a monthly review. He had got hold of a gloomy-looking old man called Herr Muller who, he said, was keenly interested. But after Herr Muller, at his own request, had been introduced to me, it soon became apparent that he was not interested in Pound and his literary review, but in me and the London *Times*, and the reason for this was that, as emerged a little later, Herr Muller operated a small and by no means thriving international espionage organisation, buying what he hoped might pass for secrets wherever he could get them cheaply, and selling them as expensively as possible in whatever market he could find. He had used Pound only as an excuse for approaching me and suggesting, at first in a suitably roundabout way and then, as I appeared obtuse, in so many words, that someone connected with *The Times* must have access to all sorts of secrets, or at any rate – which in Herr Muller's mind amounted to the same thing – could be represented as having such access. Before coming down to cases in this fashion he had taken me to the house where he lived and we were seated in a spacious and ostentatiously 'luxurious' living-room full of grandiose furniture and hung with expensive-looking tapestries. As we lit large cigars, he waved a hand to indicate the extent and character of the place.

'You see,' he said, 'the style in which I live. Not bad, you think? Quite so. In my business luxury, which in any case I insist upon, is also a business asset. For a young man like yourself – I don't suppose your salary at *The Times* is enormous, though I do not mean to suggest that it is otherwise than commensurate with the prestige of that paper – but still at the same time a young man can always use a little extra money, no? Girls from the musical comedy choruses, those little dinners with champagne in the *cabinet particulier* of some discreet cabaret?'

With leers he continued for some time to develop this sketch of Victorian delights. And at intervals he would again draw attention with his hand to the spacious apartment offering tangible proof of the profits to be made out of his business.

At length he lay back, puffing at his cigar and watching me expectantly. At this very moment the door of the apartment crashed open, and on the threshold there stood a big grey-haired woman in a quilted dressing-gown and turban, looking exactly like my conception of what is meant by the word 'harridan'. She actually stamped her foot and pointed at Herr Muller a finger which actually trembled with rage. 'How many times,' she screamed, 'have I told you, Herr Muller, that if I occasionally lend you my sitting-room to receive your guests in, you are on no account to smoke cigars in it? Kindly retire to your own room!'

Almost before she had finished speaking, Herr Muller had jumped from his chair and, babbling some frantic words of apology and farewell to myself, had pulled open the door of what I had supposed was a cupboard in the wall. Before he shot into it and slammed the door behind him, I had a glimpse of an ill-lighted closet, which seemed to be almost entirely full of bed. By this time the landlady had rushed into the room, snatched the heavy cloth from a table near the door and was whirling it round her head, like a retiarius whirling his gladiatorial net, in order to dispel the cigar smoke. It seemed best to leave as quietly as possible, smoking what remained of Herr Muller's cigar – the only profit I ever made out of the espionage business.

I returned to Berlin to find that *The Times* which, a few weeks before, had repeated its insistence that I was not to be allowed to write anything – they were afraid, Ebbutt gathered, that I was trying to chisel myself into a position where I would suddenly demand a job or a quantity of back pay – had suddenly reversed itself. Despite their injunctions I had written an article about the Hugenberg Trust, the vast newspaper, advertising and cinema combine controlled by the extreme Nationalist, Alfred Hugenberg (later a patron of Hitler), and particularly about the use of the German films of extreme Nationalist propaganda. *The Times* published it, and now had written to suggest that the best thing for me to do was to leave Berlin immediately, return to England and start going through the hoops which, by what *The Times* like to consider an unbreakable law, had to be negotiated before one could hope to become a foreign correspondent.

Theoretically, candidates deemed worthy of trial were sent first to serve an apprenticeship on some newspaper in Liverpool, Newcastle or Nottingham. If they survived that, they did a spell in the home room of *The Times* occupied with domestic reporting, and were then – assuming that worthiness was maintained – transferred to the Foreign Room. After that all was uncertainty. Some people, who had entered the Foreign Room in the belief that they would be out of it again in a year or so and on the way to *The Times* bureau in Vienna or Buenos Aires, remained there for years and years, and in the end often lost any inclination to be anywhere else.

The prospect of abandoning for Nottingham or Newcastle the Berlin which I was just beginning to discover presented itself as both distasteful and ridiculous. In particular, the violent voice I had heard for the first time by the Grundlsee kept exasperatingly ringing in my head. It was a low insistent drumming, and annoyed and disconcerted me, but it had the effect of an assurance that there existed unknown territories and horizons, which, if I were now to involve myself in regular 'gainful employment', would never be visited or viewed by me. Just then my father died, and England seemed more distastefully, more drearily alien to me than ever.

I wrote rejecting *The Times*'s offer. I thought that probably this meant I should never be a Correspondent of *The Times* at all, but Ebbutt, on information received from London, said that on the contrary the people at Printing House Square had been shocked but rather pleased – for years nobody had actually refused a job on *The Times;* they thought this showed originality. It was agreed that I might occasionally write short items of news for the paper under the strict supervision of the regular Correspondent, which was, in fact, what I had been doing for weeks past.

Then, towards the end of a blazing afternoon, tornados of rain rushed suddenly down on Berlin, and there were reports of a cloudburst on the borders of southern Saxony. The reports in the evening papers had that curious smell about them which suggests immediately that somebody somewhere is trying to conceal something. Ebbutt was away on a couple of weeks' leave and his place was being taken by a Mr Barker. He and I both had this curious impression that something rum, and possibly sensational, had taken place in the mountains down there beyond Dresden.

Since I was not a member of the staff and quite possibly nothing had happened at all, he could not take the responsibility of handing me any of *The Times*'s money so that I could go there on the off-chance. He did, however, suggest that if I could raise enough to get there, and if anything important really had happened, the gamble would have been worth while. I could raise only enough to travel fourth class, in a series of trains which moved all night at the speed of city trams. I got there at dawn, observed with satisfaction that there were no other journalists about, and found that, in one of the strangest small-scale catastrophes of the decade, the cloudburst had poured unheard-of quantities of water into mild little mountain streams, which tore down trees formerly far above their beds, jammed the broken trees against the bridges until they formed high timber dams, and, pushed higher than ever by the dams, rose and rushed along the streets of sleeping villages on the valley sides, peeling off the fronts of houses like wet cardboard, and killing more than a hundred people in a few minutes. Half a mile of that little valley smelled of death. There were corpses in the mud and in one house the table in an upper back room had been laid for breakfast. In several other houses canaries were singing or moping in their cages.

Years later, in Spain, a colleague of mine was sharply criticised for mentioning a canary as the only living creature in one of the bombed houses of a village. 'But you can't,' people said, 'use that damned canary again.' He admitted it was a bit corny and took it out of his story. I suppose the trouble is that life is a good deal cornier than it ought to be, for there really was a canary in its cage in that bombed Spanish village, and there really were canaries in the wrecked houses with breakfast laid ready, and no one to eat it, or to feed the canary.

No other newspaper in London had had a man on the spot, and their stories were scrappy compared to the column *The Times* had next day. After that *The Times* wrote again, suggesting that perhaps I might be permitted to cut out the period of apprenticeship in the English provinces and go straight into the Foreign Room in London. And, when I refused this offer too, they presently wrote a third time proposing that I should cut out the Foreign Room, too, and simply stay where I was as Assistant Correspondent in Berlin. This blithe disregard of the hoops which I had always understood it was necessary to pass through quite worried me. It seemed to me almost as though the Church of England had told someone that he could be ordained without bothering to get confirmed first. Finally I asked a visiting High Priest from Printing House Square about it. His reply was an exhilarating example of what perhaps may be called *The Times* spirit.

'That,' he said – referring to the traditional hoops – 'is our rule. Unwritten, but I hope you take it no less seriously for that.'

'Not at all,' I said hastily. 'I just wondered. . . .'

'And a very sound rule it is,' said the High Priest, sternly. 'Very sound indeed. Remember that.'

I never, as a matter of fact, heard of the rule again.

However, with every day that passed my claustrophobic distaste for immuring myself in a regular job increased, and again I refused. My resolve was strengthened, no doubt, by the fact that I had recently sold a few articles and short stories to German and American newspapers.

Even Ebbutt, always optimistic on my behalf, thought that this third refusal might have put an end to my beautiful friendship with *The Times*. However, nobody seemed to mind my continuing to occupy the centre room at the Berlin office, working there as I chose without pay except for special articles, and without any definite obligations.

A little later in the summer, rioting broke out in Vienna on a scale which caused many quite serious observers to believe that the second wave of East European revolution was beginning; the Chief Correspondent – either Ebbutt or Barker, I forgot which at the moment – had to rush off at a moment's notice, and nobody seemed to find it odd that I should be left in sole charge of the office Unter den Linden.

It was a particularly nerve-racking experience, because someone in the Head Office not only believed that this was the beginning of a new revolution in Europe, but was determined to prove it and to have *The Times* be the first to demonstrate that this was what was going to happen. I got a series of telegrams asking with increasing petulance why I had failed, for instance, to report the news that the Russian Trade Delegation in Germany had that very day been ordered by the German authorities to leave, on the ground that it had been engaged in trying to spread the 'Austrian revolt' to the Reich. The German Home Office, the Foreign Office and the members of the Russian Trade Delegation itself all denied the story and expressed bewilderment, but when I reported these denials to London at intervals throughout the afternoon and evening, the London people thought my reports were due to inexperience and went on telephoning excitedly about the matter far into the night.

The next day was worse, because I was visited by a super-V.I.P. from Printing House Square – an intimate, they said, of Cabinet Ministers – whose visit had been announced to us quite a long time before, but whom I had forgotten in the excitement of those days. I welcomed him nevertheless with enthusiasm, thinking it would be illuminating and helpful to converse at such a moment with someone right at the top of things.

What this super-V.I.P. was tremendously keen on was photography, and it turned out that what he had especially come to see was an exhibition of *Times* photographs at some gallery on the Kurfuerstendamm. He went to it and arrived later Unter den Linden much disappointed. The exhibition was poorly attended – a consequence, he opined, of inadequately energetic publicity by the Berlin staff.

I observed that Berlin, that particular day, was in a state of mass hysteria. The supposed imminence of upheaval, cataclysm and catastrophe might be distracting people's attention from our exhibits. In Vienna streets were running with blood.

He did not conceal his view that my suggestion was a puerile evasion of responsibility.

'No, no,' he said. 'The fact is, there has been a failure to make clear the nature of this exhibition. I believe people are under the impression these are simply photographs cut from the pages of *The Times*. If it were realised these are the original photographs, things would be very different.'

It was truly awe-inspiring. Mentally, as I look back, I see that man on a peak beside another dedicated soul, an antiquarian in Cumberland, who once told me that what was wrong with Lloyd George was that he utterly failed to use the trench-digging experience gained by the troops in World War I to get Hadrian's Wall properly excavated. A better man would have held up demobilisation until that had been done.

The V.I.P.'s visit to Berlin was an elevating, a climacteric experience. No statement by any V.I.P. anywhere ever surprised me again.

Quite a number of my friends and acquaintances from the party at the Kaiserhof had dashed to Vienna to see the revolution if that was what it was really going to be, or to observe at close quarters this extraordinary explosion in the midst of a relatively calm European summer. When they returned, their circle had been enlarged to include, temporarily, a lively section of the United States in the shape of Mr Sinclair Lewis. Even Herr Uhlmann, who regarded most of my friends with suspicion, as being Austrians and suchlike, lacking tempo, was wildly excited by this irruption and begged me to take him to a small party at which Mr Lewis was to be present.

His meeting with the great novelist was found by Herr Uhlmann to be exciting, but startling, too, like a first trip on the giant dipper.

Herr Uhlmann's intention had been to spend an hour or so happily cross-questioning Mr Lewis on such matters as

Americanism, Babbitry, and the Philosophy of Main Street. Lewis, however, was tired and turned up rather drunk. From beneath his jacket hung the ends of two towels clearly marked with the name of his hotel. He had them knotted round his waist to keep his trousers up. Herr Uhlmann at once thought this significant of something or other – the American revolt against convention, perhaps. But when he mentioned it to Lewis, the novelist looked at the knotted towels with an air of surprise as if he had only just noticed them and merely said he supposed his belt must have got broken or lost.

Herr Uhlmann wished to start a discussion of trends in modern world literature, and had brought an intimidating notebook in which he was going to write down his 'observations' on these matters. Lewis, for his part, was anxious to give a rendering of a song he had just heard or just composed, a parody of 'I didn't raise my Boy to be a Soldier.'

'I didn't raise my boy,' he chanted loudly, 'to be a bourgeois, I raised him to be the Third International's pride and joy. But the son of a bitch has gone and gotten rich, my boy! my boy! my boy!'

I undertook a forlorn and stumbling attempt at explaining to Herr Uhlmann the joke – starting with the origins and political character of the original song. Probably it was hopeless from the start, and in any case I had hardly begun before we were all attacked by a dog which Lewis had with him, but did not have under control. This dog was the property of the future Mrs Lewis – better known as Dorothy Thompson – who was at that time either still married to, or just divorced from, her first, Hungarian, husband. The dog, an ungainly Airedale which looked like the Mock Turtle in *Alice in Wonderland,* had apparently esteemed the first husband and did not thus esteem Lewis. Or else he regarded Lewis as the breaker of a home to which the dog had become comfortably accustomed. However that may have been, this Airedale followed Lewis about like an angry detective, literally dogging his footsteps, in what at first sight looked like devotion but was really hatred. Every now and then, exasperated possibly by the man's vigour and well-being, the dog would lose command of its temper, and bite either Lewis or one of his friends. The situation got so bad that in the end the dog was given to the biologist, Dr Wiesner, but it broke loose in the Schering chemical laboratories, where some vital experiment was in progress, and dashed about smashing things, setting back the course of science by several months before it was recaptured. Wiesner then gave it to Madame T., who, when she went to Vienna for the Christmas holidays, left it in my care.

It was a horrible Christmas for the dog, because just at that time I had run entirely out of money, and was living chiefly on expectations of a cheque from the United States which never came. To begin with, the dog fed fairly well because the butcher round the corner always had a pile of scraps – offal, bacon rind and the like – which he gave me free when I bought meat for myself. But on Christmas Eve when everyone I knew had left town for the holiday I found, distressingly, that I had only just enough money to buy a couple of drinks and some tobacco.

Feeling very low mentally and morally, I went round to that butcher and told him that I myself was, of course, invited to eat my Christmas dinner with friends, and therefore did not wish to buy anything for myself, but was anxious that the dog should have a particularly good Christmas dinner. The kindly butcher made up an unusually large and nasty-looking parcel of scraps, which I took home and cooked. The dog watched me with satisfaction. But the next day at noon, when he saw me carefuly dividing the mess into equal portions and putting only half of it on his plate, his disappointment and indignation knew no bounds. At first he watched me with an expression of sheer incredulity. Then, when he saw me actually digging my fork into that portion of his dinner which I had reserved for myself, he got up on his hind legs with his forepaws on the table, and threw back his head, howling in astonishment and despair at the pass things had come to.

During these bouts of poverty my principal amusement was visiting the theatre, for I had persuaded *The Times* to let me act as their occasional dramatic critic in Berlin, writing about once a month a half-column or so on the latest events in the German theatre.

The Times was of course unaware that, for some reason which I have never fully understood, I had until that season in Berlin been in the theatre only twice before in my life. The only two plays I had seen were a performance of *Twelfth Night* at, I think, the Court Theatre, London, to which I was taken with a group of sixth-form boys from school, and a play called *The Man from Toronto* of which I happened to see a matinée performance because it was pouring with rain in

Shaftesbury Avenue that afternoon. This gave to my dramatic criticisms a notable freshness and enthusiasm. The clever arrangement of the concealed-lighting fixtures, the way in which the curtain rose and fell so smoothly, excited my admiration. And, when there was a play about a man who fell in love with the wife of his best friend, the plot seemed to me in the highest degree striking and ingenious, and the situation packed with novelty and tension.

I was naturally rather popular with Berlin theatre managers, but later became more sophisticated and calm. Indeed, when in the early autumn of the following year I went to Paris, and continued my dramatic criticism from there, I had become so censorious that an actress actually spat at me in a café, and, later still, when I wrote about the theatre from New York I was so knowledgeable that the Shuberts at one time refused me admission to any of their theatres.

If anything could have made that winter in Paris tolerable it would have been the kindness of the two Assistant Correspondents of *The Times*, Mr Victor Cunard and Mr David Scott. (Mr Scott was the man who, many years afterwards, immortalised himself by the terms of his letter of resignation from the B.B.C. He said that to work for the B.B.C. was like having sexual relations with an elephant, for three reasons: First because there was no possible pleasure involved, secondly because of the grave danger of being overlaid, and thirdly because there was no possibility of seeing any results for twenty-one months.) However, nothing could have made it tolerable. I was miserably poor and lived in a hovel which called itself a studio on the brow of the ridge of Paris near Fontenay-aux-Roses.

The view, to be sure, was almost ridiculously sublime. The studio looked right across Paris to the Sacré Cœur, and the ridge of Montmartre on the north side, and sometimes rainbows came, and you could see their ends decorating in many colours the Odéon over to the east, and the racecourse at Auteuil on the west. But the bed was made of a couple of packing-cases, and the mattress of straw, and snow drove in through the walls and the roof, to make wet heaps on the bare boards of the floor. Also an aged Russian emigré who had occupied the lower part of the house died and, although I never saw him after his death, visitors to my studio, who knew of neither his existence nor death, saw him quite clearly sitting in the corner of my room pointing at the company in a terribly menacing manner. I lived on potato soup and

121

boiled leeks, which are delicious but became at that time so sickening to me that it was years before I could eat them again.

In the spring I was waiting anxiously for the last instalment of my Fellowship payment to arrive, and at length wrote urgently and rather irritably to Queen's College to enquire about it. The reply was disconcerting. It pointed out that the instalments had all along been paid in advance, and I had had the last one a month ago. There was nothing more to come at all. In these circumstances I wrote to *The Times* saying that although I had previously rejected their offers, I had now finished the period of my Fellowship, and would like to work as a *Times* correspondent provided, however, that I could do so in New York.

The reason for this was that by now I had widely extended the studies I had begun beside the Grundlsee, had read *Das Kapital* and the *18th Brumaire* and *Civil War in France* and other works of Marx; read Lenin's *State and Revolution,* and *Imperialism,* and *Materialism* and *Empirical Criticism,* and been particularly impressed by Bukharin's *Historical Materialism.* Yet at the same time highly informed books continued to appear in quantity, proving that what was happening in the United States in that year of boom, 1929, was making the sheerest nonsense of Marx, Lenin, Bukharin and everyone else of their way of thinking. The United States hung over my thoughts like an enormous question mark. I felt that I should never be able to make up my mind about anything unless I went there and saw for myself.

Mr Geoffrey Dawson, then Editor of *The Times,* did not have the reputation of a particularly warm-hearted or sympathetic man, but his response to my letter was a gesture which indicated a quick sensibility to my situation, and a realisation that maximum speed might be of very considerable importance to me, as indeed it was. He did not write, he simply telegraphed. 'Have no fear for to-morrow. Return at once. Job waiting.'

X PRINTING HOUSE SQUARE

NOTHING SETS A PERSON UP MORE THAN HAVING something turn out just the way it's supposed to be, like falling into a Swiss snowdrift and seeing a big dog come up with a little cask of brandy round its neck.

The first time I travelled on the Orient Express I was accosted by a woman who was later arrested and turned out to be a quite well-known international spy. When I talked with Al Capone there was a sub-machine gun poking through the transom of the door behind him. Ernest Hemingway spoke out of the corner of his mouth. In an Irish castle a sow ran right across the baronial hall. The first Minister of Government I met told me a most horrible lie almost immediately.

These things were delightful, and so was the first view of *The Times* office in London. In the Foreign Editorial Room a sub-editor was translating a passage of Plato's *Phœdo* into Chinese, for a bet. Another sub-editor had declared it could not be done without losing a certain nuance of the original. He was dictating the Greek passage aloud from memory.

That very first evening I saw the chief sub-editor hand a man a slip of Reuter's Agency 'tape' with two lines on it saying that the Duke of Gloucester on his world tour had arrived at Kuala Lumpur and held a reception. It would run to about half an inch of space, and on some newspapers I dare say might have been got ready for the printer in a matter of minutes. I was glad to see nothing of that kind happen here.

The sub-editor, a red-bearded man with blazing blue eyes, who looked like a cross between John the Baptist and Captain Kettle, had at the age of twenty or thereabouts written the definitive grammar of an obscure Polynesian language and gone on to be – a curious position for an Englishman – a professor of Chinese metaphysics in the University of Tokio. He took the slip of paper into the library and then to the

Athenæum, where he sometimes used to go for a cold snack during *The Times* dinner hour.

His work on it was completed only just in time for the ten o'clock edition. It had been a tricky job. 'There are,' he explained, 'eleven correct ways of spelling Kuala Lumpur, and it is difficult to decide which should receive the, as it were, *imprimatur* of *The Times*.'

All foreign correspondents believe sub-editors to be malevolent troglodytes, happiest when casually massacring the most significant lines of an informed, well-balanced despatch. Sub-editors believe foreign correspondents to be flibbertigibbets, uselessly squandering enormous expense accounts, lazy and verbose, and saved from making fools of themselves in print only by the vigilance of the staff in the Foreign Room.

Sharing, myself, the correspondents' views of people working at the London headquarters, I was naturally nervous. However, *The Times* people proved genial and made kindly efforts to put me at my ease. One told me that, although the London climate was lethal, one could prolong life by getting up very early three times a week and travelling to Southend for a brisk twenty minutes' walk on the sea-front.

'And of course,' he said, rather mysteriously, 'being in the train so much gives one more time for thinking and reading.'

(He was, I need hardly say, a Fellow of All Souls.)

I said I hoped to be leaving shortly for New York. He was sincerely sorry for me – such an awfully long way from healthy Southend.

This conversation took place at tea, a rather serious function performed round a large oval table in a room on the ground floor of Printing House Square. We reached the office at about four in the afternoon and went straight down to tea and a half-hour's conversation before going up to the Foreign Room, a big, well-lighted place overlooking Queen Victoria Street, furnished principally by a long narrow table, extending from the inner wall almost to the windows. Junior members of the Foreign staff like myself sat at the part of the table nearest to the Chief Foreign Sub-editor. The seniors at the far end barricaded themselves with volumes of the *Encyclopædia Britannica* or other large books and thus were able, as one of them remarked to me, to 'get on with our work without being disturbed'.

I did not at first see why this type of protection should be necessary, but later learned that several of them were engaged in writing historical works of their own, or authoritative treatises for various learned reviews, on the subject in which they were particularly expert. Mr Scott Moncrieff, the translator of Proust, worked there at one period, and I was told that the business of *The Times* was often held up for as much as a half-hour at a time while everyone present joined expertly in a discussion of the precise English word or phrase which would best convey the meaning and flavour of a passage in the *Recherche du Temps Perdu.*

For further entertainment in the long evenings, someone had invented a game – a competition with a small prize for the winner – to see who could write the dullest headline. It had to be a genuine headline, that is to say one which was actually printed in the next morning's newspaper. I won it only once with a headline which announced: 'Small Earthquake in Chile. Not many dead.'

From five until about eight o'clock work continued without a break, and then people went to eat at their clubs or the *Times* dining-room or the canteen. Unless you were on late duty you finished work at about eleven o'clock.

At first I was fascinated by the work, but after a few weeks I became bored and rather nervous because I was still afraid that someone would notice that I had not gone through any of the proper hoops, and pack me off to Newcastle instead of New York. Sometimes it seemed to me that I caught one or other of the High Priests looking at me somewhat askance, as though, perhaps, I were not, after all, worthy of *The Times.* My alarm was increased by the discovery that everyone already knew the story of something which had happened in Berlin one day when Ebbutt was on holiday and his place had been taken by a man called Pugge or something similar. Extensive unrest and street fighting were going on in Berlin at the time – I think it arose out of a demonstration on May Day. It was a confused situation and many people opposed to the unemployed demonstrators also thought the Prussian police were acting trigger-happy. Pugge, the newcomer, had no doubt that it was a straight fight of law and order versus the licentious mob. Any hesitant angels caught loitering were apt to get a sharp pushing around when Pugge rushed on to the scene.

Irked somewhat by his attitude I wrote, one afternoon when he was out watching the shooting, the despatch which I conceived Pugge would have written – From Our Own Correspondent in Jerusalem – had he been covering events there

125

approximately two thousand years ago. It was a level-headed estimate studded with well-tried *Times* phrases. 'Small disposition here,' cabled this correspondent, 'attach undue importance protests raised certain quarters result recent arrest and trial leading revolutionary agitator followed by what is known locally as "the Calvary incident".' The despatch was obviously based on an off-the-record interview with Pontius Pilate. It took the view that, so far from acting harshly, the Government had behaved with what in some quarters was criticised as 'undue clemency'. It pointed out that firm Government action had definitely eliminated this small band of extremists, whose doctrines might otherwise have represented a serious threat for the future.

I put it on Pugge's desk. Glancing rapidly through it after a tiring day and seeing familiar *Times* clichés – small disposition to attach undue importance, Government acting with firmness, band of extremists – all bowing and scraping at him from every paragraph, Pugge did not bother to read it properly, and passed it, together with his own despatch, to the telephonist.

By a piece of ill-luck it chanced that *The Times* had recently reorganised its European telephone system, with the result that the Berlin office was used as a relay centre for despatches from a number of smaller capitals which formerly had communicated direct with London.

The telephonist was already vexed by the extra work involved. Now he came rushing back from the switchboard waving my despatch in a mauve fury.

'What's all this?' he shouted. 'Are we taking flaming Jerusalem now?'

Mr Pugge was abominably shocked. I had always hoped to hear someone use the phrase 'in the worst possible taste'. Pugge did. He did his best to bring home to me the appalling character of my action.

'Do you appreciate,' he said, 'that what you have done is to attempt to play a *joke* on *The Times*?'

This he obviously felt was the most blasphemous aspect of an altogether blasphemous bit of work. And in my present state of anxiety it seemed to me that there were several people around Printing House Square who would probably share this view. I began to wonder whether the job that had been waiting for me was really the New York job or something quite different and, from my point of view, unsuitable.

It was difficult to find out, because Mr Geoffrey Dawson

had perfected a technique for not telling people anything much, and yet appearing all the time both approachable and communicative. His room had two doors. When you had been announced, and had entered, you found him standing in front of his desk, poised always on the same mark on the carpet, both hands slightly outstretched and his whole attitude that of one who has been unable to prevent himself bounding from his chair and rushing forward to meet you. Already touched and impressed, you were further overwhelmed by the warmth of his greeting and the voluble geniality of his conversation as he put his hand on your shoulder or took your arm.

There you were, pacing the floor of the sanctum of the Editor-in-Chief of *The Times*, and he concentrating on you while his secretary, you could imagine, told anxious cabinet ministers and bishops over the telephone that the editor was in conference. The effect was practically hypnotic, and in this state of partial hypnosis you were scarcely aware that with one arm across your shoulders the Editor was with the other hand opening the door at the far end of his office and pushing you gently into the corridor, bidding you a warm farewell after an interview which had lasted approximately eighty seconds.

Nothing had been promised, nothing decided; but for several hours you certainly felt that you had accomplished something or other.

As things stood I need not have bothered about my position because, without my knowing it, Sir Campbell Stuart, at that time one of the most energetic directors of *The Times*, and the man who had played a major rôle in preventing the paper being acquired by Lord Rothermere after the death of Lord Northcliffe, had been kindly watching over my interests, for he was a Canadian and a friend of my Uncle Frank. I had told my uncle that I wanted to go nowhere but New York – though I had concealed from him the full reason for so wishing. My Uncle Frank, who looked upon Europe as little more than a fascinating museum in which it was good for people on holiday to pass a certain amount of time each year, was enthusiastic about my decision, and he enlisted the help of Sir Campbell Stuart to ensure that I was not disappointed.

Sir Campbell Stuart lived with his mother in his suite at the top of the Hyde Park Hotel, and when I finally went to call on him there, he lay almost flat on his back in an armchair, and with his extremely long and angular legs extended to the fire, smiled at the ceiling in a whimsical manner as he explained to me the real reason for the delay in my appointment and the apparent inability of the Editor to make up his mind.

'They are afraid,' he said, 'of Louis Hinrichs.'

This character, of whom I had never previously heard, immediately assumed formidable proportions in my eyes. To be a man of whom *The Times* was statedly afraid was sufficiently imposing. Who and what was Louis Hinrichs? And why was *The Times* afraid of him?

Well, it appeared that Louis Hinrichs was the New York Correspondent of *The Times* and had formerly been the Wall Street Correspondent of *The Times* and the *Daily Mail* when the two papers were in the same ownership. *The Times,* said Sir Campbell Stuart, was afraid of him because he knew about finance, Wall Street, stocks and shares, things like that. Sir Campbell spoke of *The Times* with a mixture of respect and affectionate derision, as though of a distinguished but elderly uncle having venerable abilities and a good many more or less ludicrous quirks of character. Or, as I sometimes suspected, he felt himself rather in the position of the able butler when the entire family of aristocrats is marooned on a desert island and the butler, despite his comparatively lowly Colonial origins, is the only one who knows how to deal with reality and pull them through.

Smiling at the ceiling, Sir Campbell Stuart explained to me that *The Times* had a certain awe of anybody who in fact understood finance. He described to me a meeting which had taken place a couple of years previously in London between the Foreign Editor of *The Times,* Mr Louis Hinrichs, and the newly appointed Rumanian Ambassador to Washington who had stopped over in London on his way to get advice. He was, of course, attempting to negotiate a loan. The Foreign Editor had turned to Hinrichs and had asked him to sketch for the benefit of the Ambassador the situation as he saw it in the United States. Hinrichs naturally had dealt in his customary succinct detail with the situation in Wall Street, the possibilities of a bond issue. The Ambassador who, apart from other misapprehensions, confused Bernard Baruch with Senator Borah, listened to all this with distaste. He indicated that what he had hoped to hear from *The Times* Correspondent in New York was something about the inside track of high New York and Washington society, which would guide him in his search for a multi-millonairess bride. To the Ambassador this was deadly serious, but Hinrichs assumed that he was making some kind of a joke at his own expense and continued to explain the current position of the bond market. Sadly the Ambassador, on his way to Wall Street and Washington and the hopes of a loan, shrugged his shoulders and said, '*Enfin, je n'aime pas le finance.*'

'You see,' said Sir Campbell Stuart, '*The Times*'s attitude is really the same as that of that Rumanian Ambassador. They, too, do not love '*le finance*'. They think, in fact,' he began to giggle at the idea, 'that Hinrichs is a holy terror.'

The Times, in fact, liked its Correspondents to be familiar with history, archæology, the classics and the higher reaches of diplomatic society in whichever capital they happened to be established, but it was bothered by people who knew too much about money and economics and even tended to regard these subjects as of greater importance than the personal relationship existing between a cabinet minister, member of political Party A, with a politician, member of political Party B. The idea that they had a Correspondent who really understood Wall Street and positively regarded Wall Street and its problems as essential in the affairs of the world, was to *The Times* awe-inspiring. Hinrichs, in fact, was to them a Man from Mars. And in consequence one had to act pretty gingerly in deciding whom to send him as his office mate and Assistant Correspondent. Therefore everyone had to mark time until Hinrichs, in the late spring, arrived in London and could be confronted with the candidate for this office – that is to say myself.

Since I was determined to go to New York in any case, and the question of whether I went there with a comfortable amount of money and prestige as *The Times* Correspondent or had to struggle off again under my own inadequate steam, depended upon this Louis Hinrichs, I was naturally in a nervous state of mind when I went to call upon him at the Waldorf Hotel at tea-time one afternoon. I can still recall more or less clearly the brutal figure I had expected to meet, and during the first ten minutes of conversation with Louis Hinrichs I was tormented by the fear that some appalling mistake had been made and that I was talking to the wrong man.

He was one of those people whose physical appearance more or less exactly expresses their entire personality. He was unusually tall, stooped a little, and could have been considered emaciated were it not that the fineness and delicacy of his bone structure conformed perfectly to this almost spectacular leanness. His head was small but the face exquisitely aquiline, his eyes rather more luminous than the rest of him had led you to expect, and these eyes and his sensitive mouth prepared you for the otherwise disconcerting variations in the gestures of his enormously long hands and fingers, which sometimes were dryly decisive, and at others fluttered in movements of philosophic bewilderment.

The course of his life had been determined by the San Francisco earthquake of 1906. At that time he had recently come down from Harvard and was living, in New York, the quietly gay existence of an unusually well-to-do young man, interested particularly in music and literature but interested too – as a young man of his type in London at that period would hardly have been – in the American business scene and the movements of the stock market. For a couple of years he had played the market with a reasonable mixture of caution and audacity. He was attracted by the market and its environs in the way that some people are attracted by the theatre, and he used most days of the week to spend a part of the morning at his broker's watching the movements of stocks upon the board, and later lunch at one of the first-rate restaurants which at that time were common enough in the New York financial district, where in the front room a primitive ticker-tape tapped out the prices from the exchanges, and in the back room you could eat the best steaks and, above all, the best sea-food in the world.

It was his custom to glance at the ticker-tape on his way to lunch, lunch comfortably for an hour or so, and take another look at the ticker-tape on his way out after the coffee and brandy. On the day of the earthquake his first look at the ticker was appalling. There had been wild rumours of disaster, and then communication with San Francisco had been broken off, with the result that rumour magnified the disaster enormously and the repercussions were felt right through the country because if, for example, the San Francisco banks were to fail, then banks all over the Pacific Coast would fail, and this would have disastrous consequences for banks in the east. And the same thing would be true of investors and speculators in Californian stock. For a long moment Hinrichs stood puffing at the remains of his cigar and realising with perfect clarity that the proper thing for him to do was to take a further look at the figures and then abandon his lunch, dash back to his brokers and make dispositions so as to avert disaster. Then he looked around at the strained, tremulous, sweat-streaming faces of the other men gathered round that ticker. They too were preparing to abandon their normal habits and dash to their brokers.

'The sight of them,' Hinrichs said, 'rightly or wrongly convinced me that to behave like that was to render oneself a slave of the ticker-tape, to make life not worth living. I decided at that instant that the only thing to do was to pretend that nothing was happening, to eat my lunch and drink my wine as leisurely as was my usual custom, and only when I had had my coffee and brandy to come back and see what had happened.'

He did that, and what had happened, when he saw it, was that the market value of his Western holdings had crashed to nothing, and all his Eastern holdings had been sold out by his panic-stricken broker in an attempt to shore up the Western defences. The attempt had been vain, and as he lit his second cigar of the day Hinrichs admitted that he was without question penniless.

During the afternoon, and in good time for the cocktail hour at the Harvard Club, he had got himself a job as a financial expert with the *New York Evening Sun*. So far as I recall, he was for a time one of the financial editors of the *New York Herald-Tribune*, and I know that after he had gone to work for the Northcliffe organisation – as financial correspondent of *The Times* and *Daily Mail* – he was several times offered the financial editorship of the *Herald-Tribune* which at that time was one of the most influential positions of the kind in New York. He was well paid by *The Times*, but the *Herald-Tribune* was naturally in a position to offer him a great deal more, and just why he steadily refused these approaches was a question which he was never able to answer quite satisfactorily even to himself. Personally I thought that the reason probably was that his position as Wall Street Correspondent of *The Times*, and subsequently as General Correspondent in New York, offered him just that degree of detachment which he required, that same detachment which had ruined him on the day of the earthquake, and which he instinctively felt would have been impossible to preserve as Financial Editor of a leading New York newspaper.

Nevertheless English people, or people at least with English upbringing, were apt to make him nervous. And this, considering his experiences, was not surprising. As his subordinates or colleagues in New York, he had viewed a whole string of English newspapermen and had of course met on more or less intimate terms large numbers of British financiers and industrialists. Most of them had asked him to tell them what he knew, from his vast experience, of the situation in the United States, and after listening to him for an hour, a day, a week or a month, had begun to lecture him on the situation in the United States and the character of the American people.

Because he had that diffidence and capacity for genuine self-criticism which Americans of his type have in a much higher degree than Engish people, they would leap to the conclusion that being an obviously civilised and cultured man he must share all British prejudice about the United States. He was capable of criticising America savagely, but none of these people seem to have caught the peculiar intensity of his intonation when, very occasionally, he would use the phrase 'my *dear America*'.

Few of them seem to have understood – or so at least I gathered from him even in our first conversation – that he loved America in the way Europeans once used to love their countries, and the way a person might his family. At our first meeting he peered at me over a cup of China tea with a mixture of hope and despair. After all, my predecessor had been a very attractive and exceedingly able young man, and what had happened with him was that after a rather short period in *The Times* office in New York he had fallen madly in love with an actress and without notice jumped on a liner and gone to Europe in pursuit of her. It had been for Hinrichs a blow because he was a sensitive being who was incapable, if he did not actually dislike anyone, of not positively liking and cherishing them; expending himself upon them as though they were his son or brother, and building pictures of future co-operation. To me he further explained his present uncertainty and agitation by remarking that during his trip with his family to France, from which he had just returned, his elder son, then about fifteen years old, had suddenly given the family the slip in Paris, leaving a note saying that he was going to discover Andorra by himself. Hinrichs was vividly torn between a complete understanding of the romantic logic of such a boyish undertaking, and a fear that his son might inadvertently come to grief in the course of it. For a half-hour we discussed the simultaneously encouraging and distressing behaviour of his son, and he then realised that in a few minutes he was supposed to go down to *The Times* office and, in effect, tell them what he thought of me. By an extraordinarily courteous piece of acrobatics he managed to reverse our true positions.

'I do hope,' he said, 'that after this meeting you will not reconsider your wish to come to work in New York.'

As we drove down Fleet Street he said, 'You know, I wish I did not have to go to *The Times*. I wish one could simply telephone them to say that everything is all right and that I hope to see you in New York soon. *The Times* frankly terrifies me.'

Recalling vividly that he terrified *The Times,* I could think of nothing to say. He added, just as the taxi swung into Queen Victoria Street, 'You know, sometimes I feel that I really ought to write a letter to *The Times* explaining to them that I am not at all the sort of man they imagine I am.'

In Printing House Square he interviewed Mr Dawson, who was as usual delighted to find that 'everything was all right' and therefore required no supervision or attention on his part. We then went together to see Mr Ralph Deakin, entitled Foreign and Imperial News Editor. Mr Deakin was believed to be the originator of the statement that nothing was news until it had appeared in the columns of *The Times,* and at that period he gave – from his shining shoes to the beautifully brushed bowler hat on the rack behind him – an impression of mental and physical discretion and complacency which could have been offensive had it not been, in its childish way, touching. Certainly nobody could have guessed from his manner that he was the sort of man who would saddle himself with an employee of whom he so clearly disapproved.

Deakin had never made any secret of the fact that he was dubious as to whether I was the 'right type' for *The Times*. I think that he, who was a friend of Pugge, had been seriously influenced by the affair of the Special Correspondent in Jerusalem. He was obviously a little surprised that Hinrichs should accept me. He would have expected him to stand out for something a little more svelte, or else a little more businesslike in appearance. Resignedly he turned from the immediate topic of my impending journey to New York to discuss the fate of one of my predecessors, a former assistant to Hinrichs, who had been brutally murdered by the hangers-on of some Chinese war-lord under the walls of Peking. Hinrichs expressed his sorrow.

'Nevertheless,' said Deakin, 'he had his reward.'

Hinrichs and I, simultaneously startled by this observation on the death of that distinguished young man, exchanged rapid glances, each of us wondering what comment one could possibly make on such a statement. Also it occurred to each of us at the same time that this could only imply the existence of some bitter feud between Deakin and the victim of the banditti, and each of us was horrified to realise that Deakin apparently was prepared to continue this feud beyond the grave. There was a moment of danger during which either of us might have made some extraordinarily ill-placed remark had not Deakin added with a note of extreme satisfaction in his voice, 'Yes, he had his reward. I mean a column-and-a-half obituary in *The Times.*'

'You see,' said Hinrichs as we left the building, "what I mean about *The Times.*'

His son returned unscathed from Andorra, and the Hinrichs family took off for New York. I was to follow them a month later, in July. Just before I left, Geoffrey Dawson thought it proper, or at least inevitable, that we should have a thorough and extensive conversation on the subject of my future duties and responsibilities. He told me that such was his view, and invited me to dine with him one night at his club.

While we were drinking sherry he said that it seemed pointless to get down to any kind of serious business until we had gone up to dinner. At dinner he remarked that it would be a pity to interfere with our enjoyment by too much business talk, and that this kind of talk could very well wait until we were comfortably settled with our port. In the smoking-room he seemed equally incapable of approaching whatever the subject of our talk had been designed to be. At this point I realised that he in fact closely resembled in some aspects of his character my Oxford philosophy tutor and that he, having nerved himself to an unpleasant duty of this kind, secretly felt that he had really done all that could be expected of anyone by simply arranging the circumstances – setting the stage, so to speak, for such a talk – without in fact enacting anything upon the stage so set. He said vaguely that we could probably have a few words in his car on the way home, and when we reached his house he invited me in, on the ground that it would be more comfortable to conduct our conversation there. We drank a little brandy, and without anything of any bearing upon my future employment having been said, he looked suddenly at his watch and remarked that it was a pity to keep the chauffeur waiting and that perhaps I had better be getting home.

During this period I had seen very little of my Uncle Frank who, although in London, was constantly busy. But about half a minute before the boat train for Southampton was due to pull out of Waterloo Station I heard my name called, and saw my uncle's huge figure lumbering noisily along the platform, his hand waving some kind of document. His face expressed intense concern and anxiety. 'I am so glad,' he gasped, 'to have caught you. This is important. I want you to take good note of it.'

He thrust the document at me as the train actually left, and when I had time to examine it I found that it was a list of names – names of people, some of them known to my uncle personally, others taken simply from newspaper reports, who had either died or gone blind as a result of drinking impure alcohol in New York. To this list my uncle had added only two lines, which said, 'Do remember, my dear Claud: at *all* costs secure a *reliable* bootlegger.'

Already the Southampton boat train and the liner *Homeric* were ringing to the roar of the great bull market in New York. Only a few weeks before, the market had staggered momentarily in its advance. The Federal Reserve Board had attempted to get the boom under some kind of control. Now it had been defeated by the action of speculative bankers led by Charles Mitchell of the National City. Now this ship, heading past the Isle of Wight for Cherbourg, throbbed with the rhythm of Wall Street, and the people on it seemed all to be dancing to the same distant tune. There were brokers' offices aboard, and some people sat in them all the time the market was open, looking at the changing prices going up, up, up again as though they were pilgrims listening to hymns and incantations on the road to a promised land. When the broker's clerk made a special announcement, there was that kind of hush which otherwise you hear only at solemn services for the dead, or at the moment when on a racecourse they announce the runners in the succeeding race.

The ship was alive with messenger boys taking telegrams from passengers to their brokers in New York, or bringing telegrams of advice and exhortation from the men on the spot.

There were Americans who had cut short their European holiday, and were dashing back because they could not bear the thought that they might, by not being on the spot, miss the chance of doubling the paper fortunes they had already made. There were British and Europeans, some of them rich already and determined to get richer, others with strained, gaping faces, half-incredulous, yet half-convinced that at last the impossible-seeming thing was really happening – they, too, were going to be rich and happy for ever after.

At Cherbourg the American tide engulfed us altogether. I was supposed to have a stateroom to myself, but just before we sailed from Cherbourg the purser informed me apologetically that owing to an emergency he had had to put an American gentleman in the other berth in this cabin. I found him, a man about thirty years of age, sitting on the other bunk between a bottle of Scotch and a bucket of ice. He was dressed as though he had that minute walked off some expensive bathing beach. He looked at me with gloomy intensity.

'You'd think,' he said, 'on a boat of this size they'd have more space. But it isn't so. Well, naturally, on account of the market. People getting back, people going over. Listen – want a drink? Did you see what Cities Service opened at this morning? Can you imagine that?'

It was late afternoon at Cherbourg, but only around midday in New York, and the morning's quotations from the market were already available. My companion tossed off his drink and mixed himself another, looking from time to time cautiously around the cabin as though he were uncertain of its material existence.

'So,' he said, 'we finally made it.'

'You only caught the boat,' I asked, 'at the last moment?'

He gave me a long appraising stare and then hitched himself forward on the bunk with his forearms on his knees, thrusting his head towards me and speaking slowly as though this were something that it was of the highest importance for me to understand.

'Look,' he said, 'there we were at Biarritz. There I was. My name's Louis Genser, and there were Tom Holt and the Wertheims. And then Laura, she died. I'd had a little drink, and I hadn't been down there on this what they call the *plage* more than half an hour, three-quarters maybe, when they came down and told me what had happened. She'd died, see?'

'What a terrible thing. Laura was . . .?'

'I don't get you.'

'I mean she was a friend of yours, one of your party?'

'Now listen, I've known Laura five years – more. I'm talking about Laura Nehring. Well, of course when I first knew her she was Laura Price.'

'Terrible for you.'

'Well, of course first thing we did we rang up Gleneagles and we rang up the Danieli in Venice – places like that. And then there was a lot of difficulty about the mortician too. It seems in France if you die you have to go through a lot of regulations. And the casket. That was a problem too. How were we to know what sort of a casket Jack Nehring wanted her put in? Hell of a problem. And then when we had a nice casket all picked out it seemed the man had that one sold already and if we'd waited while he made another one like it we'd have missed the first boat home. That was what we wanted to get, the first boat home.'

'Naturally.'

'So we got this cheap old box and when we got to Paris we had it on the top of the cab, and we stopped off at the Ritz to get a little drink, and the first thing you know there's Jack Nehring right there in the bar having a little drink with Jack Benstead. Works in the Guaranty Trust over there in Paris. And Jack looks at us and first thing he says is, "Where's Laura?" God!'

His gaze wandered round the cabin again and he actually touched the bunk tentatively with the tips of his fingers, seemingly to assure himself that it was there and he was sitting on it.

'Well, naturally we went on up to the Majestic to see the porter there. After all, it was quite a situation. And Jack Nehring and Jack Benstead and Jack Wertheim they got in touch with the American Express and our Embassy and they all said that the boat was loaded down already, but one way and another they got it fixed, and here we are. Well, that's it, fella. Have another drink?'

The door of the cabin opened and a big man came in with a spray of orchids in one hand and a highball in the other and said,

'Say, Louis, have you seen the way Cities Service is acting this morning?'

'Certainly have,' said Mr Genser, earnestly.

A second big man with a spray of orchids and a highball was fighting his way into the cabin, and behind him there was a woman; and out in the corridor, pushing gently but purposefully, as though they believed the small stateroom

E*

was made of indiarubber and would presently expand, were another man and another woman. Through the crowd, which in that space seemed enormous, I could see that they too were calling out comments on the performance of Cities Service stock.

Mr Genser got to his feet, backed himself against the port-hole to make a little more room, and said,

'Want you to meet . . .'

He waved his highball glass in introduction.

He had already, it emerged, obtained my name and profession from the purser.

'This,' he said, 'is Mr Cockburn, the distinguished British journalist and writer. Mr Cockburn, I want you to meet my friends, Mr Jack Wertheim, of Wertheim and Driscoll, Mr Jack Nehring, I told you about him, and this is Mrs Wert-heim, and over there that's Jack Benstead of the Guaranty Trust Company and Mrs Benstead.'

For a while we stood or squatted on the bunks, drinking highballs and talking about the stock market. Mr Benstead started with the air of one who has remembered important and urgent business.

'Listen, Ethel,' he said, 'did you bring that spare orchid spray along for Louis?'

Mrs Wertheim produced an extra spray and it was handed to Mr Genser. Mr Wertheim looked at me with concern.

'I am afraid,' he said, 'we don't have an orchid spray for you, sir. We just have so many of them for each day of the voyage in the refrigerator. . . . But if you'd care to join us all the same?'

'Yes, indeed,' said Mrs Wertheim.

'We're going to see Laura,' explained Mr Genser helpfully. 'They finally got her fixed up all right.'

'And I just want to say,' said Mr Nehring over his shoulder to Mr Benstead, 'that we'd never have made it, Jack, if it hadn't been for you. It was on account of that thing you said at the Embassy. I want you to know I'm grateful, Jack.'

'Anything I can ever do, Jack,' said Mr Benstead. 'And don't forget it was you . . .'

As we moved in single file along the corridor he could be heard reminding Mr Nehring of some stock-market operation in which Mr Nehring had been of service to Mr Benstead.

'But I thought,' I said in a low voice to Mr Genser, who was walking immediately in front of me, 'I thought this Mrs Nehring – Laura – I thought she was dead?'

'Certainly she's dead,' said Mr Genser loudly over his shoulder. 'I told you that. That's why we're taking her these orchids.'

And indeed, in a distant part of the ship, there she was, in the 'cheap box' that had been obtained with such difficulty in Biarritz. The orchid sprays were laid reverently on the coffin and we spent a quarter of an hour standing round drinking a number of toasts to her memory. Mr Jack Wertheim happened to have a big flask about him, and was able to refill our glasses as required. Then the bereaved Mr Nehring made a little speech, and we went back to the main deck to get the latest news about the day's performance of Cities Service.

XI MANHATTAN MAGIC

THERE WAS A EUROPEAN WHOM I HAD NEVER SEEN before and never saw again, but the remark I overheard him make at a New York party was 'I like this, and I like that, I like it all here in New York, but what I especially like is the leisurely quality of American life'.

People around him had tittered politely at what they conceived to be a feeble paradox, but as a matter of fact he had, as the saying goes, something there. This leisurely quality is as surprising as the colour. But it is there. In the days before colour cinematography nothing prepared you for the colour of New York. You thought you were going to see a gaunt city of black and white cliffs and terraced precipices. But the brilliance of the light – after all the place is on the same latitude as Naples – turned even the white skyscrapers into precipices of colour, and all among them, as though the city were seeking to emulate the terraces and canyons of Arizona, you saw great blotches of amber and rose pink, whole streets recalling the colour-washed cottages of an Irish village, and great hotels and apartment houses where every window had its brilliantly coloured awning glowing in the sun, or crackling and sparkling in the Atlantic wind.

139

And this 'leisurely quality of American life' which the man spoke about is just as unexpected by voyagers who have a note in their books to the effect that in America what you have is 'tempo' and hustle. But in reality the tempo of New York on a day of business is like the tempo of Brighton on a day of holiday. At least it was so when I was first there in 1929, and it was the same when I was there again in the spring of 1945.

On the flight back from the Foundation Conference of the United Nations at San Francisco in 1945, my plane touched down at Cheyenne, Wyoming, at about 3.15 in the morning. The airport at Cheyenne is quite a distance out of town, but the airport restaurant was at that hour full of people. Fifty or sixty of them, I should say, mostly young men and women, not drinking, because alcohol was not served at that hour, but for the most part sitting at the long bars sucking Coca-Cola and ice-cream drinks through straws. They were not people who were travelling, not people who had come to see other people off by the plane, nor people who were meeting somebody. They were not doing anything purposeful at all. Yet long before dawn there they were, sitting on their stools, lively and mysterious, and strangely reminiscent of the crowd that is always, and equally mysteriously, present in the restaurant of a Spanish junction – say Saragossa or Valladolid – at any hour of the night.

European visitors to the United States often imagine that because an American business man tells them that the only time he can make an appointment is at 10.30 in the evening this must indicate the immense busyness and hustle of the man's life. Every so often it does, but quite equally often it simply means that the man, in his nervous, high-strung, time-squandering, lavish American way, has spent most of the day not getting on with the things that he theoretically should be getting on with, and therefore finds himself at about six in the evening with the whole day's work to do. Or at least he has to jam into the afternoon the work which he could, theoretically, have tackled in the morning, had he not spent a great deal of the morning thinking – as no Englishman would in office hours – of the meaning of life, sex problems, what would happen if there were a war, and (in this case more along English lines) what is going to happen in the ball game on Saturday?

These preoccupations cause a tension in his mind, and the tension has to be relaxed by little walks about the room to get glasses of ice-water, and every so often by trips in the elevator down to the ground floor – to get one's shoes shined, or pick out a cigar, or possibly buy the latest edition of the midday papers. In extreme cases it becomes necessary to go round the corner and have a drink or even play a little snooker. Since the trip in the elevator takes place inside the building it is not really a departure from work, but since also the trip is apt to be as lengthy as a short suburban journey – what with waiting for the elevator and then riding down in it at sixty miles an hour and jostling one's way across the lobby, all this to be repeated again on the return journey – these little excursions can take up a great deal of time.

English business men have a different system for taking care of this kind of nervous tension. Though personally I think it inferior, it has a more respectable appearance. Whenever an English business man feels an acute aversion to getting on with the job in hand he organises a business conference. This is the reason why so much less work is done in London than might be. Most of the time large numbers of people who might be doing useful work are by their own will, or the will of others, huddled in these usually futile conferences, organised for the purpose of preventing people from feeling alone with life.

In New York they have these office conferences too, but the difference between them and the Londoners' is that the Londoner cannot waste time without a sense of guilt unless he has a conference, whereas a New Yorker, in default of a conference, will waste time anyway. Also a Londoner who has wasted hours of the day himself feels guiltily censorious about other people who are visibly wasting time. Not so the New Yorker.

The first evening I was there I saw a stationary taxicab and got into it. There was no driver. As I had no idea whether it was hard or easy to get taxicabs in New York, and was afraid of not being able to find another one, I thought it best to sit where I was and await the driver's arrival, which presently occurred – he came out of a little speakeasy opposite where his cab was standing, and peered in at me in the back seat.

'Listen,' he said, 'do you want to go some place or are you just resting?'

I was enchanted, and said I was happy just to rest. The driver said that in that case he would go back and finish a

141

little conversation that he was having with some friends. When he returned he told me that he had wanted to finish the conversation because at the end of it he and his friends had got on to the subject of the stock market and several of them were seriously involved. His personal opinion was that despite a recent rise American Can was due to climb farther.

Across my conversation with the taxi driver presently fell a shadow – I felt the chill of it without knowing what threw it. Later, after a week or two in New York, I found out. It was the shadow, if you like, of a tone of voice, an attitude deemed unseemly. I had spoken, I realised afterwards, lightly of the stock market. In that turbulently pregnant summer of 1929, when people would spend an hour working out possibilities of exploiting the great stock bonanza, and then have to recuperate for two hours, drinking mint juleps in the deliciously salt-drenched air of Manhattan which had the curious quality of exhilarating and half-suffocating you at the same time, this was a shadow which could fall across any conversation, any gathering, at the most unexpected moment. I felt it at great colonial mansions out on Long Island in the Gatsby country, no less than in the striped steel box at the top of a skyscraper in Sutton Place where my friend George Busch, said to be the very smartest arbitrage broker in New York, used to lie in a half-coma after the excitements of the day, waiting impatiently for sleep and the dullness of sleep to be over and the excitement of the market to start again.

You could talk about prohibition, or Hemingway, or air conditioning, or music, or horses, but in the end you had to talk about the stock market, and that was where the conversation became serious. Unless you understood this, and it took me quite a while to understand, you caused that shadow to fall. There was a 'mystique' about the market. You could argue about the merits of this stock or that, you could analyse earnings, you could consider rationally the effects which the weather in, say, Missouri was liable to have upon the stocks of companies producing agricultural machinery. But what you could not with impunity do was to suggest, not by words only but by so much as an intonation, that there was any doubt about the fact that the market as a whole was going on up and up and up, that every 'recession' there might be in the near future would be 'temporary', 'technical', 'an adjustment', after which the new era of American life would

142

resume its swift, inevitable progress towards a hardly imaginable stratosphere of prosperity. To hint that you regarded such an assumption as in any way questionable was – whether you were talking to the Italian who kept the nearest speakeasy or to your hostess at dinner in the East Sixties – to put yourself in the unpleasant position of making some vulgarly ironic reference to the Holy Father in the house of devout Roman Catholics. There was an element of sacrilege about it, but it was worse than that. For in this 'mystique' of the market there was an element of sympathetic magic too. Deep in people's consciousness there was an instinct, like that of a primitive African, that to speak ill of the market was in itself, unlucky, a proceeding capable of bringing upon not only the speaker but all associated with him the wrath of the Market God.

Most people are capable of carrying more or less incompatible ideas in their head at the same time, and the same man who had convinced himself, by a study of innumerable market reports and statements by economists, that the level of stocks was fully justified by the underlying economic situation, and that a rise was predictable in the light of factors which could be analysed and calculated, also often believed in his heart that the whole thing was a kind of marvellous subjective trick; a séance where the table moved, and the spirits spoke, by virtue of the combined will power and capacity to believe of all present – a beneficial atmosphere which could be dissipated or seriously affected for the worse by the presence of an unbeliever. Perhaps that was only another way of stating the simple fact that if enough people started to disbelieve in the future of common stocks, common stocks would cease to have a future, but that was not the way in which most people put it to themselves. If they had, the existence of just one unbeliever would not have alarmed and wounded them so gravely.

In cold blood, and by hindsight, these attitudes can sound childish, and furthermore can support that tediously erroneous Anglo-European view of the Americans as people who are unduly – in the vulgar sense of the word – 'materialistic'. If the attitude of the Americans to the stock-market boom in the summer of '29 proved anything, it proved the opposite – for it showed that they believed in miracles. Myself I find this an endearing quality. The idea that two and two can never make anything but four is in itself depressing and limiting, and turns out, in the higher mathematical regions, to be probably untrue. This belief in miracles is simply an expression of the notion that if you try hard enough you can make wonderful things happen. The chief trouble with the Americans of 1929 was that they had their money on the wrong miracle.

The situation was no doubt absurd, and after the ball was over there were plenty of people to point out just how 'crazy' the country had been at that period. But to see it as merely absurd is to miss the pathos of what was happening there and, in the welter of greedy gamblers, to lose sight of what was tragic and even noble in this grotesque scene. For it was a scene which could have been enacted on that scale only in America, and this was so because it was a brief re-enactment of what was essentially an old American dream. They had dreamed that if you could get away from the principalities and powers of old Europe you could found a free and noble society. And when the eastern seaboard become an area oppressed by new principalities and powers, they dreamed that in the Middle West and the Far West the miracle could still happen. From the harsh necessities of millions of emigrants in the mid-nineteenth century was distilled a new and heady component of that dream-liquor, a faith that there was still room on earth for the kingdom of heaven. And the people to be pitied were perhaps not those who had that faith, however naïve, but those who had lost it. Even the most superficial student of our day is familiar with the fact that the American Civil War was an affair of inextricably confused motives, of gigantic political swindles, of meanness masquerading as patriotism, and avarice disguised as love of liberty. Yet it would be a pity to forget that there really was more to be said about John Brown than that his body was mouldering in the grave, and that the sentiments expressed later in the Battle Hymn of the Republic are not invalidated by the fact of political intrigues, however sordid. The eyes of the corrupt army contractors and later of the carpet-baggers had not 'seen the coming of the glory of the Lord', but the eyes of a lot of other people had seen something like that, and the fact that the glory of the Lord did not in the end turn up did not make the hope of it ridiculous. What it did do was to add something to the sometimes overpowering American sense of frustration.

XII GRAND SLAM

THE BIG BULL MARKET, AS FREDERICK LEWIS
Allen wrote later in *Only Yesterday*, was a compensation for
innumerable disappointments and disillusionments of the
past. And it was this which gave the atmosphere of the summer of 1929 its peculiar quality. There were moments when
you said to yourself that this was just a casino. And then
you had to admit that at the same time it reminded you of
a revivalist meeting and even of the starting of some kind of
crusade. It seemed like the pleasantest kind of crusade – one
in which the whole world was going to get happy by getting
richer and richer. It would start of course with people who
were gambling in American stocks getting rich, and then the
rest of the Americans would become prosperous too, and
pretty soon the whole world. America felt kindly towards
the world that summer – when it had a moment to think of
it at all. In any case, there was no need to think of it much, because America was going to solve all the world's problems
automatically.

The atmosphere of the great boom was savagely exciting,
but there were times when a person with my kind of European background felt alarmingly lonely. He would have liked
to believe, as these people believed, in the eternal upswing
of the big bull market, or else to meet just one person with
whom he might discuss some general doubts without being
regarded as an imbecile or a person of deliberately evil intent
– some kind of anarchist, perhaps.

I did not at all wish to be regarded as any such thing, and
I kept my doubts pretty carefully under wraps, especially as
they did not, after all, arise from any expert assessment by
me of the immediate factors in the situation, but simply from
the 'academic' theories of the Marxist and Leninist writers
whom I had studied in the apartment on the Kurfuerstendamm and my studio in Paris.

From Louis Hinrichs I was particularly anxious to conceal

my schizophrenic frame of mind, to hide from him the fact that as I read the market reports, the innumerable expert predictions of the financial writers, or listened to the talk of brokers and financial editors, I was only a little more than half-persuaded that those Marxist philosophers were wrong. I thought it would be a confession that would shock and perhaps alarm Hinrichs. I did not at that time know him very well. In any case, my comprehensive ignorance of the factual details of the present situation, as distinct from some general theory of economic movements, made it easy to avoid generalisations. I had too many questions to ask. Naturally Hinrichs's knowledge of the stock market and of the 'over-all picture' of American business conditions was encyclopædic, and in addition to that he had a fascinating sort of physical intimacy with the financial district of Manhattan. Most days we used to walk about there, going from office to office to see people who, he thought, might be useful to me later on. I had arrived with a preconceived notion of Wall Street, and that whole area, as a roaring, pulsating jungle, but under Hinrichs's gentle guidance one had, surprisingly, rather the impression of going on a conducted tour of a village; a largish village and one full of oddities and unexpected situations or characters, but still a place where you could soon learn to find your way about, and one which you could hope, after not too long, actually to comprehend. This impression was curiously deepened by the physical qualities of the financial district itself. As one approached this hub of the world's largest city one subconsciously expected a crescendo of mechanised noise. But the fact was that here traffic congestion had reached its logical paradoxical conclusion.

There was a time, I suppose, when everyone tried to drive along Wall, Pine or Cedar Street in a motor car, but what had happened by now was that since there was not conceivably room for all the mechanical wheeled traffic which wanted to use those streets, mechanical traffic had virtually abandoned them, and the crowds padded about their business on foot.

The result was that when you turned out of Lower Broadway into one of these side streets you were conscious of a kind of hush, and the noise of tens of thousands of people moving about on their feet without engines reminded you of Venice.

This powerful, towering village, the activities of whose inhabitants could tilt whole nations, was familiar to Hinrichs in all its aspects. He knew who was who now and who had been who when, and as you toured it with him you thought that here as much history had been packed into a couple of decades as had occupied a century elsewhere. We had just passed, one day, the bomb-scarred offices of the House of Morgan, its windows now heavily protected in case anyone should want to throw a bomb again – that earlier bomb had been in itself the violent expression of an earlier American dream – when Hinrichs stopped in a disconcerting manner he had when he wanted to make an important point, and spreading his fingers in the fluttering motion which expressed uneasiness and a certain bewilderment, he said.

'All the same, Claud, I don't believe it.'

In New York at that moment there was only one 'it' of which you could say that. I was as astonished as a member of some underground movement in an occupied country who discovers that the local Captain of Police is of the same opinion as himself

Strangely, for it was quite unnecessary, yet significantly – for it was an indication of the hypnotic effect of the climate we had been living in – we both of us, I noticed, as we walked along, lowered our voices. In the sixty-six-storeyed shadow of the Manhattan Bank Building Hinrichs began to explain to me what he felt about the bull market, and why he believed not only that it would not continue, but that it was a possibly monstrous delusion which could do serious harm to 'my dear America'.

We had many such conversations and from these emerged, paradoxically, the fact that, although we had reached a somewhat similar conclusion, we had reached it from premises which were diametrically opposite. Apart from the fact that I had acquired my doubts on a purely theoretical basis, whereas Hinrichs's were the result of expert practical knowledge; mine had their roots in revolutionary soil, whereas his grew from the most orthodox conservatism. He knew the form book and he went by it. He could see nothing in the history of American development to suggest that, on behalf of the American Joshua of 1929, the Lord God was going to suspend the laws of economics.

Excited by the extraordinary disclosure of Hinrichs's scepticism, I drew exaggerated conclusions.

'Then you mean,' I said, 'that you believe that the capitalist system won't work?'

But this was not what he meant at all. He meant simply that the capitalist system – a phrase he somewhat disliked, I think, because it implied the existence of other, equally valid, systems – would proceed as usual by a series of jerks frequently interrupted by catastrophes. To 'defend', so to speak, the catastrophes seemed to him unnecessary, for he considered them as inevitable as sunrise. There was not, in his view, a 'system' to blame; if one had to blame anything, then it was just life. The capitalist system was life, and therefore attempts to substitute any other type of 'system' were both nonsensical and dangerous. You could not step out of life.

He was a warm-hearted man, generous and sympathetic towards all individual miseries, but he saw no cure for the general miseries of the human race – such as want and war – and thus, at least in conversation, took the view that people who proffered such cures were mentally defective or else quacks.

Our theoretical discussions in *The Times* office were frequently broken in upon by one who might be said to have been the embodiment of the Spirit of the Boom – namely, Mr Frederick Bullock, correspondent of the *Daily Mail*. In Northcliffe's day the *Daily Mail* and *The Times* correspondents in New York had naturally shared offices, and after the papers separated no one had thought it worth while to change the layout of the office. Thus we had, on the floor above the *New York Sun,* three fair-sized rooms of which the centre one was occupied by our joint secretary, and those on either side of it by *The Times* and the *Daily Mail* respectively. It is hard to imagine how more comparatively incompatible elements could have been jammed into so small a space.

The communicating doors were usually left open, and behind Hinrichs's most delicately learned exposition of some point in the past policy of the Federal Reserve System could be heard the rising bellow of Freddie Bullock's Rabelaisian laughter, or the cheerful bark of his bullish orders being shouted into the telephone to his broker.

He was a short, enormously muscular man of sixty or so, and when you first saw him you saw a huge cigar, a pair of tufted eyebrows and hairy muzzle, combining in a face which seemed designed for durability rather than elegance. You were just deciding that what you had to deal with here was a somewhat roughly constructed cannonball, when the can-

148

nonball would come to sudden rest, the cigar smoke would cease to swirl, and you were being examined hopefully by shrewd, alertly sparkling eyes, which brimmed with amusement, eagerness and goodwill. Their expression said that if you were a member of the human race you would certainly get from Mr Frederick Bullock the benefit of any doubt your conduct might occasion. He had the candour and exuberance of a twelve-year-old schoolboy, and the theatrical instincts of a first-class clown. He smelt rather than understood Hinrichs's scepticism about the market, and as a result regarded Hinrichs with a kind of derisive compassion. He would come steaming into our office behind his cigar, launch a general discussion on the state of financial affairs, listen impatiently for a few moments while Hinrichs attempted in the most meticulous fashion to explain his point of view, and then with something between a bark and a guffaw go steaming out again, pause for a moment to tell, or attempt to tell, an indecent joke to the handsomely blonde and strictly respectable secretary, and dash into his own office where the telephone was ringing. We would hear him shouting and laughing into it, and a few minutes later he would come rushing back again, sometimes executing a burlesque dance step as he did so, and – thrusting his half-smoked cigar under Hinrichs's nose by way of emphasis – shout out the news which his broker had just given him, to the effect that some stock in which he was interested had already risen four points that morning. In his estimation this was momentarily conclusive proof that the sceptics were a lot of nervous old women who, pusillanimously, or as a result of academic inhibitions, were letting slip the opportunity to make a million dollars.

A million dollars or thereabouts was in fact the sum which Freddie Bullock had made, on paper, by gambling on the stock market during the past couple of years. He used to tell with glee, and at the same time a touch of melancholy, the story of his most recent visit to Europe where, in Paris, he had had breakfast with the then Lord Rothermere. For a time, under Lord Northcliffe, Freddie Bullock had been, so far as I recall, a director of the *Daily Mail*, and had been on intimate terms with Lord Rothermere. He had looked forward to seeing him in Europe after a separation which had lasted several years. Lord Rothermere asked him to breakfast at his hotel in Paris. There were a lot of people there, and as Bullock came into the room Lord Rothermere bounded through the crowd and gripped him by the hand, shouting, 'How much did you make? How much?' By this Bullock was somewhat vexed and disappointed – he had expected at least an enquiry after his health, or an expression of gladness at seeing him again. He shrugged.

'In your terms, nothing worth writing home about,' he said.

Lord Rothermere became almost violent in his impatience. 'I'm asking you,' he shouted, 'how much did you make?'

'But I tell you,' said Bullock, 'in your terms it's the merest bagatelle, nothing.'

'I'm not asking you for that kind of answer,' said Rothermere. 'I want the figures.'

Bullock paused to make sure that he had the full attention of the roomful of editors, financiers and politicians. 'I tell you,' he said airily, 'it's nothing – peanuts. In fact I can say that during the past three months I have not made more on the market than about six times the annual salary of a first-class man on the *Daily Mail*.'

It was his love of a really dangerous gamble which, according to his own story, had first hoisted him towards the top of the journalistic tree. That was in 1912 when he was already working as a New York Correspondent of the *Daily Mail* with office space in the offices of the *New York Times*. It was April 15th, and, a few hours before, the White Star liner, *Titanic*, had gone to the bottom in a disaster which in itself, and certainly in its impact on the minds of the public in Britain and America, was the greatest of its kind that had ever occurred. Two liners had been in a position to respond to the *Titanic's* wireless call for help and go to the rescue. One was the *Californian*, which was only eight or ten miles away, the other the *Carpathia*, seventy miles off. But on the *Californian* the wireless operator had gone to bed, and although, according to the subsequent enquiry, the *Titanic's* distress rockets were actually seen from the *Californian*, no action was taken because, as the ultimate report said, 'the incredibility of such a disaster appears to have paralysed the capacity for interference'.

All through the day the White Star authorities in New York had emphatically denied that many, if any, lives had been lost. The imputation was that all of them had been picked up by the *Carpathia*. This may have been simply a 'stall' while the White Star pulled itself together, or it may have been genuinely believed, because on learning from the

Carpathia at a fairly early moment that the *Carpathia* had picked up the *Titanic's* boats, it would have been possible to assume that this meant that all the boats were safe, with the whole of the 2,224 people on board.

Late on the afternoon of the 15th Freddie Bullock was hanging nervously about the wireless room of the *New York Times*. Owing to the difference in time between New York and London, there was not very long to go before he would have to send his message for the early London editions. Suddenly he heard one of the morse operators taking a message with a signal which to Bullock was already familiar – it was the signal of messages from the *Carpathia*. This was clearly a message from that liner, which the *New York Times* operator was intercepting. Eavesdropping frantically, Bullock thought even his inadequate knowledge of morse had read the message correctly. He persuaded the radio operator to tell him the text of it. It listed a number of boats picked up, gave a figure of about 700 and concluded 'thus accounting all saved'.

Bullock copied it down and stared at it in a frenzy of excitement. For if that message meant what it seemed to mean, then 1,500 people had been drowned. On the other hand, there was just a chance that there had been a slip in the reception of the message, and a very small slip could turn the sense of the message into something quite different – it could mean that the *Carpathia* was now accounting for the last survivors and that with their rescue all of those travelling on the *Titanic* had been saved.

It would have been easy of course to send some hedging weasel-worded telegram to London reporting, perhaps, 'rumours' that the casualty list was higher than the authorities would admit. It would be safe, but on the other hand a despatch of that kind was not going to make any journalist's reputation. Bullock admitted that he could feel his hair turning white as he took his decision. Then he sat down and deliberately wrote the most sensational despatch of the year, announcing that contrary to optimistic reports circulating, the death-roll on the *Titanic* had not been less than 1,000 people and possibly was as high as 1,500. By this time, of course, the managing editor of the *New York Times* had the radio report from the *Carpathia,* and he too was frantically working to get his tiny and ambiguous message confirmed or clarified. The White Star continued to deny that any loss of life had occurred. In the London offices of the *Daily Mail* tension was even greater and white hairs were sprouting in the editorial rooms.

The *Daily Mail* was still a comparatively young paper and it was only twelve years since it had almost wrecked itself with its publication of the false report of the massacre of the foreign delegations in Peking during the Boxer Rising. The spectre of that nearly disastrous report still stalked the offices in Carmelite Street. Like Bullock in New York, the editor in London had to decide whether to play safe or gamble. And there was very little time now before the decision had to be taken and the edition sent to press. In New York Bullock received an anguished cable from London. 'White Star,' it said, 'and all other authorities, Reuters and all other News Agencies, absolutely deny any lives lost. Are you sure?'

Quivering all over with the excitement of the gamble, Bullock cabled back, 'Absolutely sure. Go right ahead.'

The *New York Times* was in the same dilemma but it had more time in hand. Later that night the managing editor of the *New York Times* went to the New York manager of White Star and demanded a showdown. 'Unless,' he said, 'you release the full news you received from the *Carpathia,* I shall break the White Star.' The news was released in time for the *New York Times,* and Freddie Bullock, to go to bed with quiet minds.

He was a real Anglo-American. You could say that he was Americanised, yet you had to admit that he was as English as an Orange Pippin. In this Englishness of his he profoundly believed, and was proud of it. As an Englishman (he came, I think, from the West Country) he took the view that, unlike Americans, who are prone to hysteria, English people sternly control their feelings, never display emotion. In a roomful of American friends gambling like himself on the market, he would bound about shouting with excitement and begging everybody to keep perfectly calm. At dinner one day at his house – a costly penthouse apartment just off Washington Square – the talk turned on the sufferings of Great Britain following World War I. Everyone present, except myself and Bullock, was American. Bullock gave them a patriotic little lecture on how to face adversity. 'Don't think, you fellows,' he said, 'that because we English ride our feelings on a tight rein we don't feel these things deeply. It simply,' he said, his voice trembling, 'means that even when we are thinking most deeply of all our country has been through, we never show it.' His voice trembled more and more, and the glass of wine shook in his hand. 'We never,' he sobbed, 'show a trace, not a trace of emotion.' He drank deeply and two large tears rolled from his eyes.

I have read somewhere the theory – advanced possibly by an Englishman – that in the United States financial success, particularly success on the stock market, is subconsciously regarded by the male as evidence of virility, so that he boasts of it in the same way that a member of a more primitive community would boast of more directly sexual achievements. And this, the theory suggested – not too absurdly as it seems to me – could help to account for a fact which, to the truly bourgeois mind is often unintelligible: namely that when a stock-exchange gambler has made four million dollars and then loses three of them he jumps out of the window of a skyscraper. The bourgeois asks, 'But why could he not have lived comfortably enough on the remaining million?' Bullock never jumped out of a window, but he did seem to get about the same kind of pleasure out of issuing bulletins indicative of his sexual prowess as he did out of announcing each new coup he had brought off on the bull market. And it must be admitted that for a man of his age – indeed for a man of almost any age – his sexual achievements were in themselves remarkable and well worthy of report.

Together with journalism, stock-exchange gambling and women, medicine shared his keen interest. He believed that almost any time now medical science would come up with some gadget which would enable people of nearly sixty to live at top speed without the slightest ill-effect upon their health and in a general way prolong life more or less indefinitely. He was thus the victim of countless expensive quacks.

His attitude to modern medicine resembled in some respects my father's attitude in the old days to the motor car. For years, when he was younger and poorer, Bullock had pooh-poohed newfangled medical notions, as being certainly decadent and probably fatal. He spoke of 'nature's remedies', and implied that what was good enough for his father's body was good enough for his. When, however, he did start to take an interest in it his position reversed itself: his objection now was not that its pretensions and achievements were too great but that they were not great enough. Just as my father had thought that if you were going to have a motor car at all it ought to be capable of taking you from here to there

153

in virtually no time, so Bullock felt that if you were going to pay to have the wonders of science let loose on you, you ought to get something spectacular in the way of health and vigour for your money.

Though nobody formulated it quite like that, this was a notion quite common in the subconscious minds of people in New York at that time. Quacks of every description from half-trained psychiatrists to golden-tongued doctors with multi-purpose hobby-horses throve upon it. One of them, franker than most, told me that, in his opinion, this obsession with health, this nervous preoccupation with the possibilities of disease on the one hand, or of prolonging life on the other, was simply an inevitable symptom of the gambling fever and the gambling boom itself. How horrible to think that Anaconda Copper might go to 150 and you would be too ill to care; how dreadful to die and miss the universal Utopia which was just coming up. He drew my attention, this psychiatrist, to the theme in the story by Leonid Andreyev called *Grand Slam* where a man dies of a seizure at the card table just as he is about to play a grand slam in No Trumps.

An idea terrifying in its simplicity struck the emaciated little body of Jacob Ivanovitch [the dead man's partner] causing him to leap from his chair. Peering round, as though the thought had not come to him of its own accord but had been whispered by someone into his ear, he said aloud: 'But he will never know that the ace was in the pack and his hand contained a certain grand slam. Never, never.'

And it seemed to Jacob Ivanovitch that he had not understood until this moment what death really meant. Now he really understood, and the thing he saw plainly was senseless, awful, irrevocable.

'Never, never,' Jacob Ivanovitch said slowly, to convince himself that such a word existed and had meaning. The word existed and had meaning, but the meaning was so strange and so bitter that Jacob Ivanovitch again fell into a chair and wept helplessly. He pitied Nikolai Dmitrievitch in that he would never know, and he pitied himself and everyone, since this senseless cruel thing would happen to him and to everyone alike.

When Bullock was not chiding or commiserating with Louis Hinrichs for his stiff-jointed inability to grasp the opportunities offered by the stock market, he was upbraiding him on medical grounds, pleading with him not to pass up, too, the opportunities offered by modern medical science.

Significantly his feelings on this score were if possible more passionate than those he had about the stock market, and it was evident that here, too, lurked a belief in sympathetic magic – he manifested an obscure fear lest Hinrichs's lack of faith, not to mention his open derision, might be actually weakening the power of the doctors.

So it came to pass that about the middle of September a certain Dr Mayne Sturges had obtained a large symbolical stature in the conflict of the sceptics and the believers. I forget just what Dr Sturges was in favour of – whatever it was, it was drastic and miraculously effective. The practice of this cure caused Bullock physical agony four times a week, and kept him mentally elated and hopeful all the time. Hinrichs just sneered at Dr Sturges. Bullock implored him to try the cure for himself – it would make him a new man. Hinrichs said he did not wish to be made a new man. Bullock's anxiety to have us try this wonder-worker for ourselves and be forced in consequence to confess that our refusal to believe had been a monstrous error was intensified by the small break in the market which occurred early in September. Although the optimists said that the break was due solely to the Hatry crash in England, and could only be of the most temporary and limited character, at that stage every cessation of the upward movement, let alone a downward turn, was alarming.

In many stocks the drop was quite a sharp one. Thus United States Steel, which had stood at 261 on September 3rd, was down to 204 on October 3rd. On the other hand, everyone remembered that only eighteen months before you could have bought U.S Steel at 138. Back in those days of 1928 there had been people who had got scared by one thing or another and had predicted a crash. Yet what had happened to them was that they had missed the bus. The consensus was that people who now failed to buy Steel at 204 were liable to miss the next bus too, and the same argument applied with even greater force to the more volatile speculative stocks.

Nevertheless this little jar or jolt on the market – during which Bullock suspected Hinrichs of looking at him with a cynical glance – intensified, by a natural connection of thought, Bullock's desire to have us recognise unreservedly the merits of Dr Sturges.

We were at length persuaded to drive out one Saturday

155

with Bullock and Dr Sturges to lunch at the latter's large house in New Jersey. Except that he twitched like a marionette, Dr Sturges was an entirely good advertisement for himself. He looked about as sleek and agile as a film actor who is going to play the part of a champion boxer. Evidently he had been carefully briefed by Bullock, and during the drive his conversation was that of a man who is so thoroughly dedicated to his profession and the welfare of his patients that he scarcely has time to notice the world around him, let alone follow the stock market or worry about his fees. The weather was miserable and we were all hungry and longing for a drink, but by way of underlining the impression he was creating, Dr Sturges said that much to his regret duty called him to make a detour of fifteen miles or so to visit a patient of his, a Mrs Madison. She had her own regular doctor, of course, but Dr Sturges was her special adviser, and he felt himself responsible for her. He emphasised that by now Mrs Madison was really in a good state of health. He had visited her only eight days ago, and we possibly might feel that this visit was unnecessary, but it would be on his conscience if he did not just look in. Thorough and meticulous, he had to admit he was; perhaps to a fault.

Bullock looked at us sideways with an expression of triumph. We drove up to the porch of Mrs Madison's residence, and the rest of us stretched our legs on the gravel while Dr Sturges rang the bell. A maid answered. The doctor enquired for Mrs Madison. The maid looked disconcerted. 'But didn't you know?' she said. 'Mrs Madison has been dead for four days.'

We climbed silently back into the car, and lunch at Dr Sturges's was a quick, silent meal too.

XIII   THE PRIME MINISTER'S HAT

IT WAS MY BUSINESS TO WARN THE WESTERN Union operator on the floor below us that, in view of an important event now impending, we probably should be requiring special service – we should be filing more than our average number of words per day, and furthermore a Special Correspondent was coming out from London who might have particular needs.

There were three good reasons for feeling happy in the society of this Western Union operator, whose name was Joe. First he looked exactly as an American cable operator is supposed to look. He wore, at his machine, or wandering about the corridors of the *Sun* office, or standing chatting in ours, a green eyeshade and above it, tilted on the side of his head, a straw boater. He chewed two inches of an extinct cigar. He went everywhere in shirt-sleeves, sweating and looking sad. He was a first-class cable operator, and during the past eighteen months had made fifty thousand dollars speculating in the stocks of Anaconda Copper.

Secondly he had taught me to use the typewriter, a thing I had never done in my life before arriving in New York. On the third afternoon I was there Hinrichs had to leave the office on some business, and before he went we agreed on the general tenor of the despatch I was to write. Naturally I wanted my first despatch as a proper correspondent of *The Times,* a correspondent in New York at that, to be something pretty impressive – striking, though not of course 'flashy' or 'viewy'.

I lunched early and at two o'clock sat down to compose with eager anxiety. Because of the five-hour time difference between New York and London we were supposed to file as much of our day's material as possible before three o'clock, although reasonably shorter messages filed in New York up to five o'clock could still get into the first edition. Anything filed later than that had to be extraordinarily important.

This matter of the time difference had curious repercussions upon the general presentation of American events in the British press. Inevitably news presented in the editions of the New York evening papers appearing between, say, quarter-past four and five assumed a particular importance in the eyes of the correspondents in New York. When you have only a quarter of an hour in hand and all the evening papers are telling you that this or that event is the most exciting or interesting or important of the day, it is not in human nature – certainly not in journalistic human nature – to remain unaffected. Besides, even if you happen to think that this latest bit of news is less important that it appears to the New York evening papers, your competitors may think otherwise, and if they all send it, and you fail to do so, your Foreign Editor may lift his eyebrows and wonder how on earth you happened to 'miss' it. But obviously out of all the mass of news from all over the American continent, the items which the New York evening-newspaper editors are going to select for professional treatment are those which will interest the toilers of Manhattan as they stream off the island on the evening commuters' trains. To them a small bank hold-up in Manhattan is necessarily more important than almost anything, however significant, which has happened a thousand miles away in the Middle West. In this sense all city evening newspapers are more parochial in outlook than the papers are in the morning. The result is, or at least it was when I was there, that London morning papers get their news from the United States sieved through this mesh of the evening newspapers in New York, although the picture of events which entertains the Manhattan commuter is not necessarily the truest or best-balanced picture for the British reader the following morning. Even in *The Times* office we suffered somewhat from this hypnosis exercised by the late editions of the New York evening papers, though less than some other correspondents, simply because *The Times,* being less anxiety-ridden than some of the other papers, was less inclined to worry about what 'the competition' might choose to be up to.

At that time I wrote slowly and my style was erratic. Echoes of prize essays floated about in it like icebergs; or else literary flying fish which ought to have been in some quite other story got unexpectedly loose; and sometimes there were doldrums where I was unconsciously imitating a man trying to write a suitable piece for *The Times.* Sometimes it was quite difficult to see what the piece was about because a shadowy figure kept jumping up between the piece and the reader shouting, 'See me write a piece!' All these phenomena had to be looked out for, corrected or torn up.

However, at about a quarter to three that afternoon, I had a nice six hundred words written out, and took the sheets down to Joe. He held them in his hand, looking at them at first as though I had given him some blank sheets of paper for a joke, and then as though he had noticed that indeed something was written on them but was written in, perhaps, Chinese. The cigar, the eyeshade and the hat wagged slowly from side to side in sad wonder. He handed them back to me smiling gently as though I had shown him some not very

158

interesting antique. In my agitated indignation it took me all of five minutes to grasp that for years and years nobody here had filed a newspaper despatch written in longhand, and that, in fact, despatches not typewritten simply could not be despatched at all. It took Joe another five minutes to grasp that there existed grown men who actually never had used a typewriter.

However, seeing my dismay, he was consolatory. It seemed to him that to be able to use the typewriter was so natural a human attribute – like being able to walk, or strike a match – that anyone of average intelligence must be able to acquire such a skill within a few minutes. He urged me to hurry back upstairs and put the longhand copy into proper form. He even came up with me and spent a minute or so showing me how to make the space between the lines. Then, remarking that it was now five minutes to three, and I had better get on with it, he left me alone with the machine.

There was a moment during which I thought I would appeal to the secretary and get her to type out the copy, and after that I would take it down to Joe and give him a blast about the evils of a mechanical civilisation and its effects upon elegant literary composition. Then I perceived that such a course would be a blind alley from which I should never emerge, and I sat down dispiritedly to tackle that intimidating machine. Using one finger, it took me nearly an hour to copy the despatch, and the next day we had a plaintive cable from *The Times* asking us please to try to file a little earlier, but I never used longhand again and in a week could type nearly as fast as the secretary, though not nearly so accurately.

A third reason for liking to sit around talking with Joe was that if you talked with him at, say, ten o'clock in the morning you could, if you chose, go and sit in a speakeasy for the rest of the day and at the end of it you would still know about as much about 'public opinion' as you would have if you had spent your time talking with bankers, brokers and politicians. Whatever Joe said or thought turned out to be what everyone else you were going to meet was going to be saying and thinking too. In this respect he resembled the wife of a famous British newspaper correspondent in Paris. She was homely and not very smart, but she was so much the average Frenchwoman that, when he wanted to write an article on French public opinion, all he had to do was push his head through the door of the kitchen where she spent her days in toil and shout, *'Qu'est-ce-qu'on en pense?'*

The impending event about which I had to talk to Joe just now was the visit of Mr Ramsay MacDonald, Prime Minister of Britain and a Labour Prime Minister at that, and the first British Prime Minister ever to visit the United States. The London end of our concern was tremendously excited about the affair. And, where there was room, the American papers were giving it a big play too. Joe said that he thought the whole idea was kind of nice. He said that, after all, in a situation where everybody else was going ahead in a businesslike way it was about time the international statesmen got together and fixed things up. What kind of things? Well, this Anglo-American relations, and world peace and suchlike. If they could do that it would be kind of nice, or if they found it impossible then it would be merely just too bad.

To the reader of today it is perhaps necessary to explain that there was nothing by way of what we would call an international crisis on hand at the time, and that the principal international friction then existing was between Britain and the United States. The British, it is true, had for some time been making menacing gestures in the direction of the Soviet Union but, after doing so, and believing, as they always did, that they must have the Americans at their back in such a demonstration, they suddenly discovered that the Americans without any official recognition of the Soviet Government had, through the Standard Oil Company, established excellent trading relations with it, and the place where you could read the most favourable description of the life and progress of the Soviet Union was in the *New York Times*. When the Standard Oil got into action – shortly after the British had become involved in the Arcos Raid – wise people realised that within a couple of years a change in American-Russian relations must be about to occur. As the German essayist Tucholsky once wrote in reply to people who were speaking of the power of the Third International: 'There are at the moment, and in reality, only three effective international powers in the world, namely the Roman Catholic Church, the homosexuals, and the Standard Oil.'

With fifty thousand dollars in Anaconda Copper under his belt, Joe felt that several alternative things were all of them kind of nice. On the one hand anything that was wrong with international relations was simply a left-over from the world war. He often said to me that in his view the Treaty of Versailles and all this imperialism were the cause of whatever trouble there might be. On the other hand the United States

160

was in any case so much bigger and stronger than everybody else now that if any of these old imperialist powers like Britain and France started anything, why the United States was in a position to push them back into line. (In this Joe was in agreement with Ludwell Denny, who wrote a book called *America Conquers Britain* which, after a sapient analysis of the financial and commercial situation of the world, concluded with the words: 'What chance has Britain against America? What chance has the world?')

And then, after on the one hand and on the other hand, the fact was that the whole thing was relatively unimportant. Joe thought there were two possible views to be held about Ramsay MacDonald. He might of course be a genuine socialist, one of these reds. In that case on arrival in the United States he would see that his theories were false and that there was no future or percentage in that line of country and go back a converted man, which would be a good thing. Or else, Joe opined, he was not much of a socialist, because in Joe's view all these people were simply on the make and therefore there would be no need to convert him to anything. All he needed was the prestige of having been to Washington and sat down with President Hoover.

In addition Joe was hospitable and there were points which worried him. He wanted New York to give a good welcome to this Ramsay MacDonald regardless of the fact that he was a Labour Prime Minister. He said it would be a sin and a shame if they were to snoot him on that ground. It would not be nice. Kind of nice, however, was the news in the paper that Mr Hoover and Mr McDonald were not going to conduct their talks in the formal atmosphere of the White House, but on the contrary were going up to Mr Hoover's camp at Rapidan where it was announced they would sit on a log together and discuss the problems of the world. Sitting on a log, Joe thought, was about what statesmen ought to do, because it would in some way help them to get together. He would say this off, so to speak, the top of his mind, and then under the brim of the hat and the eyeshade and behind the cigar he would give you a look which said, 'What difference does it make whether they're sitting in chairs or on a log? Who do they think they're fooling?' I said, 'So you think really it's a phoney.'

'Don't see how it can do any harm,' Joe said, 'and, say listen, excuse me, I'm busy.'

And he was indeed. He was busy getting off a despatch,

and then he had to dash over to the stock-exchange ticker in the *Sun* office and see what Anaconda Copper was doing today.

I never found anybody who, except in statements for the record, took any other view of the MacDonald visit than that advanced by Joe, and the whole affair was farcical to the point where one wondered at what stage the public would notice that the two statesmen principally concerned – Mr Hoover and Mr MacDonald – were cocking snooks at the said public in the interest of their respective political careers. However, as Joe would have wished, New York gave the Labour Prime Minister a fine welcome. The Tenement Commissioner went down to Quarantine at the head of a Welcoming Committee. The Sanitation Band played 'God Save the King' and 'Rule, Britannia!' over and over again. The raft belonging to the Fire Department put on a display, pumping fountains of water into the air from all its hoses simultaneously.

But on board the ship itself there was crisis. A perplexity darkened momentarily the mind of the visiting Prime Minister. On landing at New York should he, as the first Labour Prime Minister of England to visit the United States, or should he not, wear a top-hat? The issue involved was to his mind serious. The smallest false step might have a serious effect on the goodwill of the citizenry and, via the resultant publicity, on the whole population. One knew that the Americans were on the one hand democratic. On the other hand they were anti-socialist. In this prickly situation the wrong sort of hat might easily be as disastrous as the wrong sort of policy. MacDonald, who could not decide the question of whether he wanted his eggs hard or lightly boiled without falling mentally into the pose of Rodin's *Thinker,* was thinking deeply. He consulted the staff of advisers he had with him on the boat. Expert as they were in observing and noting every changing nuance of America opinion and taste, they yet did not feel entirely competent to decide the question on their own responsibility. The boat was already leaving Quarantine and proceeding up the bay. Urgently they radioed the Foreign Office. The Prime Minister, they said, wanted to know whether he should wear a top-hat or a cloth cap in the Keir Hardie manner. With hardly more than a few seconds' hesitation the Foreign Office replied that the Prime Minister should certainly wear a morning coat and top-hat. This he did.

The demonstration accompanying his parade up Broadway

was adequate but not extravagantly enthusiastic. The volume of ticker-tape was by no means huge. As luck would have it, the office staffs of the speculators whose windows lined the route were on that day occupied with matters rather less festive than the Prime Minister's little trip, but no less closely connected with the course of international affairs. It happened that the Bank of England had on the previous afternoon at last decided to raise its discount rate in an effort to arrest the flow of speculative capital to the New York Stock Market. This action, following other warning squalls, gave the market a further nasty jar, and brokers were more intent on reading the ticker-tape than on throwing it out of the windows.

Not that it matterd. The newspapers of both countries were genially determined that the visit should be a howling success and an unexampled good time had by all. Ticker-tape or no ticker-tape, Bank of England or no Bank of England, the story of the welcome to MacDonald had to be one of the biggest, jolliest, heartiest stories of the month, even of the year; and it was. The public, reading the accounts, was delighted, and comfortably convinced that Anglo-American relations were on a thoroughly sound basis of mutual friendship and co-operation. A detachment of the Young Socialist League injected what might have been something of a sour note into the proceedings by stationing itself on the corner of City Hall Plaza singing 'The Internationale' and waving banners with socialist slogans. The Prime Minister, aware of the welcoming Government's attitude to socialism, and determined to do nothing that might impair the hope of international goodwill, disappointed them by refraining from looking in their direction, instead waving his top-hat in the general direction of the people looking out of the windows of the Bank of America.

The incident passed almost unnoticed, for in those days the Young Socialist League represented practically nobody. The prevailing mood of American Labour was contented and mannerly, and as for the fact that Mr MacDonald had once been a socialist himself, his hosts were prepared to treat that as a kind of frenzy, an almost amusing wild oat.

It was true that only a few days before his arrival six workers in the textile mills of North Carolina had had to be killed for trying to organise in favour of better conditions and wages. But that was an accident incidental to the industrialisation of the new South. In its search for cheap labour and low production costs Capital was deserting New England and finding employment in the South. The Chambers of Commerce in the Southern States were spilling the glad news that labour was to be bought, comparatively speaking, dirt cheap. Even British and European capital had begun to take advantage of American cheap labour in the South. Naturally since the whole point of capital investment in the textile industries of the South was to get the competitive benefit of cheap production costs, including labour, people who tried to raise the cost of labour there by organising unions had to be driven out or jailed or killed. They were running against the trend, and the consequences were obvious.

I had been interested in the situation down there and had taken a little trip to North Carolina. I had seen several leading textile manufacturers who explained to me about the trend, and I had seen a Presbyterian minister kneeling beside the open graves of the trade unionists shot by the Company guards, his hair tousled by the wind, his arms raised above his head and his voice crying:

'Oh God, what would Jesus do if He came to Carolina?'

He too seemed to be betting on the wrong sort of miracle.

To people who had been disturbed by the events in North Carolina it was refreshing to hear the rich religious voice of Britain's Labour Prime Minister booming thousands of encouraging words into the microphone. He went to Washington and appeared on the floor of the Senate. His appeal to the optimism of the American people was irresistible. In New York he went to tea with the Foreign Policy Association at the Commodore Hotel, and made a speech in which he said that wars occurred because people got into a certain state of mind. Afterwards he and his daughter Ishbel sat in a roped-off space like creatures in a museum while the adoring public filed past to pay its respects.

The stairways and environs of the hotel were crowded with people assembled to see him leave. They wanted to see this leader of the British Empire, who had so repeatedly and sonorously denounced and renounced imperialism, and was going, they thought, to create a situation in which all the conflicts and problems of imperialism would be dissolved in a strong solution of common sense and goodwill.

As he appeared on the stairs the band of the Commodore Hotel, with sublime ironic inspiration, stopped playing a tango and struck up the ever-swelling theme-song of imperialism, 'Land of Hope and Glory'. MacDonald descended.

'Wider yet and wider may thy bounds be set' – as he crossed the lounge.

Women waved handkerchiefs, the leaders of the Foreign Policy Association bowed and smiled, bows and smiles came from the Foreign Office Attachés.

'God who made thee mighty, make thee mightier yet!'

The band ended, and MacDonald was gone.

It had all been, Joe felt, nice, and in an obscure way comforting too. And comfort was something that was beginning to be needed, because the stray squalls on the Stock Exchange had now begun to fall into an almost menacing pattern and we were moving into the fateful third week of October 1929.

XIV DAY OF BATTLE

THE MORNING OF THURSDAY, OCTOBER 24TH, WAS like the morning of a battle which people are beginning for the first time to realise may be lost. Until soon after the opening of the market on the previous day, nobody had thought of such a thing. It was assumed, as it had been assumed on each previous occasion when a break in the market had occurred, that this was a temporary setback, a 'readjustment' – the bulls were losing a skirmish or two but they were not going to lose the battle.

But by the close of Wednesday's market the *New York Times* averages for fifty leading industrial stocks had lost over eighteen points, Joe had lost ten thousand dollars, and long after the close Freddie Bullock, in the intervals of trying to reach his brokers on the jammed telephone lines, kept coming into our office talking, arguing and listening for the first time to Hinrichs with a kind of nervous awe. Bullock came across from his apartment to have breakfast with me that Thursday in the café of the Hotel Lafayette. He needed company, and I dare say, too, he needed the peculiar atmosphere of the Hotel Lafayette which took you a little bit out of this world. It was owned by Raymond Orteig, who had put

165

up the original prize of twenty-five thousand dollars for the non-stop flight between New York and Paris ultimately won by Colonel Charles Lindbergh. The Lafayette was no mere curiosity, a French hotel in New York. It was, on the contrary, a first-class hotel and one which was simultaneously as French and as American as the French district of New Orleans. The food was the best in New York, and if you were a resident and took your meals in your own apartment you could get the benefit of one of the best cellars in New York too – the management of the Lafayette taking the view that prohibition did not apply to resident guests.

We had breakfast at a marble-topped table in the café at the end of which there was a ticker machine. Bullock kept jumping up and walking over to it by force of simply nervous habit, because at that hour the ticker could tell us nothing that we did not know already. Yet that morning there was a stream of men trotting up to the ticker and standing for a few minutes gazing at it in an unusual silence.

It takes nothing less than a major air raid to produce any visible change in the social 'atmosphere' of London, but New York lives more externally, and on the subway to the City Hall Square the change was as evident as a notable change in the weather. At the *Sun* office there was just that nip in the emotional air which you get on the day after a big air raid, when people have grasped that the bombers really did get through last night and may do so again today. It was a situation in which nobody says much but everyone knows what everyone else is thinking and knows that everyone else is a little frightened too.

As the electric clocks ticked off the minutes until the opening of the market, the tension was nearly intolerable. I do not mean that any of us had much idea of what was really going to happen except perhaps Louis Hinrichs. None of us, I am sure, thought, 'This is a turning-point one way or another in the history of the twentieth century.' None of us was sapient enough to reflect, 'Upon what happens today hangs the fate of nations. A way of life is going to survive or is going down the drain. After today, either everything will be as it was, or else nothing will ever be quite the same again.'

There were some very smart people hanging over the ticker at the opening of the market that morning in the *Sun* office, but none of them was quite smart enough to know that, as they saw in those first few astounding minutes shares of

Kennecott and General Motors thrown on the market in blocks of five, ten and fifteen thousand, they were looking at the beginning of a road which was going to lead to the British collapse of 1931, to the collapse of Austria, to the collapse of Germany, and at the end of it there was going to be a situation with Adolf Hitler in the middle of it, a situation in which no amount of get-togethers on a log at Rapidan was going to do much good, a situation in fact which was going to look very much like the fulfilment of the most lurid predictions of Marx and Lenin.

I kept being reminded of the old story about the enthusiastic American who took his phlegmatic British friend to see Niagara.

'Isn't that amazing?' said the American. 'Look at that vast mass of water dashing over that enormous cliff!'

'But what,' said the Englishman, 'is to stop it?'

There was nothing much to do that morning except just to watch Niagara. It seemed pointless to go through the usual routine of telephoning to 'contacts' and informants and asking for their comments on the situation. There was no sensible comment that anyone could make, and furthermore you had the feeling that there was no question you could ask which would not strike the man at the other end as some kind of affront. Even so I scarcely began to guess how bad the situation really was until Hinrichs, in a low voice, said to me: 'Remember when we're writing this story the word 'panic' is not to be used.'

At length we left the crazy-looking ticker and started to walk through the bright streets towards Wall Street, walking in silence because, in the light of the enormity of the event, anything that one could say seemed intolerably trivial. Thousands of other people were streaming towards Wall Street and they were walking in silence too.

In the Street itself there was an enormous murmuring crowd, and the people pressed close around us were talking, when one listened to them, almost in whispers. Every now and then you could hear quite distinctly a hysterical laugh. As time passed, the crowd grew thicker and noisier, and then there was an eddy in the middle of it and a man in shirtsleeves was pushing his way across the street in the direction of the Morgan offices. Hinrichs nudged me sharply. This was an easily recognisable denizen of the Village, namely Charles E. Mitchell, Chairman of the National City Bank, the leader of the bull market and the champion of the 'expansionists' against the 'restrictive' efforts of the Federal Reserve Board. He pushed his way into the offices of the house of Morgan and a little later we learned what he had gone for. He and the other leading bankers of Wall Street had been summoned there to establish a multi-million-dollar pool in an attempt to steady the market.

Silver-haired Mr Lamont received us with a manner so reassuring that, upon me and many others, it had the same effect as Hinrichs's warning against the use of the word 'panic'. It was like the manner of the man who comes on the stage of a burning theatre and urges everyone to keep perfectly cool, stating there is no cause for alarm. He made soft, soothing gesticulations with his pince-nez as softly, gently, almost stammeringly, he deprecated anything in the nature of sensationalism. His first sentence has been aptly described as one of the most remarkable under-statements of all time.

'There has been a little distress selling on the Stock Exchange,' he said, 'and we have held a meeting of the heads of several financial institutions to discuss the situation. We have found that there are no Houses in difficulty and the reports from brokers indicate that margins are being maintained satisfactorily.'

The pince-nez gently waved away ill-informed rumours of the disaster, moving to and fro in the dim light from the high window heavily covered with anti-bomb steel netting. Nothing fundamental, he said, had changed. There was nothing basically wrong with the country's economy. What had occurred was due simply to 'a technical condition of the market'.

Since becoming a journalist I had often heard the advice to 'believe nothing until it has been officially denied'. But, despite this, even the ominous blandness of Mr Lamont did not shake me into full awareness of what was going on. The shake came a little later at lunch with the Edgar Speyers.

'Edwardian' was the adjective which inevitably occurred to you in the presence of Edgar Speyer, and equally inevitably he recalled to me the Rothschilds as I had seen them in my boyhood days at Tring. He was an American now, had been an American for years, and he and his brother were not only millionaires but had made themselves powerful figures in the cut and thrust of Wall Street, but the aroma of Edwardianism still hung about him like the scent of a good cigar. This was natural enough since it was in Edwardian England that this originally German Jew had risen to wealth and prominence.

He had been Sir Edgar Speyer then, and a Privy Councillor. Then he was caught in the storm of indignation against Germans in high places in England which at the beginning of World War I swept even Prince Louis of Battenberg out of the Admiralty. He could afford to recall what for many people might have been a disaster with an amiable shrug. His enforced good-bye to all that had by no means been disastrous for him. He just got on a boat and went to Boston and made a couple of million dollars. Later he advanced triumphantly on New York and, at the time I knew him, lived in one of the lovely rose-coloured houses on the north side of Washington Square. It housed, not in any special gallery but as part of its furnishings, a small but luminously beautiful art collection composed chiefly of Chinese paintings and porcelain. The atmosphere was one of elegant calm in which the rich odour emanating from pots and pots of money was naturally, but not disagreeably, perceptible. It was at that time one of the few houses I visited in New York where you did not have to talk about the Stock Market or any other form of business, and the food and wine were so good that nobody thought it odd if at lunch or dinner you were perfectly silent for minutes on end. There were a middle-aged English butler and a youthful English footman, but, except for their age, one might have supposed that they had been trained in Edwardian England and come over with Speyer on the boat to Boston in 1914. Their only departure from an older tradition was that they both of them left the room as soon as each course had been served by the footman under the butler's supervision.

Leonora Speyer was a writer. She had, as I recall, recently published a volume of poems, and on this October 24th of 1929 the Speyers and their four guests were talking about modern American poetry. I was eating pompano and listening to somebody telling something about some poet I had not yet heard of, when I perceived to my astonishment that some kind of disturbance was going on at the other side of the dining-room door, which faced me as I sat at the table. Something had certainly bumped against the door. I heard a very faint thump, and I saw the door shiver slightly. The idea of anything, as it were, untoward occurring in the Speyer household was nearly inconceivable. I concluded that they must be the owners of some large dog which I had never seen, and that this dog had escaped and was probably at this moment being hauled off to its proper place by the footman. And then just as I was about to give full attention again to the conversation, something else happened.

The handle of the door turned very very slowly, the door shuddered again and moved an inch or so inwards. Then it closed again, and again the handle very very slowly turned in the direction opposite to its direction before. There was no longer any doubt about it. Either somebody in an ecstasy of indecision was trying to make up his mind to come into the room, or else, as seemed more likely, two people were struggling over the handle of the door, one of them trying to open it and the other to keep it closed.

In any other house there might have been a dozen explanations for this – children loose in the passage, for instance. Perhaps children playing with a big dog. But in the Speyer household things were so ordered that a disturbance of this kind was as startling as it would have been to find the dining-room too hot or too cold, or to have a draught blowing down one's neck. Fascinated by the mysterious struggle behind the door, I found myself gazing at the man who was talking intelligently about this poet with an expression, as I could see from the surprised look he gave me, of absolutely idiotic vacancy. I was so placed that I was the only one at the table who, when the door opened, could see right down the corridor outside, and what I saw, when the two manservants came in to put a saddle of lamb in front of Speyer, was that at the end of the corridor either four or five maidservants of various ages were grouped together in what seemed to be an excited attitude and one of them – unless I was under some kind of hallucination – had actually shaken her fist at the footman as he came through the door.

Within a few minutes the butler and footman had again withdrawn, but we had swallowed no more than a mouthful or two of lamb when the noise in the passage became so loud that nobody in the dining-room could even pretend to ignore it. A woman shouted, 'Go on – or else! — ' and then the door was burst open and the butler, very red in the face, nearly bounced into the room as though he had been pushed violently from behind at the last moment.

He closed the door and as collectedly as possible marched across the room to Speyer and in low apologetic tones begged him to come outside for a moment. Listening with an air of astonishment, Speyer, after a few seconds' amazed hesitation, left the room with him. Almost immediately Speyer came back again looking a little dismayed. He begged us to excuse him. The staff, he explained, had of course their own ticker-tape in the kitchen premises and of course they were all heavily engaged on the Stock Market. And now the ticker was recording incredible things. In point of fact the ticker was by that time running just over an hour and a half late, owing to the enormous volume of trading, so that the prices which the Speyer staff were reading with horror at a quarter to two were the prices at which stocks had changed hands at the very worst moment of the morning before the bankers had met and the formation of the bankers' pool had been announced.

The staff saw their savings going down in chaos; since they were certainly operating on margin, they might at this moment already have been wiped out. Among the stock in which all of them had speculated was that of Montgomery Ward, and that had dropped from an opening price of 83 to around 50 before noon. And all this was going on before their eyes while their employer, reputedly one of the shrewdest financiers in New York, was calmly sitting upstairs eating pompano and saddle of lamb. They absolutely insisted that he go at once with them to the kitchen, study the situation, make telephone calls if necessary, and advise them what to do for the best.

Speyer left the rest of his lunch uneaten, and his wife and her guests finished the meal under conditions of confusion and makeshift which probably had never been seen in the Speyer household before. I left as soon as I decently could and did not see Mr Speyer to say good-bye. He was still in the kitchen. I hurried to the office to write my story, beginning at last to be aware of what the great crash meant.

By this time everyone else was beginning to be aware of it too, most of them more fully than myself. Whereas in the morning the atmosphere had been in the main one of incredulous excitement, now there was a strong smell of fear in the air too.

Our office had begun to look as though the waves were going over the bridge. Naturally we all of us had to write several thousand words to London describing the great crash. But at the same time everybody was either emotionally or financially so deeply engaged that there were constant little conferences in the corners, where people were trying to figure out what really had happened. Every now and then forlorn telephone calls came in from other people who were also trying to figure that out. And, as always happens at times like these, the element of low farce walked in in the shape of a little man whose name I remember so poorly that I can only describe him as Colonel X. Colonel X was some kind of dilapidated British peer who had spent years of his life in the Intelligence Service in India. He was now in New York, had been in New York for some time and had repeatedly come into *The Times* office suggesting that we buy from him for a large price a story he had, which told that a new anti-British revolution in India was being planned among the Indian students of Columbia University. He was a dirty little Lord, and it was obvious to the least experienced observer that he was reeking with heroin. However, he had at one point somewhat endeared himself to me by showing a really extraordinary knowledge of the English hymn-book. He could at any moment recite any hymn in the English hymn-book of which you gave him the number, and this seemed to me a very remarkable accomplishment. He had also once borrowed from me a sum of money after I had determined never to lend him any more money at all. He had said to me, gazing into a battered straw hat which he wore, 'You know, laddie, what I need is five thousand dollars.'

I, who had been so sure that I never would lend him any money at all, had said laughingly, 'Well, that is unfortunately too bad. I don't have more than ten dollars available.'

To which he had replied, 'That will do, laddie. That will be sufficient for the moment.' And of course there had been nothing to do but to give him the ten dollars.

He stank so badly that normally one did not care to see him otherwise than on the public street, but on this occasion, on the day of the great crash, one stench seemed no worse than another. I could not at first focus upon the little man. I could not make out what on earth he was doing in this *galère*. Then I realised that he was standing on his bow legs with his little cane and his busted straw hat on the side of his head, looking at everyone with an air of enormous superiority. At last he, so to speak, 'cut me out' in the way that a cowboy cuts out a cow, and he said to me, 'You know, all these people are worrying, worrying, worrying. They are worrying about the crash in America, about some crash they think is going to happen in consequence in Britain; they think that we shall all go off the gold standard or something of the kind. And what I want to say to you, laddie, is just simply this. Don't worry, don't worry, don't worry.'

I said to him that there were grounds for worry. He said,

'I thought you would say that, laddie, and that is why I am going to tell you something. Let me tell you that to me, and just a very few people in the Intelligence Service, is known the fact that in the heart of Africa, right in Zululand, we have a mountain of gold. Yes, laddie, a mountain of gold. And that gold – that mountain of gold – is patrolled day by day and night by night by a great troop of the finest Zulus in the world. Loyal chaps, laddie, yes, loyal chaps.'

At this point his voice had risen to such a screech that even the Financial Editor of the *New York Sun* was peering to see where it came from.

'And these Zulus,' he said, 'splendid physical specimens, magnificent men, they go round and round this mountain once at dawn and once at night. At dawn they run up the Union Jack on the mountain, and the chief of this magnificent tribe drives in a carriage round it, with, laddie, cream-coloured ponies – cream-coloured ponies like Queen Victoria had. And if any one of the magnificent Zulu guards is not in his place, that guard is taken out and lashed – lashed practically to death, laddie, because these are loyal fellows. And that means that whatever happens – whatever happens to America, whatever happens to Germany or Russia or this kind of nonsense, we've got this mountain of gold and we are going to survive. Do you see what I mean, laddie?'

I saw just what he meant, and it was the end of that day.

XV THE KNIGHT OF NEW HAMPSHIRE AVENUE

THE NEXT WEEK WAS JUST THE SAME AND EVERY day people said that everything was going to get better, and every day it got worse. Things reached a point where it became almost impossible to face one's friends or acquaintances in New York because everything that had happened or was happening seemed to make them out to be fools, and just because at one time or another one had questioned their judgment in the grand old times of ten days ago, one seemed to be swaggering with superior knowledge. Superior knowledge which of course one did not possess.

I was thus both happy and tremulous when I suddenly received the news that *The Times* Correspondent in Washington, Mr Wilmott Lewis, had been summoned to London to attend some international conference or other, and the plan was that I should immediately go to Washington and take over his job. I was elated because I was glad to get away from the gloomy atmosphere of New York at this period, and to get also to the political centre of affairs. On the other hand, I was nearly unnerved by the thought that I was suddenly, at so brief a notice, and with such minimal knowledge and journalistic experience, to take over what by this time had become the major political bureau of the London *Times*. I left for Washington on the night of December 31st, 1929.

Sliding into Union Station, Washington, in the darkness of New Year's Eve, I reflected momentarily that the last member of my family to visit the American capital was Admiral Sir George Cockburn, who had burned the White House and the Capitol, and much else of Washington besides, in 1814. Not, I had always thought, a very nice kind of man. For example, when he was in command near Annapolis before the assault on the city, he considered the food and drink available in the camp not up to the mark. He had also heard that there was an excellent restaurant on Pennsylvania Avenue in the enemy capital. Sensibly enough, he made arrangements to visit this restaurant every evening in disguise. However, no memory of these pleasant little soirées prevented him later from cantering up and down Pennsylvania Avenue on his horse urging the soldiery to further acts of rape and arson. The proprietress of the restaurant is said to have been very much wounded by his behaviour.

As I left Union Station there was a considerable glare in the sky. The dome of the Capitol had just burst into flames.

Startled, I drove to the house of Wilmott Lewis where I was to stay. It was our first meeting. He was entranced by the occurrence at the Capitol. Holding both my hands in his he beamed upon me and, 'Now,' he said, 'one sees at once that you have been born under the right star. You have luck – and that is the most important thing in life.

'Even with your outstanding abilities – which I may say I

have for some time been noting from afar with admiration – it might have taken you weeks to make your mark, to become any kind of a lion in the Washington Zoo. Now, as a result of this happy concatenation of events – call it luck, call it destiny, call it what you will – you will be at least a lion cub no later than tomorrow morning.'

Before he had even finished speaking he had lifted the receiver of the telephone in the hall and communicated the story, decorated with some remarkable grace notes of his own, to all the columnists in Washington, and to two in New York. In the brief intervals between the calls he gave me a little lecture on the values of publicity in facilitating one's serious work, and smoothing the path towards one's real objectives.

'Do any of the people you have been talking to,' I asked, 'know what actually caused this fire tonight?'

'They suppose,' he said, 'that it was a painter. The inside of the dome is being redecorated. One of the painters, no doubt drunk, since it is New Year's Eve, probably dropped a cigar among the paint and varnish and so on. However, it is what one may call the 'Cockburn angle' that really makes the story.'

Still talking, he led me into the drawing-room, where an exhilarating symphony of noise and almost overpowering volume of sound proved after a time to be composed of the Philharmonic Orchestra playing something rowdy on an enormous radiogram, about thirty of the best-informed people in Washington rattling the tall windows with their gossip, and the yells and incantations of two senators, a Congressman, several journalists, and the then Mrs Lewis, daughter of the owner of the Associated Press, who were on their knees shooting craps in the middle of the carpet.

'Curiously enough,' said Lewis, towards five in the morning when the party was beginning to break up, 'I feel a little tired. I must be getting old.'

He was then in his early fifties. For all these hours he had 'conducted' that party of star performers as a conductor conducts a band. Reeling to bed when the last guests had gone, I passed the open door of his study and saw him in his shirt-sleeves, his dinner-jacket draped over the back of his chair, thoughtfully beginning to tap out two or three pages of notes recording impressions, potentially significant pieces of information, dropped into his attentive ear in the course of the evening.

'There are a million pieces in the jigsaw,' he said. 'At any moment you may unexpectedly find that you have just picked up the one you need.'

I had met a lot of colourful and impressive personalities that evening, but before I finally got to bed I could not feel that any of them was quite as impressive as my host. Nothing in the years that I knew him altered that opinion.

Strangers thought he must be a famous actor or Envoy Extraordinary of some very civilised state. In the grey dawn of an all-night poker session he seemed, rather, the phantom of the original Mississippi Gambler, so sardonic, debonair and quick on the draw. Or smiling thoughtfully in the inner circle round the President at a White House reception, he suggested an angularly handsome Mephisto, wondering whether or not to wave a conjuring hand and transform the company into swans and bullfrogs.

High-placed Americans insisted he was the secret Chief of the British Intelligence Service in the United States, and years before he became officially 'Sir' Wilmott Lewis. American colleagues recognised the panache of his personality by referring to Wilmott Harsant Lewis as the Knight of New Hampshire Avenue, where his big house was situated. When he was knighted they asked him whether they should address him in some new way.

'You will continue,' he said, 'to address me as "You old s.o.b.," but from now on you have to smile as you say that.'

Up-to-the-minute as a portable voice recorder, he yet had about him a flavour which evoked Europe of the late '90s. In his teens he had been at the universities of both Heidelberg and Paris, and one of a group of *avant garde* poets and critics who met at the Closerie des Lilas. He admitted occasional nostalgia for the continent he had scarcely seen in twenty-five years.

'Nevertheless,' he said, in his habitual style of faultlessly elaborate parenthesis, 'Washington – which Viviani, when he led the French delegation to the Disarmament Conference, was tactless enough to describe as *"un Versailles nègre"*, thus (for you figure to yourself the reactions of Southern senators to whom his ill-timed if apt remark was, I need hardly tell you, instantly communicated) stabbing himself in the back, a performance singularly otiose in a city where so many stand only too eagerly ready to do it for you – Washington has many amenities and compensations, not least among

176

them the fact that it is the last world capital still resisting Americanisation.'

Among the amenities he enjoyed were the rare, perhaps unique, local prestige and international influence his ability had achieved for him during his first years in the capital. He had come to be regarded generally as more important than most Ambassadors most of the time and always much more fun. It was a situation he appreciated without illusions.

'The advantage,' he remarked to me once, as we sat eating enormous oysters in a tiny yacht on the Potomac, 'of having spent a good deal of one's early life on – not to put too fine a point on it – the bum, is that one learns never to take even a square meal entirely for granted.'

As a very young man he had been for a time an actor, down and nearly out. He had sat up at night in an Eastbourne lodging-house writing fresh material for the bankrupt troupe, himself among them, to act next day. It was presumably during this period that he had acquired a kind of barnstorming fruitiness and floridity of tone and gesture which sometimes disconcerted the stolid.

'As you gaze, Mr President,' I once heard him say to President Hoover, 'into the future, as you peer down the grey vista of the years, do you not apprehend, sir, that the problems of the United States are problems not only of growth, but' – the voice sank to a vibrant whisper – 'of decay?'

The President seemed bemused alike by the question itself and by the sudden extension of arm and hand which accompanied it, the index finger pointing menacingly down the grey vista. The incident must have disturbed him, for later he made a speech in which he said the problems of the United States were those of growth only – not of decay.

Lewis would describe as poignantly as though it had happened yesterday the occasion when after starving for nearly four days in London he had found a shilling or so in the lining of his jacket and rushed out to buy a tin of beef or something of the kind. When he got it back to his room and had hacked it open, with the saliva running down his chin, he found that the beef was hopelessly maggot-ridden.

'It is a good thing,' he said, 'to remember, that, however nicely we may be doing, to millions and millions of people all over the world, privations and disappointments of that kind are happening all the time.'

He told me when I came to know him well that he thought probably the most 'formative' influence in his early life had been the occasion when as a very junior reporter he had been assigned by the *Daily News* to write a preliminary 'feature' story about the Diamond Jubilee Review to be held at Aldershot by Queen Victoria in 1897.

'I went to Aldershot and viewed the sand-dunes, the broad driveway where the Royal cortège and the whole pomp and panoply of empire, the Kings and Queens and Princes, were to be assembled, where troops from twenty races and from every continent were to pass in view. As my mind's eye envisaged the superb spectacle, my physical eye detected an unexpected movement among the sand-hills on the other side of the reviewing place. Mildly curious, I moved in that direction. I soon saw that the movement was caused by human figures.

'Approaching still nearer, I perceived these to be the figures of women in rags and horribly decayed. At that time, you know, there was in the British Army no proper system of education and instruction on the subject of venereal disease – it was thought that to introduce such a system officially might be offensive to the "respectable" public, and perhaps to the Queen herself. These women, then, were former prostitutes of Aldershot, so diseased as now to be unable to pursue the practice of their profession and living in the most miserable shacks and shanties among the sand-dunes. One must admit, of course, that they were excellently placed to enjoy the prospect of the great Diamond Jubilee Review.'

An abruptly switch-backing course took young Mr Lewis from London to the Far East, where he was alternately on top of the world and reduced to helping to manage a tough bar at the Shanghai racecourse. Soon after that his astounding energy shoved him to a point where he was internationally recognised as one of the most ingenious and brilliant war correspondents in the Russo-Japanese War.

He edited a newspaper in Manila, worked as a sports writer in San Francisco, was 'hard pressed' again in New York, emerged penultimately in Paris at the moment of the Versailles Conference. Deeply impressed, Mr Wickham Steed, then editor of *The Times*, introduced him to Lord Northcliffe. The meeting was in a sense a failure. Apparently Lewis, as was his habit, illustrated his conversation with rather frequent quotations from the French minor poets. Lord Northcliffe complained that the man was a damned foreigner. He compromised by agreeing that he be hired, provided he was sent

178

somewhere far off. They thought first of Tokyo, finally agreed on Washington.

By the time I met him his prestige was alarming, and his despatches were misleadingly described as models of what such things should be – misleading because anyone trying to imitate these superbly individual works of art would have come a nasty cropper. Sometimes he spent three or four days or even a week preparing and polishing a despatch on some aspect of American affairs which would be filed to London at a moment when an event, foreseen by Lewis, occurred to form the 'news peg' upon which the rest of the carefully prepared message was to be hung. More often he wrote his despatches or articles very fast, but this was only because he was, so to speak, permanently 'in rehearsal'. He was always rehearsing, mentally or in conversation, the formulations or comments which would be appropriate to this or that development of the situation, so that when the development actually occurred, the polished phrases and considered judgments poured from the typewriter at a pace which, but for the unending 'rehearsals,' would have been incredible.

I was to have only forty-eight hours with him in Washington before he left for London. Considering my ignorance of this vast and complex stage, the experience would have been very alarming had not Wilmott Lewis, by a kind of courteous hypnosis, succeeded in creating for myself and almost everyone else the illusion that I was a person of such enormous experience and ability that – with a hint or two, probably unnecessary, from him – I could effortlessly take charge of the situation.

Comment flowed briskly as he hurried me on a conducted tour of personalities and situations. ('In fairness to Senator Cole Blease, old boy, it must be said that he has the unique distinction of combining in his sole person *all* the disadvantages attaching to the democratic form of government.' 'One should perhaps avoid being hypercritical of acts of high policy. Take the charitable view, bearing in mind that every government will do as much harm as it can and as much good as it must.' 'He is one of those American politicians who believe that the women of his country are more virtuous and its diplomats more stupid than those of any other. Since he is wrong on both these counts, it is reasonable to assume that he is wrong on every other, too.' 'Do not under-estimate his capacity for snatching defeat from the very jaws of victory.'

'Inspiring, is it not, to see eyes so ablaze with insincerity?' 'He will always be happy to advise you. You may rely upon him to maintain a firm grip on the obvious.')

Just before leaving, he suddenly presented me with the first of two pieces of journalistic advice which were the best I had ever had.

'I think it well,' he said, 'to remember that, when writing for the newspapers, we are writing for an elderly lady in Hastings who has two cats of which she is passionately fond. Unless our stuff can successfully compete for her interest with those cats, it is no good.'

Months later, when he was back in Washington, I once submitted to him a two-column article for *The Times* on which I had worked hard and of which I was extremely proud. Lewis read it with close attention. As he nodded appreciatively my pride and pleasure increased. He read it for the second time. Then, holding it between his finger and thumb, he said, 'Old boy, this piece is not only informed but erudite. Its material is solid and accurately observed; its style polished – and, in my estimation, witty. In fact it is everything which one imagines to oneself an article in *The Times* should be. Yet I'm afraid – my instinct tells me – that,' he opened his finger and thumb and the pages dropped into the waste-paper basket, 'the cats will have it.'

Despite the intensive forty-eight-hour course in Washington affairs which I had gone through under his guidance, I was uneasy. Left to myself, I thought, I should write something terribly mistaken, causing panic in London and upsetting the empire. Sensing my emotion, Lewis pushed head and shoulders out of his departing taxi and gave me the second piece of admirable advice.

'Whatever happens,' he shouted, 'don't be nervous. Remember, old boy' – the taxi was moving faster now and he had to shout through the driving sleet – 'whatever happens, you are right and London is wrong.'

He had been away many weeks, was in fact just returning, before I grasped the full extent of his own faith in this statement. He had invited me to stay in his house and also use it as my office. He had omitted even to mention that there was in fact a *Times* office in Washington. I found it by accident one day when I was wandering through a downtown office building looking for something else. It was locked. I obtained a pass-key. The door moved with difficulty. When I did get inside, I found the door had been jammed by a cascade of cablegrams and letters pushed daily for weeks and weeks through the letter slip.

Most of the cables were from *The Times,* some of them sent since I had taken over, most of them of earlier date. They said 'Urgently require 700 words on . . .' and 'Please cable most urgently full coverage of . . .' 'Must have tomorrow latest . . .'

Appalled, I met Lewis on his return with the dreadful news; I supposed it to be due to some ghastly mistake by the Cable Company. He looked at the cables distastefully.

'Ah yes,' he said, 'perhaps I should have told you about that office. London, you know, *does* these things. I've always found it best to maintain a certain distance. Better to decide for oneself what to send and when to send it.'

I found out later that a couple of years previously *The Times* really had made a determined attempt to get him to respond to their cabled enquiries and demands. When he was in London on a brief visit they waited until the last day of his stay in order to make the *démarche* the more impressive and memorable, and then a number of the High Priests cornered him in a small room somewhere in the labyrinth of Printing House Square, and Mr Deakin, Foreign and Imperial News Editor, made an impressive statement. It was, he said, intolerable that *The Times* should launch urgent cablegrams across the Atlantic and hear no more of them than if they had launched their messages upon the bosom of the ocean. He depicted movingly the distress and confusion thus occasioned. Could not Lewis promise solemnly, here and now, that, in future, cables sent at urgent rates, and signed personally by the editor, would at least be acknowledged? He went so far as to suggest that in return for such a promise *The Times* might be inclined to consider a bonus or a rise in salary as compensation for the trouble involved. While Deakin was speaking Lewis had got to his feet, and seemed to be beating his breast and to be making other mysterious gestures with his hands.

'I am,' he said, the moment Deakin concluded his remarks, 'a sinful man, my dear Deakin. I feel like a San Sebastian – every word of yours is an arrow in my heart.'

By now everyone's attention was concentrated on Lewis's theatrically trained hands plucking imaginary arrows from his heart. As he plucked, he strode about the room. For about five seconds too long his audience sat bemused or hypnotised by the performance, and too late saw the door closing behind him, and heard the words, 'arrow in my heart, my dear fellows' floating down the corridor outside, as Lewis hastened towards the exit and to the taxi which would hurry him to the Southampton boat train, still uncommitted to answering even urgent cables signed by the editor.

Relieved by his explanation of the business of *The Times* office in Washington, I asked him why he had refused the Foreign Editorship of *The Times,* which I knew had been offered him during his most recent visit to London.

'I am too scabrous an individual,' he said, 'to survive for long the rarefied air of Printing House Square. I did, however, offer to become their *London* Correspondent – reporting, you know, on the motives and personalities of political activity in England with the same interest and detachment that one seeks to display here. Would it not, I suggested, be an excellent idea for *The Times* to be as informative, and when necessary as candid, about people and events in Westminster, Whitehall and the City as it is about goings on in Washington or Paris? They didn't,' he said, looking happily out at Washington, his expression more Machiavellian than usual, 'seem awfully keen on the idea. I wonder why not?'

The roar of the Press Club dining-room engulfed me. Lewis, listening to a fierce political discussion, seemed a little tired. He said he kept remembering the dream a French poet friend of his had once had, in which he saw the whole world covered by an inundation. Only the tops of the highest spires and steeples peeped above the flood, and the only survivors were some parrots which perched on these and, taught by man, kept screeching out 'Justice, Progress, Freedom!'

Somebody said, 'Bill, you're a nasty old cynic.'

Wilmott Lewis looked at him shortly. 'Cynic? Not at all, old boy. If humanity leaves such memories to the birds, it will have been a considerable achievement, something of which we may all be proud.'

During the first two and a half years of that decade, when I was in Washington, sometimes for months at a time, sometimes only for a few weeks or even hours, things to take pride in seemed to be what we were rather short of. First we had a crisis which no one would admit officially existed, so that – somewhat like the prostitutes at Aldershot who became diseased because the army did not dare officially to admit the existence of syphilis – unemployed men in Chicago had to fight one another for first grab at the garbage cans put out at the back doors of the great hotels because a full and proper system of unemployment relief would have been 'socialistic', and above all would have been an admission of the existence of a crisis of scarcely believable proportions.

Later the crisis was admitted all right, and what we had then was something very like chaos. It was one of those situations in which deterioration and collapse are so rapid that even quite sensible policies always seem to be put into operation too late. There were flashes of hope and optimism which as they flickered out only emphasised the surrounding gloom. It seems odd, almost ludicrous, perhaps, by hindsight, that the so-called Hoover moratorium – the suspension of payment on all international government debts – should have appeared to enormous numbers of people as equivalent to an announcement that salvation after all is just around the corner, that God, after some agonising stumbles, is once again marching on. Yet it was so. The atmosphere of those sweat-soaked summer days when the moratorium was announced throbbed anew with the electric impulses of American evangelism, of that enthusiasm for the crusade which in America can be touched off so easily because the American heart feels so deeply the need of it.

Austria was going to be saved from financial collapse and Germany from Communist revolution and Hitler. All Europe was to be saved from financial collapse, or from the preventive war which it was then commonly supposed in Washington the French were about to undertake. For a few days Washington felt itself the headquarters of salvation. The New World was going into action to put the Old World on its feet. America was going once again to assume its natural leadership as the champion of peace, unity and common sense – its policies could be seen by all to be far-sighted, generous and altruistic. And since Heaven must surely be on the side of the good, and the good need to eat, Heaven would certainly see to it that the idealism of the good paid off pretty damn quickly, rewarding America by ending its depression, restoring its prosperity and getting things back to normal before the hire-purchase men finally came to repossess the car.

I saw President Hoover several times at that period, and if ever a man was transfigured with pleasure and a sense both of rightness and righteousness, it was he. Secretaries used to run in and out of his office with the latest quotations from stock markets all over the world – Berlin, New York, Chicago, London, New Orleans, Tokyo and Sydney. For long years

183

Mr Hoover had accepted the view that the way things look on the ticker is as important as the way things really are, or, rather, is the same as the way they really are. Now everything was going up. The depression was over. If it was not over, why was everything going up? I noted at the time that 'it was just the sort of public mood that the President likes best: *carte blanche* and no maddening interruptions from the blundering crowd. He is the Great Executive again, the Great Engineer of modern society, and he has pulled the right lever at last.'

The shock was naturally all the more severe when it became evident that the declaration of American policy had solved almost nothing, and the optimism and enthusiasm petered out in a long and violent wrangle over the exact terms of the moratorium between Washington and Paris. When 'agreement in principle' was finally reached, M Paul Claudel invited a number of American officials and others to the French Embassy to celebrate the event. Worn out with quarrelling and heat, the guests looked forward to the ceremony with gloom. There would be rhetoric and platitudes, speeches dripping with false optimism like the leading articles in the newspapers.

In the drawing-room at the Embassy M Claudel greeted them.

'Gentlemen,' he said simply, 'in the little moment that remains to us between the crisis and the catastrophe, we may as well take a glass of champagne.'

The familiar element of low farce was also present in the diplomatic international melodrama of the day. In this case the sub-plot had for its theme a romantic attachment formed between the Alsatian valet of M Claudel and my old Berlin acquaintance Wolfgang Putlitz, who had turned up in Washington as Third Secretary at the German Embassy. With Germany lurching towards a catastrophe, Putlitz mentally and physically seemed more and more some vast symbolic illustration to *Der Untergang des Abendlandes*. His emotions sang '*betrunken und hymnisch, wie Dmitri Karamazov sang am Weg zum Chaos*'. He had the air of a man attending a non-stop performance of *Götterdämmerung*, and his profound Prussian sense of doom, his Teutonic taste for disaster, were sharpened and exacerbated by the bitter flavour of America. To him America was a kind of Caliban – enormously strong, hopelessly uncivilised, and, in its blundering way, quite liable callously to burn, so to speak, all the books in which were recorded European traditions, scholarship, sense of history and – above all – sense of aristocracy. Just instinctively, and without what is ordinarily called conceit, he felt himself a superior being virtually alone on Wild Animal Island.

Moving in half-contemptuous intimacy among the bar boys of Berlin, Putlitz had been used to tell one with a kind of wondering pride, 'Nobody knows who I really am.' And he felt the same sensations in America. Nobody, he felt, knew who he really was, and that was very hard luck, but it made him feel lonely too.

A couple of times a week we would lunch or dine on the roof of an hotel on Pennsylvania Avenue in Washington, or at one of the fish bars down on the river. In Berlin he had thought me naïve because I took seriously, and as though they were as interesting as events in European history, the activities and trends of the North American continent.

Driven to an over-simplification, he would declare that indeed in his opinion the Americans and their institutions were childish and unpleasantly childish at that. He took the view, still quite common among Europeans at that date, that America is 'a young country'. Myself, I thought at the time that it was probably an old country – old because into less than two hundred years of history the American people had crammed the experience of Europeans acquired in thousands of years, and old because precisely this forcing process tends in itself to age people prematurely.

'Well, there you are,' Putlitz would say. 'I say they are suffering from retarded development, and you say that they suffer from over-development – children already weaned, young in years but already raddled and cunning. It comes in the end to the same thing.'

As the news from Germany grew worse he became more and more restless. One day when we met for lunch on the roof of the hotel on Pennsylvania Avenue to discuss particularly ominous reports from Germany, the weather – as curiously enough, it so often does – co-operated. Thunder rumbled round the hazy horizon, pale lightning made occasional livid patterns on the copper sky, and every so often, in the breathless heat, a tiny puff of wind – like a hand delivering a secret message – softly lifted a table-napkin or a flower and dropped it again. Perhaps influenced by these surroundings Putlitz told me that he was on the verge of a decision. He considered that at any moment now the situation in Germany might reach a point where he would feel it essential for him to return to his native land and 'do what is to be done'.

As I have said, he was a man without ordinary conceit but of enormous inbred arrogance of mind. As a Prussian aristocrat he would return to Germany in the capacity of a leader. He meant this, I think, in a partially mystical sense. He conceived it possible, of course, that he would form some kind of group, rally some kind of support and be a leader in the material sense of the word. On the other hand, if he landed in Germany and nobody rallied to him at all, he would not be disappointed. It would make no difference to his attitude to himself as a leader. He would still be spiritually 'as' a leader. He thought that if this course became necessary it was certain that by the time he arrived in Germany the currency would have collapsed. It would be necessary to carry concealed about one's person the maximum number of gold dollars. He had been told that anyone who wears a money-belt heavy with gold is liable during the first couple of weeks to be spotted at once by any experienced eye as one who is carrying a lot of metal around his waist – his gait and general posture give him away. For the past fortnight, Putlitz confided, he had been practising – he had acquired as many gold dollars as he could carry and had been wearing them all the time in a money-belt. He had also learned from a Negro smuggler at Annapolis of other ways in which additional supply of gold coins could be concealed about the body. These methods required practice and entailed a great deal more physical discomfort. However, Putlitz had been practising and had, he claimed, been able considerably to increase his storage capacity. As heat, humidity and excitement over the future of Germany made him stir abruptly on his chair I heard distinctly the chink of metal.

With the valet of the French Ambassador, I gathered, he really let himself go. This Alsatian was in Putlitz's eyes virtually a peasant, one at any rate with whom it was unnecessary to exercise that discretion in emotion and sentiment which was desirable in converse with one's equals. The valet in turn was evidently entranced by the romantic melancholy, the sonorous despair and the volcanically grandiose plans of his noble but unhappy Prussian pal. As he listened to Putlitz speaking aloud his thoughts about the fate and sufferings of Germany, the valet identified himself with Germany and with Putlitz and there painted itself in his mind's eye a picture of France as a typically venomous and treacherous

186

female tearing at the flesh of the helpless German hero, tying him up in cords of diplomatic intrigue, driving frightful political tent-pegs through his noble head. And here was he, the valet, personal attendant upon the diplomatic representative of the French monster. Determined to prove that he too could take his part in the fight for the good cause, the valet committed a number of small acts of sabotage designed to irritate the Ambassador, put him off his stroke, lower his morale and efficiency in diplomatic dealings. To Putlitz he said nothing of these acts of silent service, but when they appeared to be ineffective he conceived a more drastic plan. He ascertained the date of some crucial meeting of ambassadors with the United States Secretary of State, and a few minutes before M Claudel was due to leave for the meeting the valet was going to say that his trousers needed pressing. He would wait until the very last moment and then he would heat the iron to burning-point and burn out the whole seat of the Ambassador's trousers. He would do it very cunningly – he prided himself on being a tip-top valet – so that the burnt cloth would remain momentarily in place, at least until M Claudel sat down in the car on the way to the State Department. After that it would be too late, and it was the valet's opinion that the shock and humiliation of finding himself attending a high diplomatic gathering with his shirt-tails hanging out of the seat of his striped pants would virtually prostrate the Ambassador, rendering him incapable of prosecuting effectively whatever baleful diplomatic designs he might have. The valet was so proud of this idea that he could not resist communicating it to Putlitz. He had bottled up the great news until the last moment of a more or less clandestine *tête-à-tête* between himself and the German Third Secretary, and Putlitz had to rush back to the Embassy on some vital appointment without having had time to consider or comment upon the proposed undertaking. When he did get around to considering it, he was horrified. He had a prevision of the scene in which the valet, successful but detected and sacked, would in a romantic fervour strike his breast and declare that he had done it all for Germany. He tried to send messages to the valet, but failed to reach him.

The conference at the State Department was to take place at eleven-thirty the following morning, and soon after breakfast on that day the staff of the French Embassy was astounded to encounter the haggard Third Secretary of the German

Embassy passionately demanding an audience not with the Ambassador but the his valet. The audience was successful, and the Ambassador left for the conference with his pants unsinged. The French Embassy staff, however, considered that German indiscretion had surpassed the limits of what was supportable. One knew that certain people had certain peculiar tastes, but was that a reason for flaunting them in the entrance hall of the Embassy at ten o'clock in the morning?

XVI   MR CAPONE'S AMERICA

IN CHICAGO THE DIRECTOR OF THE ILLINOIS Central Bank, to whom I had been putting solemn questions on the subject of car loadings, commodity prices and the like, said moodily, 'Hell, boy, the capitalist system's on the skids anyway, let's go and get a drink.' I was glad of this attitude on his part because I had not really come to Chicago to discuss commodity prices in the Middle West, but to report the background to a murder. A couple of days before, we in New York had read the news of the killing in broad daylight of Jake Lingle, then crime reporter of the *Chicago Tribune* and – as emerged later – an important liaison officer between the Capone gang and the police department. It was one of the most spectacular and, for many reasons, looked like being one of the most revealing Chicago killings of the period when Al Capone was at approximately the height of his power. From a friend in New York who knew Chicago I learned enough of the background of the crime to make me very eager to go to Chicago myself. Hinrichs, who thought it would be a splendid story, was nevertheless hesitant. He explained to me that whenever *The Times* published a crime story from the United States somebody from the American Embassy or the English-Speaking Union or some other agency for promoting Anglo-American relations would ring up or would attack the editor at dinner, saying how much he had always previously admired *The Times's* treatment of American affairs, and could there not be at least one British news-paper which did not represent the United States as a land dominated by gunmen and hoodlums? Hinrichs thought we had better cable London asking whether they wished me to go to Chicago.

As an assignment to report a murder the reply from *The Times* was probably a classic. 'By all means,' it said, 'Cock-burn Chicagowards. Welcome stories ex-Chicago not unduly emphasising crime.'

By the time I was in the air over Cleveland the difficulty of carrying out this directive successfully had notably increased. Ex-Ambassador Charlie Gates Dawes had impetuously been 'drafted' or had drafted himself to act as 'strong man' of the situation, to put himself, it was stated, at the head of 'the better element' and to 'clean up' Chicago. Before I touched down at Chicago Airport he had arrested nearly six hundred people and a number of others had been wounded in indis-criminate gunplay. I drove to the Criminal Courts Building and sought the advice of the dean of Chicago crime reporters, the original, I believe, of one of the central characters in Ben Hecht's play *The Front Page*. I showed him my cable. His deep laughter shook the desk. What, he asked, did I want to do? I said I supposed the first thing to do was to interview Mr Capone. He suggested that I listen in on an extension while he telephoned Mr Capone at the Lexington Hotel where he then had his offices. Presently I heard Capone's voice on the wire asking what went on. The crime reporter explained that there was a Limey from the London *Times* who wanted to talk with him. They fixed up an appointment for the follow-ing afternoon and just before he rang off the crime reporter said, 'Listen, Al, there's just one thing. You know this bird's assignment says he's to cover all this "not unduly emphasising crime".' Bewilderment exploded at the other end of the line. 'Not what?' Capone said. 'You heard me,' said the crime re-porter. 'Not unduly emphasising crime.'

The Lexington Hotel had once, I think, been a rather grand family hotel, but now its large and gloomy lobby was deserted except for a couple of bulging Sicilians and a reception clerk who looked at one across the counter with the expression of a speakeasy proprietor looking through the grille at a poten-tial detective. He checked on my appointment with some superior upstairs, and as I stepped into the elevator I felt my hips and sides being gently frisked by the tapping hands of one of the lounging civilians. There were a couple of anterooms to be passed before you got to Capone's office and in the first of them I had to wait for a quarter of an hour or so, drinking whisky poured by a man who used his left hand for the bottle and kept the other in his pocket.

Except that there was a sub-machine gun, operated by a man called MacGurn – whom I later got to know and somewhat esteem – poking through the transom of a door behind the big desk, Capone's own room was nearly indistinguishable from that of – say – a 'newly arrived' Texan oil millionaire. Apart from the jowly young murderer on the far side of the desk, what took the eye were a number of large, flattish, solid silver bowls upon the desk, each filled with roses. They were nice to look at, and they had another purpose too, for Capone when agitated stood up and dipped the tips of his fingers in the water in which floated the roses.

I had been a little embarrassed as to how the interview was to be launched. Naturally the nub of all such interviews is somehow to get around to the question 'What makes you tick?' but in the case of this millionaire killer the approach to this central question seemed mined with dangerous impediments. However, on the way down to the Lexington Hotel I had had the good fortune to see, in I think the *Chicago Daily News,* some statistics offered by an insurance company which dealt with the average expectation of life of gangsters in Chicago. I forgot exactly what the average expectation was, and also what was the exact age of Capone at that time – I think he was in his very early thirties. The point was, however, that in any case he was four years older than the upper limit considered by the insurance company to be the proper average expectation of life for a Chicago gangster. This seemed to offer a more or less neutral and academic line of approach, and after the ordinary greetings I asked Capone whether he had read this piece of statistics in the paper. He said that he had. I asked him whether he considered the estimate reasonably accurate. He said that he thought that the insurance companies and the newspaper boys probably knew their stuff. 'In that case,' I asked him, 'how does it feel to be, say, four years over the age?'

He took the question quite seriously and spoke of the matter with neither more nor less excitement or agitation than a man would who, let us say, had been asked whether he, as the rear machine-gunner of a bomber, was aware of the average incidence of casualties in that occupation. He apparently assumed that sooner or later he would be shot despite the elaborate precautions which he regularly took. The idea that – as afterwards turned out to be the case – he would be arrested by the Federal authorities for income-tax evasion had not, I think, at that time so much as crossed his mind. And, after all, he said with a little bit of corn-and-ham somewhere at the back of his throat, supposing he had not gone into this racket? What would he have been doing? He would, he said, 'have been selling newspapers barefoot on the street in Brooklyn'.

He stood up as he spoke, cooling his finger-tips in the rose bowl in front of him. He sat down again, brooding and sighing. Despite the ham-and-corn, what he said was quite probably true and I said so, sympathetically. A little bit too sympathetically, as immediately emerged, for as I spoke I saw him looking at me suspiciously, not to say censoriously. My remarks about the harsh way the world treats barefoot boys in Brooklyn were interrupted by an urgent angry waggle of his podgy hand.

'Listen,' he said, 'don't you get the idea I'm one of these goddam radicals. Don't get the idea I'm knocking the American system. The American system. . . .' As though an invisible chairman had called upon him for a few words, he broke into an oration upon the theme. He praised freedom, enterprise and the pioneers. He spoke of 'our heritage'. He referred with contemptuous disgust to Socialism and Anarchism. 'My rackets,' he repeated several times, 'are run on strictly American lines and they're going to stay that way.' This turned out to be a reference to the fact that he had recently been elected the President of the Unione Siciliano, a slightly mysterious, partially criminal society which certainly had its roots in the Mafia. Its power and importance varied sharply from year to year. Sometimes there did seem to be evidence that it was a secret society of real power, and at other times it seemed more in the nature of a mutual benefit association not essentially much more menacing than, say, the Elks. Capone's complaint just now was that the Unione was what he called 'lousy with black-hand stuff.' 'Can you imagine,' he said, 'people going in for what they call these blood feuds – some guy's grandfather was killed by some other guy's grandfather, and this guy thinks that's good enough reason to kill the other.' It was, he said, entirely unbusinesslike. His vision of the American system began to excite him profoundly and now he was on his feet again, leaning across the desk like the chairman of a board meeting, his fingers plunged in the rose bowls.

'This American system of ours,' he shouted, 'call it Americanism, call it Capitalism, call it what you like, gives to each and every one of us a great opportunity if we only seize it with both hands and make the most of it.' He held out his hands towards me, the fingers dripping a little, and stared at me sternly for a few seconds before reseating himself.

A month later in New York I was telling this story to Mr John Walter, minority owner of *The Times*. He asked me why I had not written the Capone interview for the paper. I explained that when I had come to put my notes together I saw that most of what Capone had said was in essence identical with what was being said in the leading articles of *The Times* itself, and I doubted whether the paper would be best pleased to find itself seeing eye to eye with the most notorious gangster in Chicago. Mr Walter, after a moment's wry reflection, admitted that probably my idea had been correct.

Even so, when I did start writing my thesis from Chicago – not unduly emphasising crime – I became aware, really for the first time, that about fifty per cent of what seemed to me to be the truth about the situation in Chicago would certainly be unpalatable and perhaps in parts unintelligible to *The Times*. I struggled with the article, produced a couple of readable pieces, and *The Times* wired me quite a large and much-needed bonus on the strength of it.

As for Capone, one could say of course that he was politically a buffoon, and the fact that his views coincided with those of the leader writers on the paper was a clownish and insignificant accident. But I knew then, and I felt more deeply still in the time that followed, that the incident had only expressed in terms of farce a genuine situation and a genuine problem. *The Times* of the early 1930s was of course a great deal farther to the Right than it is today. It is hard to recall so many years later the tenacity with which people hung on to notions and principles which their successors might still consider theoretically desirable but have come to recognise as untenable for any practical purpose. I remember the disconcerting feeling that myself and nearly every serious person that I met in the United States were growing up under the tremendous pressure of the great crisis much faster than the people in Printing House Square. It is true that in many respects *The Times* was a good deal more open-minded, or at least more prepared to consider possible novelties in the situation, than many of the other London newspapers. I can recall very few occasions indeed when it would have been possible to have accused *The Times* of deliberate distortion, suppression or invention of 'favourable' news by means of pressure upon the correspondent.

Once in New York when I was covering for a colleague on another paper who had gone off on a more or less illicit holiday, I was astonished to receive a cable from London in the following terms: 'Good woman story today.' (This in the jargon of the Foreign Editor meant alternatively a story about women likely to interest men, or a story about women for women.) 'Send sensational story today illustrating futility Hoover's efforts arrest market decline emphasising possibility bottom imminently outcrash.'

When the colleague returned he was quite annoyed to find that I had failed to respond to this directive. I asked him why I should help to make money for somebody in London who was evidently short of the market in a big way, and trying to use the paper to accelerate the decline in stocks. Somebody responds to a request like that and what happens? The despatch under the date-line New York appears on the front page of the paper in London, and somewhere in the financial columns, or perhaps even in a leading article, there is a reference to it. 'Our New York correspondent in his exclusive and significant story today,' etc., etc. And that section of the public which pays attention to such things starts to unload.

'What beats me,' I said, 'is why they bother to have an office in New York and a correspondent, and pay the rent and your salary, when they could just as easily write the whole stuff in London and simply put "from our New York correspondent" on top of it.'

My colleague, a thoughtful man who understood the form better than I did, said, 'They would never do that. They wouldn't think it at all honest.'

The Times never did anything like that, and to tell the truth I should not have been shocked or startled if they had. It seemed to me that a newspaper is always a weapon in somebody's hands, and I never could see why it should be shocking that the weapon should be used in what its owner conceived to be his best interests. The hired journalist, I thought, ought to realise that he is partly in the entertainment business and partly in the advertising business – advertising either goods, or a cause, or a government. He just has to make up his mind whom he wants to entertain, and what he wants to advertise. The humbug and hypocrisy of the press begin only when newspapers pretend to be 'impartial' or 'servants of the public'. And this only becomes dangerous as well as laughable when the public is fool enough to believe it.

Such 'pressure' and 'guidance' as *The Times* did attempt to exercise were usually of a subtle and more amusing sort and caused me neither trouble nor vexation. The pressure of events in the United States – where the prophecies of the Marxist classics were being fulfilled with the punctuality of minute guns – was of a different kind. (When I speak of 'prophecies' I am not of course referring to the quick-firers of contemporary day-to-day controversy who necessarily and for obvious morale-building purposes prophesied that the current crisis in America was the final crisis of American capitalism, and that a revolution might confidently be expected in a year or two. I knew the United States fairly well by that time and I agreed with Mr Capone that the American system would get by for a lot longer that that.)

But the American 'way of life' of the past decade was changing before one's eyes, and the exhilarating sense of change, of history on the march, of new possibilities opening, was all-pervading. There was nowhere you could go in the United States and feel that things were as they had been or as they would be again.

I was privileged to view what I suppose might be called 'the dawn of social consciousness' in the mind of a Middle Western millionaire who had the reputation of being what was then called an 'economic royalist', a political troglodyte, a foe to progress. He was known to his friends as 'Mr Pop', on account of the way in which he had made his first pile of money. At that time – at the time, I mean, when Mr Pop was a fairly young man – big developments were taking place in the popcorn-vending industry. There was a continuous effort by inventors and manufacturers to modernise and streamline the machines in which popcorn was visibly popped and sold to the onlookers. As he went about the streets and occasionally stood watching corn being popped in one of these machines, Mr Pop was aware of a sense of disappointment. Ruminating, he at last got his finger on the cause of it – these machines were not like the machines used to be when he was a boy. There were not so many wheels, not so many lathes, not so much to watch. Being evidently a man of humble mind, Mr Pop decided that, if he felt this disappointment, millions of other people must be feeling it too. Acting on this assumption, he went around buying up the patents on the old types of machine – the patents could of course now be had for a song, since the machines, totally unfunctional, were supposed to be obsolete. Mr Pop manufactured these machines by the thousand and put them on the streets, and pretty soon the news came in from the street vendors that the public was flocking to them, happy indeed to watch all those nostalgically whirring wheels and writhing lathes and to buy their corn from the vintage models rather than from the modern types. With the packet of money he made out of that Mr Pop went on and made a lot more, and now he had a big house in Southern Indiana with a stream and a road bridge, with towers, which was a model of something he had seen on his travels about the world, I think in Southern Germany.

As a result of some muddle in the instructions given to the architect, the house had, as a matter of fact, got built the wrong way round, with its back to the stream. This was unfortunate, but Mr Pop reasoned that it was no ground for piling one misfortune on another, and losing his bridge. In consequence, when one approached the house, one did so by a mile or so of perfectly flat driveway which suddenly humped itself up between the towers of the bridge, and from the top of the bridge you looked down and saw the green grass growing beneath you. Inside, the house was full of 'finds' of archæological and artistic interest made by Mr Pop on his world travels. Beside each of them was fixed an elaborate bronze plaque describing the nature of the object, its age, and so on. One of them was a tile from the Summer Palace at Peking, which was described on the plaque as being three thousand years old. Rather oddly, when I visited Mr Pop he explained emphatically to myself and the other guests that there was no doubt whatever that this tile was a fake – manufactured probably strictly for the tourist trade.

The guests on this occasion were for the most part politicians – there was a Republican senator from Washington and a couple of Republican congressmen, the Republican governor of Indiana or his deputy – I forget which – and two or three members of the Indiana legislature. At dinner the talk naturally enough was all of the crisis, of unemployment, of threatened hunger strikes, of the bread lines, and of the need for the organisation and extension of relief measures. It was the kind of talk which Mr Pop hitherto had supposed was only to be heard among anarchists, socialists, and the long-haired agitators of one kind and another. Coming from leaders and fellow-members of the Republican Party it hit Mr Pop like a blow on the head. After dinner he was sitting with me a little apart from the others, and he presently began to move about uneasily and peer at me with the air of a man preparing to propound a question of supreme importance. At last, peering into his glass, he said: 'Mr Cockburn, may I ask you something?'

I bowed.

'Would you,' said Mr Pop, 'see anything wrong in being the fourth richest man in Indiana?'

I made some incoherent reply.

'Well that,' said Mr Pop, 'is what I am. I am the fourth richest man in Indiana.'

I had sympathised with Capone in his human and social predicament, although I had not found him a particularly likeable man. And I sympathised now with Mr Pop, who I had grown to like, at the moment of his confrontation with the possibility that there might be some snag, something historically or morally not absolutely nice, about being the fourth richest man in Indiana in the year 1931. I sympathised with *The Times*, too, but it did not make the situation any easier or solve any problem.

In a sense *The Times* entered into the matter only incidentally – in the sense, I mean, that we were all engaged in the newspaper business. Had *The Times* been a firm of automobile exporters, and I their salesman, the problem would not have arisen in the same form. An automobile salesman can go about – mentally speaking – in disguise, and I believe many of them do. He can believe passionately that the earth is flat without causing a drop in sales. He can even secretly hold, and secretly propagate, some unpopular political or religious opinion without going to pieces and without – if he is careful – being caught at it. For the journalist things are more difficult.

Essentially, the late Lord Northcliffe was right when he said to some intellectual who thought himself so very smart that he could 'write popular' and get away with it, 'You can never successfully seek to put upon the table of Demos what you would not put on your own table.'

A lot of people, perhaps influenced directly or indirectly by the late C. E. Montague's book *A Hind Let Loose*, where the same man writes the leading articles for two newspapers of fiercely opposed opinion, believe that newspaper offices are full of successful journalists who write with their tongue in their cheek. When such people get journalists alone, they say, 'I know that's what you wrote, but what do you really think?'

It is of course possible to write for two newspapers of opposed opinions at the same time, I have even done so myself, but for the writer – and I am talking here of the journalist who is really a writer, and not a failed politician, diplomat or lawyer, or defrocked clergyman – it is a dangerous business It turns him from a creative writer into a lawyer. Lawyers can be creative writers too, but there is no identity between the two sides of their activity. Or else this kind of double game – the kind described in *A Hind Let Loose* – is only an expression of the writer's probably genuine scorn and derision for both his clients and for all their readers too. And that also is a risky attitude.

Naturally the aeroplanes and sleeping-cars are filled with people who have 'journalist' written on their passport, but are really only secretly prospecting for uranium, or going to assassinate the Chief of Police, or filling in time until they can meet such interesting people as will marry them and let them settle down. But these are not writers either.

Evidently there are plenty of people in journalism who have neither got what they liked nor quite grown to like what they get. They write pieces they do not much enjoy writing, for papers they totally despise, and the sad process ends by ruining their style and disintegrating their personality, two developments which in a writer cannot be separated, since his personality and style must progress or deteriorate together, like a married couple in a country where death is the only permissible divorce. It is a fate which through incompetence or economic necessity may overtake anyone, but one does not wish to start out by accepting it as one's own.

Although by the beginning of 1932 I was secretly bootlegging quite a number of pieces of news and articles to various extreme Left American newspapers and news services, I was conscious that my style – in the narrow and in the wider sense of the word – was deteriorating.

I decided to make a change. The relief of having taken this decision was such that I probably should have dithered about for months without actually doing anything had not my elbow been jogged by an external event.

What had happened was that Wilmott Lewis, whose doctors had at last succeeded in causing him some mild anxiety about the state of his heart muscle, was beginning to entertain the idea of a partial retirement. He had suggested to *The Times*, and *The Times*, he told me, had agreed *en principe*, that I should be transferred from New York to Washington and there take over the ordinary or day-by-day and week-by-week operation of the Washington bureau. He would retreat to a beautiful winter residence he had his eye on in Georgetown, and in the summer he would live on the Blue Ridge Mountains. He would be 'available for consultation', and occasionally, perhaps once a month, write an article for the paper. He would also read all the books he had never had time to read, and write, he surmised, at least one of the books he had never had time to write. It was a wonderful prospect and his eyes shone with enthusiasm as he first unfolded it to me. Particularly characteristic of Wilmott Lewis and particularly moving was the fact that a great part of his pleasure in this plan was that, as he saw it, the scheme would be as splendid a thing for me as it would be for him. His excitement and his solicitude for my career were so touching that for a moment I felt that it might even be humanly better to abandon my own plans and fall in with his. However, short of that, there was not a moment to be lost in disillusioning him.

He sat for a few seconds in an aghast silence, watching the house in Georgetown, the summer place on the Blue Ridge and all the books fade into thin air. I asked desperately whether somebody else could not take over the rôle proposed by himself and *The Times* for me. He said it was quite impossible, and I knew that this was in fact the case. Within a minute or two he had entirely recovered himself and with his native, and extraordinary, delicacy was consoling me as though it were I whose plans had been upset and not himself. He guessed, of course, that I felt a certain sense of guilt *vis-à-vis* himself, as though I had betrayed the years during which he had taught me so much of what I knew about the United States.

'My dear boy,' he said, 'any small debt you may have owed me has been long ago repaid over and over again. And if you insist on regarding yourself as my pupil, reflect how far more agreeable it must be for me to have produced one who now moves freely under his own steam rather than being stuck, my dear boy,' he made the last words sound like death, 'in the mud.'

After an equally melancholy explanation to Hinrichs, who tried to take the sadness out of our parting by remarking that for several months he had expected that something of the kind must happen, I wrote to *The Times* announcing my decision. To my vexation they treated my big gesture simply as a sign of a slight over-strain, and wrote back suggesting that I take a couple of months' paid holiday in Mexico. I had to write again in more vigorous terms, explaining, by way of putting an end to any discussion, that my motives were largely political. I was horribly disconcerted to find that *The Times* did not take this very seriously either. Mr Dawson wrote me a letter in which he said that it was foolish in his opinion to give up working for *The Times* simply on account of one's political views. *The Times*, he said, was a vehicle which could be used by people of the most varied opinions. 'For myself,' he concluded, 'I have always regarded *The Times* as something of an organ of the Left.' There followed in brackets a classic qualification. 'Though never,' wrote Mr Dawson, 'I hope of the extreme Left.'

I had to abandon my naïve belief that however difficult anything else may be, the one thing that is easy, and makes everyone happy, is when you resign. Resigning was proving a lot more difficult than I had expected. A short while after the exchange of letters Mr Dawson, Mr Deakin, the Foreign and Imperial News Editor, and one or two other of the High Priests who had been to Ottawa for the Conference, came down to New York and took it in turns to explain to me the folly of my attitude. One view was that the thing to do was settle the whole business quickly on a cash basis, and there was talk of something in the way of a bonus, plus an early rise in salary. I was humiliated to find that my important decision had been interpreted in these quarters as an act of vulgar blackmail. Others, probably reflecting that they had to do with a wild-eyed intellectual, thought that a more spiritual approach would be the right ticket. They spoke of the good which a first-rate correspondent of *The Times* could do to mankind. When these and other suggestions, which had been made separately, had all failed, we gathered one morning in *The Times* office in New York and were joined by Wilmott Lewis, who admitted to me privately that he had not been able to resist coming up for the final scene. Sitting at what until now had been my desk, Dawson swung his tortoiseshell spectacles lugubriously and remarked, looking at me with a puzzled frown, 'It does seem rather bad luck that you of all people should "go red on us".' His voice put audible inverted commas around the phrase 'go red on us'. At this point Wilmott Lewis, his sense of the theatre overcoming any discretion he may have had, moved to the centre of the stage, or rather of the office, and with a gesture which in some indefinable way suggested that he was flaunting the black cloak of a magician, gazed down upon Dawson and raised his hand in a familiar gesture.

'You speak, my dear Dawson,' he said, 'of luck. Speak rather of history. Throw your mind forward along the path of history. Envisage, my dear Deakin, with the eye of imagination the not too distant future. The time will come, my dear fellows, when you will hire as correspondents elderly men who will be conservatives. But many of them, mark you, may well be suffering from heart attacks when the great story breaks. Or, my dear fellows, you may hire young men who will also be conservative but, note this! many of them may well be too stupid even to know when the great story is breaking. Or you may hire men who are both young and intelligent, and quite a lot of *them*, my dear fellows,' his voice dropped to a menacing whisper, 'will be Reds.'

Dawson, who had put on his spectacles to watch the performance, now peered up at Lewis over the top of them. He gave a small acid-sounding laugh.

'I'm afraid,' he said, 'you have been talking too much to your *ex*-assistant.'

Then I knew that I had resigned at last.

XVII ON WITH THE NEW

ROARS OF APPLAUSE ARE NICE TOO, BUT THERE IS historical evidence for the belief that you get, in the end, better service out of a sound piece of denunciation and insult by some properly accredited reviler. I learned this personally from the late Ramsay MacDonald, then Prime Minister, at the time of the World Economic Conference in London, in

1933. He reviled me in the crypt of the Geological Museum, South Kensington.

The route from *The Times* office in New York to this encounter with the angry Prime Minister in South Kensington had been bumpy and somewhat circuitous.

My intention had been to walk out of *The Times* office on to a boat, tour Europe, and then see what was best to be done. There was a hitch at the very outset. I had supposed – reasonably enough considering the amount of money I had been making during the past two and a half years – that I must surely have enough money in the bank to finance me for at least the next three or four months. This was a miscalculation, for there was an amount in the bank of only about a hundred dollars.

Fortunately there happened to be at this time a boom in books about the 'inside' of Washington politics, and a leading American publisher offered me an advance of five or six hundred pounds, plus expenses, to write anonymously such a book on condition that the manuscript was completed and delivered within six weeks. I had to go down to Washington in the heat of one of Washington's hottest known summers to do it, but at the end of six weeks it was ready and I could collect the money and sail for Europe.

When we got there I was so much excited at seeing Europe again that I could not wait for the boat (it was a freighter) to dock at Le Havre – where also there would be endless delays with Customs – and jumped from the deck on to one of the locks as we passed through. This jump sprained an ankle, and I spent my first few days in Europe immobilised on the edge of it.

The delay, as it turned out, was fortunate, because while hobbling about Le Havre I came across a party of dock workers who were on their way to an anti-war congress being held in Amsterdam. In exchange for a promise to send them occasional free articles, I had secured in America a journalist's card from the American Federated Press – a news agency organised, so far as I remember, by the trades unions. The dockers from Le Havre said they would be happy to have an American journalist go along with them to the congress, and it seemed as good a way as another of getting back fast into European life. It was.

The special train which took us from Paris to Amsterdam was bulging with delegates from all over France and some who had crossed illegally from Spain. About half of them

G*

were peasants and a large number of these had never before travelled more than a few miles from their own villages. They carried baskets and bundles full of enough good food to last them for a week in case the food in foreign Holland proved inadequate or unpalatable. I found, after a time, one who was a native of the Cévennes and knew intimately the village where I had lived seven years before. He assured me that nothing there had changed, but I thought that it must have, because at that time nobody in the neighbourhood would have thought of electing a delegate to an anti-war congress at Amsterdam. Our conversation was limited because he wanted to concentrate on peering out of the window, which he did in a state of evident anxiety and agitation. I asked him why. He said he feared that the railway authorities would in some way sabotage the trip – run the train into a siding and keep it there until the congress was over. I said it seemed unlikely they would dare to do such a thing, there would be too great an uproar.

'Still,' he said, 'it's best for all of us to keep a sharp look-out.'

He began to recount some of the swindles that had been practised upon him by 'authorities' in the course of his hard life. He was contemptuous of my foolish attitude towards the railway authorities, and I knew that soon I was going to hear a phrase very familiar to me from my days in the Cévennes, and soon I heard it.

'I don't know,' he said, 'how it may be where you come from, but in my experience people have bad characters.'

We crossed the old battlefields of Compiègne, St Quentin, Cambrai, Mons, and at stations all along the line workers waiting for local trains waved and cheered as the special train went by, its carriages chalked with huge slogans against Fascism and war, and the windows jammed with the heads of delegates singing the Carmagnole.

Outside the main station at Brussels men on the way to early shifts in the factories dropped their bicycles, came swarming over the railway embankments and rushed on to the line singing and cheering and waving red flags.

The congress, attended by thousands of delegates from all over Europe, lasted several days, and by the end of it I had a more lively picture of the state of the anti-Fascist forces of Europe than I could have acquired elsewhere in two months. I went on to Vienna and Budapest, spent a few weeks in the

Austrian Alps, and returned to Berlin intending to spend the winter there.

To come to Berlin just then, after New York, was to be whisked down suddenly from the gallery of a badly lit theatre and pushed against the flaring footlights to see that what you thought you saw from back there is really going on. The act is coming to its horrible climax, and furthermore the man who is playing the part of the murderer really is a murderer. His knife is not a familiar stage property but a real one and he is going to kill people with it.

Already the Storm Troopers were slashing and smashing up and down the Kurfuerstendamm, and there were beatings and unequal battles in the city streets. The toads beside the Charlottenburger Chaussee looked more menacing than ever. The newspapers and the 'thoughtful observers' and the pro and con men went humbugging along, but no one with any feeling for the situation believed them. I several times met Herr Willi Muenzenberg, who was popularly believed to be the real brains and driving force of the German Communist Party, and once I had the opportunity for a short private conversation with General Schleicher, then Chancellor. Each spoke in terms of reasoned optimism, and each gave the impression that he did not give a damn whether you believed a word he said because he did not believe it himself. (Schleicher was murdered sooner than Muenzenberg, who survived until the early 1940s, when he was strangled – on suspicions of being a secret Nazi agent – in the forest of Fontainebleau.) A situation in which even the professional humbugs cannot keep a straight face is always somewhat exhilarating, but, as one always finds in those situations, the naked truth can be a chilly, nobbly kind of companion too. Also, just as in New York and Chicago, it had gradually begun to seem absurd that one should spend one's time going about writing articles for *The Times*, so now in Berlin it rapidly began to seem even more absurd to sit observing events and trends, writing an occasional short story or articles for Leftish American newspapers, and news agencies. If one were not going to disintegrate under the pressure of events, the thing to do seemed to be to organise oneself into something coherent and effective.

Once again I might have dithered about for weeks or even months had not something jogged my elbow. This time it was Hitler. He came to power.

For weeks friends had been advising me to get out of

203

Germany well in advance of that event. The Nazis, they said, had me on a black list. It was true, I said, that I had gone around a good deal with Communists, but what did that matter? I had a British passport. I had a perfect right to stay as long as I liked. In reply to which an American correspondent quoted to me the rhyme about William Gay, who 'died asserting his rights of way. He was right, dead right, as he sped along, but he's just as dead as if he'd been wrong.' Furthermore, he pointed out, I had failed to take the elementary precautions desirable in such a situation, above all the precaution of putting on some kind of recognisable fancy dress. If I had said from the outset that I was here to organise propaganda for popcorn machines in Germany or was spying for the Chinese, I would have been in a safer position. Everyone suspects, and no one will protect, the person who is not avowedly up to anything in particular. The only thing known about me was that I was what later came to be described as 'a premature anti-Nazi'. I reflected that were I to be beaten to death accidentally by Storm Troopers in the first ugly rush, there would certainly be a protest from the Foreign Office, and Mr Deakin might even reward me by getting me, say, three paragraphs of obituary in *The Times;* and so on the day when it became certain that Hitler would become Chancellor within twenty-four hours, I took the first train to Vienna. There I sat down to consider seriously a notion which had been buzzing in my mind for some time. It had started buzzing when I worked – off the record – with a publicity expert in Washington who was conducting a one-man battle against what was known as the Radio Trust. I had noted at the time, and the note appears in the book which I wrote just before leaving Washington, that 'among the technical devices which as everyone knows are revolutionising the workings of modern government, the humble mimeograph machine is seldom mentioned. Less spectacular than the other wonders of the age, as for instance the mass-production newspaper, the telephone, the radio and the talking picture, it exercises, in its cheap and incessant activity, an influence scarcely less than theirs, and seems to have reached the peak of its activity in Washington, D.C., at the present period. Washington is in many respects the ideal field for a mimeograph machine to work in. For this little device requires for its most effective functioning the smallest possible geographical area, containing the largest number of persons who are influential, either because of the position they hold, or the money they have, or because like newspapermen they are sitting at the feeding end of a pipe-line with millions of people at the other end of it. . . . It is commonly agreed that the press, the radio and the moving picture are the most powerful forces in existence for moulding public opinion. To control any or all of them, or even to get the opportunity to use them as a medium, requires a great deal of money. The people who have enough money to control them are therefore sitting pretty in the democracy, but not nearly so pretty as they would be sitting were it not for the mimeograph machine. Naturally they have mimeographs too, but here for the first time their competitors find themselves on an equal footing. The police force can supply itself from larger sources with tanks and armoured cars and laboratories for the manufacture of tear gas. It is only in the possession of the automatic pistol that the enemy of the police finds himself on a level with his opponents. A mimeograph machine is one of the few remaining weapons which still gives small and comparatively poor organisations a sporting chance in a scrap with large and wealthy ones.'

The general idea which I had had then was revived in my mind later in Berlin by, of all people, General Schleicher, who ran, in his own interests, a weekly mimeographed sheet of information and comment which circulated by mail and was not sold on bookstalls. The total circulation was very small, and of course it did not do General Schleicher very much good in the end, but from my viewpoint the important thing about it was that it exercised an influence out of all proportion to its circulation. That is to say, in terms of influence, one reader of Schleicher's sheet was, on an average, worth about five thousand readers of one of the daily newspapers. (It was, for example, 'must reading' for all foreign newspaper correspondents in Berlin, and for all the embassies and legations.)

This phenomenon had reminded me of another aspect of the situation which I had often discussed with Wilmott Lewis in Washington. The discussion had arisen over the late Hamilton Fyfe's *Life of Northcliffe,* in which he makes this central point:

When Northcliffe started the *Daily Mail* in the '90s, Fyfe suggests, he was not 'playing a hunch' but tapping a mathematical certainty. He argued: The Education Acts of the 1860s have changed the entire character and extent of the literate public. But in the years since the 1860s the newspapers have not changed at all. Therefore there must exist somewhere a new pool of potential readers not taken care of by the existing newspapers. And this pool, if correctly tapped, could provide a new multi-million readership.

This proposition and its consequences were often discussed by Lewis and myself, and it seemed to us that the success of the Northcliffe idea had by now produced a quite new sort of 'untapped pool'. This had happened because the vast extension of the readership of a daily newspaper – and the swallowing of relatively small newspapers like the *Westminster Gazette,* simply because they could not produce such huge dividends as the others – meant that what might be called the Highest Common Factor of reader-interest had become lower and lower. You interest a million readers a little – but very few readers a lot. As you increase your 'extension' you decrease your 'intention'.

'The more the cobbler plies his trade the broader grows his thumb', with the result that presently he is capable of turning out a lot of cheap objects which will pass for shoes, and can be worn with more or less satisfaction by people who just want something to put between their socks and the roadway, but no longer capable of catering for the customer who wants something specially fitted to his own individual feet, something like Father used to wear. There are too few such people. Yet there are probably enough of them to provide a market for a specialist.

In the same way, it seemed, the economic necessities of the modern daily newspaper which require that it should cater for an almost inconceivable variety of people simultaneously – people with an almost inconceivable variety of background and taste – involve also the creation of a kind of vacuum which could be filled, the pool which could be tapped.

There was not much doubt in my mind as to the sort of people who would constitute the 'pool'. Anyone in, for instance, London or New York or Berlin or Vienna who frequented any kind of club or other meeting-place where, say, diplomats, lawyers, bankers and newspapermen gathered together and talked, must have been deeply aware of the strange contrast between the colourful information and significant rumours – for rumours can often be as significant as facts – circulating in the clubs, and the awfully tight-lipped drabness of the newspapers being sold on the club doorstep.

I got most of the English daily newspapers in Vienna and

was struck once again by the fact that what informed people were really saying – and equally importantly, the tone of voice they were saying it in – were scarcely reflected at all in the newspapers, and that these people themselves were more or less acutely aware of this lack in the newspapers.

A further conclusion followed. It was that such 'pools' could only be effectively tapped by a paper run 'on a shoe-string'.

The moment any kind of big financial commitment came in question – even the investment that would be needed to launch a printed weekly paper – it would begin to be necessary to 'broaden the base', 'extend the appeal', in fact lower the Highest Common Factor. The advertisers alone would see to that.

What all this added up to was that I had better go to London and start a weekly paper of a new type. For the third time, extraneous circumstances precipitated a decision. I discovered with dismay that the money I had had from the American publisher was almost gone. It was evident that, if I waited any longer, I should scarcely have the fare from Vienna to London, let alone enough to support me during the two or three weeks which I felt sure would be needed for the organisation of the paper.

It took in point of fact nearly six weeks, the result, I suppose, chiefly of the fact that since out of the past six years I had spent only a little over two months in England, and that had been three and a half years ago, I knew almost nobody, and I had forgotten how important people think it in England to know not only where you are going but where you have come from. Also when the news of where I had come from did get bruited it was not always an advantage – learning of my resignation from *The Times*, people on the Right thought that I must be a Red and shied off, and the Reds, since I was not a member of any known Left organisation, were if possible more suspicious still.

The atmosphere was both depressing and exhilarating. Even the most detached citizen must find it occasionally depressing to find his country so reduced in circumstances that it had to have such a man as the late Ramsay MacDonald for its Prime Minister. It was, on the other hand, exhilarating because the smug smog in which the press of that time enveloped the political realities of the moment was even thicker than I had anticipated, and thus offered even better conditions for the conduct of my experiment. The one or two

207

old friends I had, and the people I presently got to know, were for the most part sympathetic but discouraging. And many of my few acquaintances who expressed a flattering and uplifting interest in the idea turned out to be firm believers in the axiom that one should never put off till tomorrow what one might possibly be able to do the month after next.

It is hard to imagine what justification the English suppose themselves to have when they sneer gently at the Spaniards for their alleged *mañana, mañana*. Probably the fact is that everyone is much lazier than he likes to admit, and, when he finds himself procrastinating wildly, comforts himself with the thought that someone across the seas is lazier still. I remember remarking bitterly at the time that if I wrote a book about England I should call it *What About Wednesday Week?* which is what English people say when they are making what they believe to be an urgent appointment.

I was constantly frustrated too by the habit people have got into of considering that nothing important can be done without going through the ritual of 'a conference' and for two pins they will set up a committee. In my experience all but the very rarest kind of committee meeting can be placed in one of two categories. There is the committee meeting at which everything has been decided in advance so that the whole meeting is unnecessary anyway, and the meeting at which nothing has been decided in advance, nothing is decided at the committee meeting, and when everyone is leaving the building two men get together in the corner of the lift and fix up what is to be done next. Several times during that six weeks I had to tuck my idea under my arm and run with it to prevent it being suffocated by some well-intentioned conference or by a committee.

Frustrating and even alarming though all this was, it was at the same time amusing, helped me to extend my 'contacts' and to pick up a smattering of information about the state of affairs in Britain. But after the first three weeks or so I realised clearly enough that until I actually produced my paper 'of a new type' I should never be able to explain to anyone what it was I had in mind – and I realised too that a lot of them would not like it if I did.

Everyone had been well-meaningly discouraging about the money. Some said that even the smallest weekly paper could not possibly cost less than £5,000; others said £10,000. It was agreed that such a sum could probably be raised, but I understood now that to raise it would involve introducing the very frets I was seeking to avoid. There would be advertisers and shareholders and even, it was hinted on several sides, some kind of editorial board, and what we should end up with would be just another weekly newspaper.

In any case I had not left *The Times* for the purpose of saddling myself with another editorial board and some more shareholders and advertisers. After thirty days of patient investigation I had grasped more firmly than ever the truth that what one must do was to ensure that this paper was all of a piece and all under one control. That it should express one viewpoint and one viewpoint only – my own. In other words, size must be sacrificed to coherence and to unity of style. Thus after four weeks of bumbling more or less agreeably about London I came to the conclusion that the thing to do was to cut the cackle and start the paper regardless of what anybody might say, warn or advise.

I went out to Berkshire and found an old Oxford friend – a novelist who had for some time been vegetating unwholesomely in that section of the home counties. By this time I personally had only five pounds left, and I had reckoned that we would need at least forty pounds to start the paper. I suggested to him that it would be good for both of us if he lent me forty pounds for the paper, in exchange for which he would have a job on it as a kind of manager. This was not merely an inducement to him to part with his forty pounds, but was based on a genuine feeling that it would do him good to come back into circulation in London, and also on the knowledge I had of his habits – he was an extraordinarily neat man and I thought that some neatness in our office would be desirable. He agreed.

Fortunately he had been quite out of touch with the sort of people I had been talking to in London, so that to him it seemed no more improbable than it did to me that one could start a weekly newspaper of importance for forty pounds. He agreed to return to London with me that evening and start to get things going. On the return journey I explained to him all over again my precise purpose.

G. K. Chesterton, I reminded him, had written of editors that they lived in the shadow of three fears – fear of misprints, fear of libel actions and fear of the sack. We would aim, I said, to disregard all considerations of that kind, more particularly the second, because what we had in mind was a revival of the uninhibited eighteenth-century English tradition of the Newsletter. It was going to give the customers the sort of facts – political, diplomatic, financial – which were freely discussed in embassies and clubs but considered to be too adult to be left about for newspaper readers to get at them.

In our Newsletter anything interesting could get a U certificate. The slogan was, '*Mais si, devant les enfants!*'

I pointed out to him that by the method we proposed to use – that of the mimeograph machine – we should kill two birds with one stone: we should on the one hand ensure that we were in total control of our own paper, and on the other that people who wanted to bring libel actions could of course do so, but probably would not, because most libel actions are brought for the purpose of getting money, and it would be evident to one and all that we had no money of any kind.

After that things moved at a fairly brisk rate. We found an attic in Victoria Street approached first by a shaky lift and later by a staircase which was rather more of a ladder than a stair. There was room in it for a kitchen table, four chairs and a smaller table on which we installed a duplicating machine bought on the hire-purchase system so that the libel-mongers would have even less to gain than they might have hoped. We found a brilliant and devoted secretary – again a person who had not been involved in the type of calculation which was so common in London, and at once saw the possibilities of the idea.

At that stage we had only two troubles. The first was a row between myself and my partner, who hoped that the sheet would look clean and dignified. I, on the other hand, thought that the important thing was that it should be noticeable. Given the price of paper and duplicating ink, there seemed no possibility that it could be both. In the end we made it noticeable. It was mimeographed in dark brown ink on buff-coloured foolscap. It was not merely noticeable, it was unquestionably the nastiest-looking bit of work that ever dropped on to a breakfast-table.

The other trouble we had was from people who had heard what we were about to do and wanted to help. There was a man from Vancouver who knew about business and insisted he could get a lot of advertising for the paper. I told him we did not want advertising, but it did not diminish his enthusiasm. He quite evidently regarded me as a kind of babe in the wood who must be protected from the wild animals that are loose. In view of this touching solicitude it was impossible to turn him out of the office, and he used to stand there for hours talking and explaining his general plan for making us more money than anybody could have dreamed of. He stayed with us, in fact, throughout the launching of the paper and for three weeks after it had begun to come out, but then he went out of his mind just outside the Army and Navy Stores where he knelt on the pavement one morning, addressing me as his Brother in the Sun. As I drove him to the nursing home I realised I had been right all along about advertising.

Lawyers volunteered to help too, but I had to point out to them that either they were good lawyers, in which case they would have to keep saying, 'You can't publish that, it's libellous,' or bad lawyers, ignorant of whether things were libellous or not. In either case what use would they be? It was sad having to fight off so many well-intentioned offers of assistance, but I had to keep firmly in mind that what we were running was a pirate craft and we could not burden ourselves with conventional navigators and mates, however skilled and knowledgeable.

I had decided early on that we would not attempt to sell the paper on the bookstalls and news-stands. To begin with I did not want to get involved in a distributive organisation which would be beyond one's own personal control. Also under English law, so far as I understood it, the wholesale newsagent can be held responsible for damages awarded in a libel suit against a paper distributed by him. For this reason the wholesale distributors are forced or encouraged to exercise a kind of long-term censorship over the products they handle. (That was why some time later we had the ridiculous situation in which the people who handled the London circulation of *Time Magazine* had to spend hours with scissors snipping out of the paper, when it arrived from New York, those stories which might be considered libellous in England; that was how it happened that when the British papers were keeping mum about the abdication crisis of 1936 and *Time Magazine* was running constant stories about the King and Mrs Simpson, *Time* reached the British bookstalls full of holes where the most interesting stories ought to have been. Yet even then you could meet people who would declare that there is no press censorship in England.)

It seemed to me that we could turn this circumstance to

account and use it to deepen the 'confidential' atmosphere around our paper. For the same reason I preferred, although it cost three times as much to do so, to mail the paper to subscribers in closed envelopes.

All these questions of production and circulation, interesting as they were, took up a good deal of my time. My partner, as I have said, was a novelist and short-story writer who had a positive horror of business, and was totally ignorant of it. He scarcely knew where to buy a stamp. Also it had been part of our bargain that I should not bother him with anything of that kind – what he wanted to get in exchange for his forty pounds was, so to speak, a tiny airstrip in London from which he could take off for social and literary trips about the town.

The secretary was a young married woman, daughter of a backwoods baronet living somewhere in East Anglia, and until about this time her idea of a major event in Home Affairs had been the exclusion of some friend from the Royal Enclosure at Ascot, and when I once expressed regret that I did not have time to dash down to Rome to take a look at what was going on there, she looked at me with surprise and said that surely it was the wrong time of year to go to Rome. She was pretty, energetic, intelligent and loyal, but she could not type and most of the people who dashed in and out of the attic in Victoria Street were as alien to her as though they had escaped from the Zoo.

However, in addition to her other qualities she had a great deal of commonsense, and the business of occasionally explaining to her what we thought we were up to helped to clarify one's mind. All the same, it was difficult in the circumstances to spend as much time as I should have liked on the organisation of our news sources. By this time of course I had a lot of 'contacts' in London – particularly in the City. But we could hardly have come out when we did had it not been for the co-operation of a number of foreign correspondents in London, many of whom I had known in Berlin or Washington, chief among them Mr Negley Farson, then London Correspondent of the *Chicago Daily News*. I met him only a couple of weeks before *The Week* was due to come out, but he was immediately enthusiastic. He shared, so far as I know, none of my political ideas, but he liked the idea of *The Week* as such, and at that time was one of the very few people who at once grasped the possibility of something so small becoming, in its effects, big.

Zero hour was a Wednesday in the mid-spring of 1933. We had chosen Wednesday as 'press day', so that *The Week* would reach people ahead of the existing weekly newspapers. I had had a great deal of difficulty in getting hold of a mailing list. There was no money to hire one of the lists which were available, and instead I had borrowed one which contained names of the subscribers to the then temporarily defunct weekly paper *Foreign Affairs*.

It was a list of about 1,200 names. Myself, the manager, the secretary and the man from Vancouver had spent the previous night addressing foolscap envelopes, and in the very early morning, in order to make our deadline as late as possible, I wrote the entire issue covering three sheets of foolscap written on both sides, and then cut the stencils.

All the things that always happen on such occasions happend. None of us had ever used a duplicating machine before and stencils cracked like sails in a gale and the place was bespattered with sticky brown ink. The valuable Pekinese dog belonging to the secretary became disgusted and spitefully chewed up the reserve tubes of ink. The man from Vancouver was already showing signs of the mental unbalance from which he later suffered more spectacularly. Also the manager's highly developed sense of neatness was offended by the way in which we were folding the foolscap sheets and shoving then into the envelopes and he kept taking them out in order to refold them in a neater but rather delaying manner. By early evening we had the whole lot enveloped and mailed and staggered to the Café Royal to drink champagne.

To my companions and fellow-workers I pointed out that the whole thing was absolutely sure-fire. Here we had a list of 1,200 names. Our product, *The Week*, was sensational, brilliant, irresistible. However, let us be cautious and assume that some of the people on that list are ill – too ill to fill in a subscription form – or they are dead. Say 300 of them. Then assume that there are some fools among them – boneheads or embittered maniacs who will not be charmed by *The Week*. Say 100 of them. That leaves a residue of 800 people who by tomorrow evening will be sitting down to send off their twelve-shilling postal orders for the Annual Subscription.

Unfortunately no one had warned me that the *Foreign Affairs* list was years old. Forty per cent of the people on it were dead, indifferent, or had radically changed their attitude to world affairs. Also there had been a serious miscalculation

213

regarding the mentality of the British public – its readiness to jump for something new or love the highest when the editor saw it.

The number of paying customers secured by that first circularisation was seven. Just seven.

The news spread rapidly among my friends and acquaintances that my big idea had misfired.

Personally, since I regarded the existence of the 'pool' as a mathematical certainty, I was not discouraged, although I could think of no convincing reason to offer anyone else as an explanation of my continued optimism.

And yet little less than two years later this small monstrosity, *The Week*, was one of the half-dozen British publications most often quoted in the press of the entire world. It included among its subscribers the Foreign Ministers of eleven nations, all the Embassies and Legations in London, all diplomatic correspondents of the principal newspapers in three continents, the Foreign Correspondents of all the leading newspapers stationed in London, the leading banking and brokerage houses in London, Paris, Amsterdam and New York, a dozen members of the United States Senate, twenty or thirty members of the House of Representatives, about fifty members of the House of Commons and a hundred or so in the House of Lords, King Edward VIII, the secretaries of most of the leading trades unions, Charlie Chaplin and the Nizam of Hyderabad.

Blum read it and Goebbels read it, and a mysterious warlord in China read it. Senator Borah quoted it repeatedly in the American Senate and Herr von Ribbentrop, Hitler's Ambassador in London, on two separate occasions demanded its suppression on the ground that it was the source of all anti-Nazi evil.

Admittedly none of this seemed at all probable at the end of that first week when the total circulation stood at seven. Apart from the moral shock – disclosure of low mental level all round, nation sunk in apathy – this lack of response left hardly any money to circularise anyone else and raised the whole question of how to go on living at all.

I was forced to live meagrely on the twelve-shilling postal orders which occasionally came in, spending much of my time at the Café Royal, then in its last phase as a gathering-place of just the kind of people who ought to be reading and talking about *The Week*.

It made – since a bottle of good wine cost three shillings –

a fine, nearly free, place to do business in. People coming in for drinks who had vaguely heard of *The Week* would often pay over their subscription money in cash, though they probably would never have got around to sending in a subscription form and a postal order. The late Professor Joad brought in quite a freshet one night by shouting his congratulations on *The Week* all over the Café Royal and declaring that no man in the place could claim to have any idea upon what was going on unless he were a subscriber to *The Week*.

Even so, things remained extremely difficult for several weeks, until one day, with the circulation awfully steady at thirty-six, the Prime Minister intervened.

The World Economic Conference – some joker had housed it among the fossils in the Geological Museum – was a big thing in his life. Figuratively speaking, he had his name in lights all over it. Yet, the Premier excepted, almost everyone from Leadenhall Street to the Afghan Legation knew that the Conference was dying on its feet. But it was thought not very good taste to point in public. 'Useful spadework' was what the newspapers said was going on.

The Week, in a special issue, reported extensively upon what was really being said *sotto voce* by informed observers. It remarked that the only spade at work on the Conference was the grave-digger's. Quoting Charles Dickens, it saw fit to liken the position of the Conference leadership to that of the Dover Mail, which 'was in its usual genial position that the guard suspected the passengers, the passengers suspected one another and the guard, they all suspected everybody else, and the coachman was sure of nothing but the horses; as to which cattle he could with a clear conscience have taken his oath on the two Testaments that they were not fit for the journey'.

On the day this appeared Mr MacDonald came down to the Conference looking, as someone remarked, as though he were on his way to Clarkson's to hire a crown of thorns. He convened a special off-the-record press conference in the crypt. He said he had a private warning to utter. Foreign and diplomatic correspondents from all over the world jostled past mementoes of the Ice Age to hear him. For as a warning-utterer he was really tip-top. In his unique style, suggestive of soup being brewed on a foggy Sunday evening in the West Highlands, he said that what we saw on every hand was plotting and conspiracy, of this, that and the other kind, in the larger sense, and here in his hand was a case in point, tantamount to just that sort of thing.

Everyone pushed and stared, and what he had in his hand was that issue of *The Week;* and he went on to quote from it, and to warn one and all to pay no heed to the false prophets of disaster, activated by motives of this or that or the other thing. This was good strong stuff and stimulating to these people who hitherto had never heard of *The Week,* and, but for this, possibly never would have.

Regrettably I had to miss a good deal of it. I recalled that this was the hour when the manager would be sitting in a barber's shop in Curzon Street where he spent a rather large part of each morning, and that the secretary was away attending some society wedding. The office was deserted. I urgently desired to know what else Mr MacDonald had to say, but equally I urgently needed to dash back to Victoria Street so as to be there in time to answer the telephone which, as could easily be foreseen, would soon be vibrating with voices of the anxious *cognoscenti* of international affairs.

It was ringing all right. 'This is the diplomatic correspondent of *Le Matin.* I want . . .' 'Here is the diplomatic correspondent of *Frankfurter Zeitung* I require immediately . . .' By tea-time the circulation was in the seventies, with Pertinax and Mme Tabouis, then in their heyday, well up there with the leaders.

And then to prove that it wasn't just raining manna, it was pouring it, another big shower of it fell.

While I was still scribbling down the names of the new subscribers, I heard afar off a muttering and puffing, and then upon the ladderlike stair leading to our attic I heard the thunder and crack of impetuous feet. In a split trice the place was heaving and bulging with enormously moustachioed men, and women with mauve veils, speaking excitedly of the Prophet Isaiah. What did they want? They wanted subscriptions to *The Week*. Why? Because at a neighbouring hall – Caxton or Central – there was in session a congress of citizens taking the view that the future may readily be foretold by measuring the Pyramids and that the British (even, stretching a point, the Americans) are the lost tribes of Israel. Someone had read aloud to this gathering a passage from an earlier issue of *The Week,* and it absolutely confirmed, apparently, something Isaiah had said. It could be that *The Week* was divinely inspired by the prophet. In any case they wanted forty subscriptions quick.

216

They were solid people with cash in their hands, and I could hardly refrain from taking time off to telephone the café manager at the Café Royal to tell him that in an hour or two it would be in order to wipe clean my terribly congested slate.

One of these enthusiasts, a secretary from the organisation somewhere in the north, waited to talk with me. He had the air of maintaining an – how shall one say? – if possibly more normal relationship to reality than some of his co-believers. Trading on this, I ventured to ask him whether he was not a good deal pestered by the sort of person who really thought he only had to look up the length of some gallery in the Great Pyramid to know what was going to happen in the middle of next year. That, he said, was quite frankly only too often the case.

'You get,' he said, 'a lot of these people who rush in expecting an answer to such a question right away. People cannot realise that to work out a thing like that accurately often takes several days.'

XVIII RIBBENTROP DISLIKES ME

'IF YOU GO ON LIKE THIS,' SAID MR JOHN WHEELER-Bennett, then head of the Royal Institute of International Affairs at Chatham House, 'you will soon, I should think, be either quite famous or in gaol.'

'Lots of people,' I said, 'have been both.'

'That,' he said, turning upon me his luminous smile, and beaming as though an awkward question had now been satisfactorily resolved, 'is so.'

A lot of people who, by constantly talking of *The Week*, complaining of it, denouncing it as a horrible liar, and even praising it, were helping to make this tiny sheet 'quite famous', were also of the opinion that something terrible must be going to happen to *The Week* pretty soon. Mr. Kingsley Martin, editor of the *New Stateesman*, who had been very kind to me personally and wished us well, was one of these.

Once he wrote in his column in the *New Statesman* that he had been waiting for a fortnight for 'the heavens to fall' as a result of a particular disclosure in *The Week* – it was fairly clear from the context that what the heavens were going to fall upon was me. Another time he came briefly to my office to tell me that he had just read the current issue and wanted to warn me that to his mind the only doubt as to the result was whether I should get out with a heavy fine or suffer a sharp gaol sentence into the bargain.

The Criminal Libel Law and the Official Secrets Act, one or other of which we apparently infringed about twice a month, were the instruments which people imagined were going to send me to gaol. Since, as I have said, I had no lawyer to bother me about such things, and since nobody but myself could possibly be involved in whatever unpleasantness might arise, I was saved all the advance worry which nags at people on other types of paper when they are handling dynamite, and by being simply ignorant of whether I was infringing some law or not, saved myself from the temptation which otherwise I make no doubt would have often been irresistible – to omit or tone down reports of facts and reports of rumours merely on the ground that to publish them might land one in the Courts. We were of course repeatedly threatened with libel actions, but none of them was ever brought and none was ever settled out of Court. When deciding whether or not to write a story which was obviously, in the legal sense, libellous, but which I believed to be true and of some public interest, I used instead of a lawyer a simple criterion of my own.

In case he brings an action, I asked myself, which of us in the end will look more ridiculous? On the whole, this criterion worked fairly well. When the emissaries of the libelled came to see me with threats and menaces, they were immediately discouraged by the evident poverty of our organisation. Their usual technique was then to demand an unqualified apology. This I invariably refused on principle, although always expressing readiness to write another story on the same subject giving any facts they might choose to supply tending to show that the earlier story had been baseless. It was at this point that one could usually detect from their expression that the thought passing through their minds was that which had passed through mine earlier – namely that if their client took the case to Court he would probably make more of a monkey out of himself than he was likely to make out of me.

How often we really infringed the Official Secrets Act, or were suspected by the authorities of espionage or improper relations with public servants for the purpose of extracting state secrets, I have no idea. For the first eighteen months or so, at any rate, we were highly suspect – naturally, and for the same reason that I had been suspect in Berlin, namely that we had no easily recognisable fancy dress and the authorities were somewhat in the position of the drunken Dutchman in the musical comedy who gets by accident into the middle of a fancy-dress ball and runs frantically from person to person imploring them, 'Do please tell me once and for each what are you *as*?'

Obviously the authorities would much rather deal with people who are visibly members of some recognised political organisation, and I had a lot of evidence that they were considerably worried by not knowing what I was 'as'.

Long ago Wilmott Lewis had drawn my attention to what he called 'the factual heresy' or 'the illusion of spot news'.

It would be tedious to examine the historical phenomena which had produced in the public mind a belief that the desirable thing to read in a newspaper is 'the inside news', and still more the illusion in the public mind that the newspaper, or rather the reporter, really has 'inside news'.

Wilmott Lewis, who was usually right about such matters, took the view that about ninety per cent of what the public conceived to be 'inside news' or 'spot news' is either something so trivial or obvious that it is not worth writing about, or else is not 'inside news' at all in the sense of being something secret and confidential, but is the kind of information which any highly informed and reasonably intelligent person could piece together from, say, a week's reading of all available newspapers and a week's conversation with all available sources. And even this, he used to insist, is not enough. News, he used to say, is in itself nothing. Presentation is almost everything. The entire question, he would insist, is a question of style.

I have seen people who, as he made these observations, came rapidly to the idiotic conclusion that the creative journalistic process is much simpler than it really is – you could see them beginning to imagine that all the man had to do was to sit about reading and talking and presently, having developed his 'style', present the matter in coruscating prose. This of course is untrue too, and the reason why Lewis, for example, leaned over backwards talking about style, and the reason why it is necessary to do so repeatedly, is that, although in the early days of journalism style was emphasised to the point where the rôle of the 'facts' was merely forgotten, nowadays the 'factual heresy' is a dangerous one.

To hear people talking about the facts you would think that they lay about like pieces of gold ore in the Yukon days waiting to be picked up – arduously, it is true, but still definitely and visibly – by strenuous prospectors whose subsequent problem was only to get them to market.

Such a view is evidently and dangerously naïve. There are no such facts. Or if there are, they are meaningless and entirely ineffective; they might, in fact, just as well not be lying about at all until the prospector – the journalist – puts them into relation with other facts: presents them, in other words. Then they become as much a part of a pattern created by him as if he were writing a novel. In that sense all stories are written backwards – they are supposed to begin with the facts and develop from there, but in reality they begin with a journalist's point of view, a conception, and it is the point of view from which the facts are subsequently organised. Journalistically speaking, 'in the beginning is the word'. All this is difficult and even rather unwholesome to explain to the layman, because he gets the impression that you are saying that truth does not matter and that you are publicly admitting what he long ago suspected, that journalism is a way of 'cooking' the facts. Really cunning journalists, realising this, and anxious to raise the status of journalism in the esteem of the general public, positively encourage the layman in his mistaken views. They like him to have the picture of these nuggety facts lying about on maybe frozen ground, and a lot of noble and utterly unprejudiced journalists with no idea whatever of what they are looking for scrabbling in the iron-bound earth and presently bringing home the pure gold of Truth.

When I had to start explaining what *The Week* was trying to do, I did myself a good deal of harm by being rather too frank about this matter. To make matters worse, I went about saying that rumours were just as important, just as significant, just as – in the last analysis – 'valid' as 'facts'.

This shocked people horribly, although if you pressed them and asked whether it was not true that ninety per cent of 'information received' by such serious persons as Ambassadors and Chiefs of Police really consists in significant rumours which can be interpreted by the person who knows enough rumours, they were usually bound to admit that this is indeed the case. Contemporaries on the existing weekly newspapers used to complain that *The Week* published rumours which they themselves refused to publish until they were confirmed. One was reminded of the atheistic young man who told the believer that he would never believe anything that he did not understand, to which the believer replied, 'Young man, your beliefs are likely to be small.'

In the same way people who refused to print anything that was not a confirmed fact were likely to print very little of general interest And I found that attitude arrogant, for, unless one imagines one is God, how on earth can one tell truth from rumour in less than perhaps fifty years? And fifty years is too long to wait if one is in the business of issuing a weekly newspaper.

So far as *The Week*'s news-gathering operations were concerned they were conducted for the most part on a barter basis with a group of what were then the best-informed and most lively-minded correspondents in London.

They included Mr Farson, correspondent of the *Chicago Daily News;* Mr Stefan Litauer, correspondent of the Polish News Agency; Mr Paul Scheffer, correspondent of the *Berliner Tageblatt,* and a varying group of French correspondents.

Two or three times a week we met around noon in Mr Farson's office at Bush House and pooled our information. And on the days we did not meet we pooled information over the telephone. To describe this pool as a 'group' would be to use too formal a word, but – owing, I think, to Mr Farson's guidance – we all of us came to realise that there was something to be said for regular exchanges even when there seemed to be no news at all. The mere fact of each in turn going through a kind of 'total recall' of what had been said by informants – diplomats, financiers and others – during the course of the past forty-eight hours was clarificatory and often produced a piece of the great jigsaw which otherwise could have been overlooked or forgotten. Usually of course there was plenty of news. There was news which – for example – Mr Farson could not handle for his paper but which was exactly suited to *The Week*. Everyone had something to contribute, everyone picked out of the bag what suited his own requirements. Apart from what *The Week* could directly contribute to the pool, it had a special rôle to play, a special utility. There were innumerable stories which, for example, Mr Farson or Mr Litauer could not venture to send directly to their papers or news agencies but which they could send if they had just appeared in *The Week* and could thus be quoted instead of being sent on the responsibility of the correspondents.

The French were particularly good at playing this game. And, as time went on, this group – every member of which had his own special contacts with news sources in London, his own confidential sources of news in his own country and a lively awareness of the difference between the apparently significant news and the news that really was significant in the light of knowledge of the basic trends – made up a pretty formidable information centre.

And then naturally the whole business 'snowballed'. When it was seen what kind of stories *The Week* uniquely would handle, all sorts of people – for motives sometimes noble and quite often vile – would approach *The Week* to draw its attention to the most extraordinary pieces of more or less confidential information. Sometimes it came from frustrated newspapermen who could not get what they considered vital news into their own papers. More often such confidences were the outcome of obscure financial or diplomatic duels. They would come, for instance, from the Councillor of an Embassy who was convinced of the wrong-headed policy of the Foreign Office and the Ambassador, and wished, without exposing himself, to put a spoke in their wheel.

The savage tensions of the 1930s naturally produced a situation favourable to this type of development. Under the frightful overhanging menace of Hitlerism, there roamed through the capitals of Western Europe people who were half saint and half bandit – the sort of people who would commit a murder for twenty pounds and suicide for a good idea.

For many months one of *The Week's* principal informants in Berlin was a principal secretary of Herr von Papen. This man, who at times acted as von Papen's Chef de Cabinet, was an energetically devout Catholic and an astute anti-Nazi.

At that time it was still necessary for Hitler to treat von Papen with caution and a kind of respect, so that it was impossible to conceal from the von Papen bureau more than about thirty per cent of what the Nazis were really up to.

It was of course impossible for this secretary to send his information through the mails and I had, in fact, insisted that nothing must be written down at all. I had a messenger – a former sports writer of the Ullstein press – whom nobody suspected of being anything but a damn fool, travel to and from Berlin to talk with this secretary, memorise his information and bring it back to London.

Unfortunately the secretary was less careful than he should have been. He kept a file of *The Week* in order to check up on the way in which we were handling the information which he gave us. One day in June my messenger, who generally had very little interest in politics and was not particularly alert to what was going on, arrived in Berlin and went to see the secretary.

The copies of *The Week* were covered in blood – the man had been shot at close range by the S.S. assassins who had just invaded the house. Our liaison man escaped, by an estimated four minutes, before they returned to the lower floors after a search of the bedrooms to find someone else they might like to kill.

Probably this was one of the reasons – this event and its repercussions – why Herr von Ribbentrop, German Ambassador, thought that I and *The Week* were the centre of all anti-Nazi intrigue and propaganda in London.

The fact that he thought so – that he could be such a fool as to think so – helped to give me a measure of the Third Reich which could employ such an Ambassador. One is not much alarmed about people who are what is called 'sinister' – one is never alarmed about people who are reasonably intelligent. What was terrifying about this man was that he was a damn fool – and could only have been employed by a régime of, basically, damn fools, who could blow up half the world out of sheer stupidity.

A satisfactory thing about Herr von Ribbentrop was that you did not have to waste time wondering whether there was some latent streak of goodness in him somewhere. He was all of a piece. He had me followed about London by enormous blondes. From the fact that *The Week* often spoke disobligingly of the Foreign Office, too, he of course deduced that it must be secretly run by the Foreign Office. The disobliging remarks were a clever blind, and there was Ambassador Ribbentrop seeing right through it. Vansittart foiled again.

Also, to help mould his ideas, I had arranged to have conveyed to him the information that my real name – now clumsily translated from the German – was Hahnbrandt, and that my father came from Czernowitz. Supposing that this piece of intelligence had been treacherously sold to one of his agents by a friend of mine, Ribbentrop was inclined to think it true. He never really believed any report honestly come by.

The blondes were sometimes female, sometimes male. One of the males had the job of getting a seat beside me on one of those plush-covered benches by the marble-topped tables in the old Café Royal, which at that time I used as an alternative to my office, on account of the superior amenities. Most of the full-time Nordic representatives one encountered were swarthy chaps about five and a half feet high, but this fellow was a true chip off the Herrenvolk. He would have made Lohengrin look quite a dago. Often he got so close that you could see the tiny yellow hairs quivering deep inside his ear.

Not wanting anyone's time to get wasted, I arranged for use on these occasions some informative little dialogues with whichever friend happened to be sitting with me.

Me: Say what you will, you cannot deny the Gentiles started the last war. Wormed themselves into key positions everywhere. Asquith, Bethmann-Hollweg, the Hohenzollerns, Poincaré – all Gentiles, old boy.

Friend: But look at the thing broadly – think of their contribution to literature, culture in general. Look at Shakespeare.

Me: Shakespeare I grant you – if he really was a Gentile. But if you want to talk about writers, what about Wells, and Shaw? Typically disruptive, *negative* Gentile mentalities. Mind you, I've many good Gentile friends myself. But taken in the *mass*. . . . Besides, I always think there's something queer about their eyes.

Ten minutes of this, and the horrified Wandervogel had had about all he could hold, and was off to the little door on the Duke of York's steps to report on the swelling arrogance of crypto-Jewish conspirators, and add another page or so to my dossier.

XIX CRISIS AND CHAMPAGNE

PERSONALLY, I WOULD HAVE LIKED TO KEEP OUT
of internal English politics altogether – I felt I could understand the international relations of the English, but I never
could very well accustom myself to their internal affairs.

Yet, in the situation I was in, running this news-sheet which
got itself more and more talked about – and I naturally wanted it to be talked about and be effective – it was impossible
not to become to some extent involved in these concerns.

Forming committees is, as I have said, a kind of occupa-
tional disease of the English – they regard it as a substitute
for action. Inevitably I became engaged in the formation of
the National Council for Civil Liberties – and I mention this
because it was the experience here gained which, in a very
short space of time, caused me to feel bewildered by the
English.

A girl I knew from Ohio who wanted to see the real England took me straight from a polo game on some suitably
green sward to a meeting of a Society dedicated to the task
of preventing people getting buried alive.

She said it was typically British to bother so much about
such a possibility. I said that, come to think of it, it was a
bothersome thing to have happen to one. She said but only
the British had Societies – it seemed there were several of
them, hating one another for being on entirely the wrong
lines and not understanding properly the underlying principles of the thing – to prevent it. We ought to see how they
operated.

Subject of discussion at the meeting we attended was a proposal – rather sound, I thought – for having all the cemeteries
in the country centrally heated; so then, if you did get prematurely buried you'd be perfectly cosy and come to in good
shape to ring the bell for the attendant to hurry over and
get you out of there.

Almost everyone on the platform spoke in favour of the

scheme, many taking the view that not having such installations was a blot of large size on our national copybook.

Then a chap, a member of the Committee, rather a business type, made a very damping speech indeed, saying that the whole project would cost a minimum of two or three hundred million pounds, and where was that coming from, he would like to know?

Naturally he was shouted down, but at several later stages of the discussion he bobbed up and made other remarks along the same lines – wet-blanket talk about labour, and cost of materials and stuff like that.

The girl from Ohio passed the somewhat crude and sweeping remark that this business type was obviously the only sane person on the platform, and she said that if we wanted to know more about this organisation he was clearly the man we had to talk to after the meeting.

We buttonholed him, and she sugared him in that dreadful journalist way, congratulating him on the stand he had taken. Realistic. Said she thought some of the other speakers were a little lacking in realism.

He said, 'Of course they are,' and he looked like a bank manager turning down a loan request from some visionary fellow. 'How,' he asked sternly, 'can you expect to persuade the Government to put a sum like two or three hundred million pounds in a project like this when there isn't, so far as I am aware, a single vegetarian in the whole Cabinet?'

This whetted the girl's appetite for this kind of British life, and whenever we saw announced a meeting of a Society for getting this and that done more, or that and this done less, we had to rush off and attend it. Kept us busy. For it is a fact, and personally I'm in favour of it as showing everyone we have nice characters and deplore evil, that there are more organisations shouting 'Stop it, you brutes!' per square mile in the British Isles than anywhere else in the world.

(Never mind that business of saying with a sneer, What effect does it have on the brutes? That's not the point at all.)

This is why I am glad to have been in at the literally cryptic birth of one of the most vigorous of them: I mean 'literally' literally, because where this birth occurred was the crypt of the church of St Martin-in-the-Fields, north-east of the Nelson Column and south of the Coliseum.

Assuming that you are one of those people who think it jolly unlikely you personally are going to be batoned without cause by the gendarmerie, wrongfully arrested, mistakenly detained in a mental home, stoned in Belfast for looking like a Roman Catholic, prevented by some fool bit of bureaucracy from showing a film of outstanding cultural merit, or thrown off a soap-box when you have a perfect right to stand on it and made a speech, and nobody ought to stop you unless you speak blasphemy or the sheerest sedition, you may greet with fairly academic interest the news that this Council for Civil Liberties, which in such an event would come bustling up to your aid, has been thus bustling for over twenty-one years now. I am in no position to assess just what the current standing of this organisation may be: it has had its ups and, I don't suppose anyone would deny, downs.

You would look at it one day and there would be a list of Vice-Presidents as long as your arm, half of them consisting of the spryest kind of peer, and the kind of publisher you met in some of the best restaurants in London, and a man famous for having been thrown in the river by roughs on Mafeking Night for saying, in the middle of the Strand, that he thought the whole carousal was based on a political and moral misconception.

And then the heat would go on from somewhere, and next time you dropped in it turned out that the peers and publishers were dashing for cover because someone had said that the whole thing had been captured by the Reds, or else it was the stooge of the Labour Party, or, they said, was being used as the merest stalking-horse for the Liberals.

So far as I can recall, this birth of the Council for Civil Liberties was brought about by a saint-like man called Ronald Kidd, who thought things could be done about things. He organised this meeting in the crypt of St Martin's, and before we had to clear out to make room for the meeting of some other Society we had a Society ourselves.

Kidd, who looked like a canon of some rather forward-looking diocese, had a hovel-like dwelling opposite a public convenience in a mews, called Dansey Place, a half-block or so from Shaftesbury Avenue. Without much thought for what on earth he was going to use for money, he had offered his whole-time services free to the Council, and thus the only way to keep anyone alive at all seemed to be to use this dwelling of his as the Council's offices and the Council would pay the rent, which was about the lowest anywhere in the centre of London and would have been cheap at about half the price.

At that time we had people on the Committee or Council or whatever we called it such as the novelist E. M. Forster and Editor Kingsley Martin, and a lot of lawyers who later made good and are Q.C.s now, or well on the way. (The Shaftesbury Avenue sojourn was experienced in the mid-nineteen-thirties.) Membership extended from Communists in reasonably good standing to Liberals, and the man that thing happened to on Mafeking Night. All of which led to a certain amount of misunderstanding. There was a time when I was arguing so passionately in favour of doing something or other to prevent something or other – it seemed pretty vital at the time – that one of the Elder Liberals suddenly jumped to his feet and cried: 'It's getting to be time to arm the masses.'

I was a bit taken aback by the effect of my words, and sought to soothe him. But he had already reseated, and was looking a bit bewildered. 'By the way,' he said, peering round at the company, 'how, exactly, *does* one "arm the masses"?'

One of our first tasks was to organise a lot of 'observers' to go to Hyde Park on the day when a demonstration of Hunger Marchers was being held there. At the last demonstration they had, there had been 'allegations of undue violence' against the police, and although the Hunger Marchers had said 'Yes, they did' the police kept saying 'No, we didn't' and nobody could finally agree what occurred.

This time we were going to have Publisher Victor Gollancz, and Professor Harold Laski, and Author H. G. Wells, and a lot more of the same big-calibre figures right there in the park, observing, and in that way the truth would emerge.

Kidd was nervous lest some of our big guns would fail to turn up – the day being one of the chilliest of London Sunday afternoons. Members of the Committee were detailed to go and fetch them at the proper time, and the one I was to fetch was Mr Wells. He had been ill, and after he had loyally abandoned a good lunch we trotted down the draught-torn passage of his apartment house, with the Baroness Budberg loyally trotting too, wrapping mufflers round him and pushing his umbrella into his hand.

In the park itself the mounted police were drawn up on the grey horizon, and our observers – flower, you could nearly say, of cultural London – strolled across the huge space intervening between them and the temporary platforms from which the Hunger Marchers were to speak.

Suddenly Mr Wells dug his umbrella into the mud and said, 'I refuse to go any farther. I detect,' he said, turning to me, 'your plan. At any moment now, as a result of some pre-arranged signal on your part, the situation will get out of hand, the police will charge, a dozen prominent authors and legislators will be borne to the ground, and you will have the incident you desire.'

Just at that moment it looked to me like quite an idea, and I was sorry I hadn't thought of it earlier.

However, nothing whatever happened, and since nobody could say what on earth might not have happened if our Council had not been on the spot, we became nationally known overnight, and people from far and wide who felt themselves spurned by bureaucrats, menaced by tyrannical authorities or just generally kicked about and done down, came rushing to Dansey Place with such enthusiasm that part of the staircase gave way and people looking for Civil Liberty had to jump.

Kidd, who liked order and was surrounded by something awfully like chaos, was the only person who had a diary or engagement book or list of things to do, and – no doubt in self-protection – adhered rigidly to this, whatever might be going on. One of his most frequent engagements was to go to a place called Braintree, which is somewhere in Essex, and prevent the people of Braintree being prevented from assembling in some place they wanted to assemble in for public meetings, but from which they were in some manner being debarred.

If the Blackshirts had seized power, or Hitler suddenly come over, on a day when Kidd was due to go to Braintree, Braintree would have been where he would have gone to.

I thought this an admirably cool way of dealing with things until one day when, in order to 'test' some new police regulation preventing people making speeches near Labour Exchanges, I went down to South London and made a speech in a prohibited section of the street and got arrested.

When I was being put in the cell at the police station a rather nasty know-it-all sort of a policeman who was in charge said with a sneer: 'Don't suppose you'll be here long. Your friends that organised this'll be along in double quick time to bail you out.'

Secretly I was happy to agree with him. Ronald Kidd, Secretary of the Council for Civil Liberties, would be along to take care of this important sector of the fight for freedom.

It was particularly important to me because when they locked the cell I found I was out of cigarettes.

Only after a couple of hours did I remember with a shock of horror – seeing the long smokeless hours till morning stretching ahead of me – that it was one of Kidd's days for Braintree.

It was at about this time that Mr Pollitt, Secretary of the Communist Party of Great Britain, whom I had never met, was suddenly announced on the telephone – would I, he asked, take the next train, in twenty minutes or half an hour, and report a mine disaster at Gresford, North Wales. Why? Because he had a feeling that there was a lot more in it than met the eye. But why I in particular? Well, because, it seemed, Mr Pollitt – who was worrying at the time about what he believed to be a lack of 'reader appeal' in the *Daily Worker* – had been reading *The Week* and thought I might do a good job.

I like sudden decisions, and went, and I did a good job.

And a few days after it Mr Pollitt asked me to call on him and said to me, 'How much d'you make?' I told him I had never figured it out – I kept getting new jobs, like being newly appointed first London Correspondent of *Times Magazine*, and then, as a result of a complex journalistic phantasy, first London Correspondent of *Fortune* – magazine of American Big Business.

(The short list had got shortened to two names – so at least I was told by Mr Ralph McAllister Ingersoll, then Managing Editor of *Fortune*. There was myself, and there was Mr Randolph Churchill – who had the backing, it appeared, of Mr Brendan Bracken. We made the deal in the foyer of the Savoy Hotel and took off for Brussels in a specially chartered plane to see the head of the Belgian Radium Trust who, when we got to Brussels, turned out to be in the Savoy Hotel, London.)

Mr Pollitt said, 'Well, anyway, do you make more than thirty pounds a week?' I said that, at least, I could certainly deny.

To this Mr Pollitt replied, 'Well, how'd you like to work for about four pounds a week – and half the time you won't get even that? How'd you like to work for the *Daily Worker*?'

This suggestion would probably have been in any case irresistible – and it was the more so because of my experiences among the British Labour people and Liberals. I was as certain as I ever have been of anything that I could never possibly appreciate their viewpoint – not, that is to say, to the extent of becoming enthusiastic about it, writing honestly and creatively in favour of it. To put it in slang, the Labour people seemed to me to be about where I had come in in Germany years and years before. And if there were things to disagree with the Communists about, what I felt at the time was that they were a lot nearer being a creative force in British politics than any other that I could see.

Also they were a force that was small, poor and adventurous, and the distance between their thoughts and their actions appeared to me to be a lot shorter than it was when you came to the Labour people, the 'progressive intellectuals'.

Decisive in this situation was that I had, for a short time – some months before Mr Pollitt made his offer – worked for a weekly newspaper called the *Clarion*, run by Odhams Press, owners of the *Daily Herald*. I wrote a weekly page of paragraphs on foreign affairs. It was not a bad page, but it had something false and brittle about it, and I knew the reason – the things I really thought were happening could not be expressed directly in that Labour-organised newspaper, and once again I faced the same inhibitions and distortions of expression, of style, as I had faced at *The Times*.

Misled, probably, by sensational literature and the motion pictures, people said one thing was certain, and that was that it would be very, very different from *The Times*. They said they could hardly imagine a bigger change than going from *The Times* to work for the *Daily Worker*. Like most statements made without fear of successful contradiction, this one turned out to be full of error.

True, the plain-clothes detectives of the Special Branch of the C.I.D., bulging in the saloon bar just across the street, struck a note unusual in Printing House Square. So did the social viewpoint of the cartoons presented to the publican by a former artist of the paper in payment for services rendered.

Then I noticed the expression upon the face of the van-driver waiting to rush next day's paper to the stations, and became aware of something at once rare and familiar. I had seen it on the faces of *Times* drivers, but – until now – nowhere else.

It was an expression which said the edition was going to come off the press long behind schedule, and he was going to risk his neck tearing along the streets to Euston and Paddington, and if he caught the trains at all it was going to be a flaming miracle. And just why was the paper going to be late? Not, you could bet your life, because a big murder story broke at the last minute, or floods menaced thousands, or heiress's secret wedding exclusive, or any of that class of caper, but because the leader-writer – the flaming *leader-writer*, well, I ask you – was still batting out a pronouncement on something or other and they were holding the whole edition for him while he reached for the *mot* flaming *juste*.

A nice state of affairs in the middle of the twentieth century. Who did he think he was? Gladstone?

Within the building, at the entrance to the editorial offices, the sense of familiarity, of *déjà vu*, deepened. This was not entirely due to the fact that at that date the offices of both newspapers looked, in contrast to Fleet Street, like something Dickens had set out to describe, and then left to be continued by someone who was just starting to read up on this new-fangled steel construction you heard about. Functional they were not. They reminded me of Boston. But, more than this, it was an organisational detail which evoked a memory of Printing House Square.

Naturally, all newspapers have guardians whose business it is to prevent eager but irrelevant people bursting in and disturbing the editorial inmates at their tasks. At *The Times,* when I worked there, this protection had been considered particularly important. And I had been told that as for the *Daily Worker* I should find it guarded, they said, like a fortress.

Of course, the character of the most probable intruders differed, up to a point, in each case. *The Times,* I had always been given to understand, was protecting the editorial staff against the onset of people with plans to reorganise the Church of England, people who wanted it to publish a five-column letter demanding State subsidies for otter-hunting, and people who were going to beat up the racing correspondent because of the ruinously misleading thing he foreshadowed about the third race at Newmarket.

At the *Daily Worker* the job of the man on the door was rather to keep out people with plans to reorganise the Communist Party, people who wanted to get a five-column letter published demanding State subsidies for Esperanto, and people who were going to beat up the racing correspondent because of the ruinously misleading thing he foreshadowed about the fourth race at Wolverhampton.

First time I called at *The Times*, I got right to the editor's door without being questioned, and learned that the obvious reason for that must have been that the person who kept people out had had to slip away for a minute to make some tea. At the *Daily Worker* the arrangements were, in truth, more elaborate. There was a cubby-hole for the guardian to sit in, and a small *guichet* for him to peer out of, and a door which would open only when he was satisfied and pulled a string. On this occasion the door had been wedged open with a piece of wood, the cubbyhole was empty, and as one walked unchallenged up the stairs one caught, at the end of a passage, a glimpse of the guardian's back as he pored over a gasring, making some tea.

On the voyage to the interior, other well-remembered sights were witnessed. That man, half-crazed by worry and frustration, shouting about trains leaving and peering over his shoulder towards the leader-writer's room with the mixed rage and awe of one who is trying to get an archdeacon to step on the gas, must obviously be the manager. These chaps, eruditely discussing in a mood of high-minded levity the racial composition of the Saar and that business about the M.C.C., can be none other than the Foreign Editor and the Diplomatic Correspondent. And clearly the tense-looking man scribbling away at the end of the table is the world's greatest expert on something and, though ostensibly subediting a small item of late news, is really writing a definitive article for a quarterly or monthly review.

After all this, the sight of the leader-writer himself, a Scotsman, it need hardly be said, or at any rate one of Nature's Scotsmen, came as no surprise at all. One had seen virtually the same man coolly holding up production of *The Times* while his sinewy pen wrestled mightily with Unrighteousness, a spiritual descendant of Covenanters and of the sort of preacher who held that if a full and proper exposition of The Word was going to cause the sermon to go on for five hours, then five hours was what the sermon was going to go on for. Feather-pates might babble of parishioners falling exhausted in the aisles, or trains leaving the termini without the paper. That was just too bad about the parishioners and the disappointed readers.

Occasionally, in those early days at the *Daily Worker*, the readers at the far end of the long-distance lines would get together in protest, claiming they would rather have a paper with a political howler in paragraph four of the leader than no paper at all. These explosions shook the building. Campaigns were initiated for more hustle, modernity and snappy popular journalism all round. People sat gazing sadly at the *Daily Express*, with a view to imitating it. Over the problem of how to get snappier there raged discussions comparable to those at *The Times* office when some ruthless modernist, shouting for the Common Touch and plenty of it, came in with that shockingly vulgar suggestion about sticking in a crossword puzzle.

In the midst of one of these periods of controversy, I came down to the office to find a big section of the library space occupied by a broodingly thoughtful Burman, the entire table before him covered with books, brochures and manuscript documents. It looked as though the article he was evidently going to write on the situation in Burma was going to cover the subject pretty comprehensively. Next day he was still there, writing down figures in long columns – statistics of rice production, I supposed. His books and papers now took up so much room that it was hard to move about the library at all. It seemed it must be going to be quite a series of articles. And about all this research there was something impressive and solemn, making one feel that any other article written for the paper was going to look trivial and superficial.

On the third day I took alarm and placed the whole question squarely before the editor.

I yielded, I said, to no one in my appreciation of the gravity and world importance of the situation in Burma. A couple of rousing pieces about it were, I did most profoundly realise, what the paper needed as badly as anything. But, so far as I could judge, our friend aimed at turning out a minimum of twenty such articles, and frankly, and without in any way seeking to minimise the vital urgency of getting the facts in front of the public, was this project entirely in line with decisions recently taken about developing more zing, zip and popular appeal? Would a series of twenty articles on Burma To-day be the snappiest thing imaginable? As a circulation-getter, was it just what the *Daily Express* would do?

The editor, who personally would rather have enjoyed reading twenty longish articles subjecting the Burmese situation to an exhaustive analysis, listened with an air of melancholy. Painfully, as though revealing that in the rush for the Common Touch we had decided to go in for some kind of pornography, he explained the position. The Burman was not, in fact, writing an article about Burma. He was not an expert on that country. What he was an expert on was greyhound racing. And what he was doing with all those books and papers was working out greyhound form for the coming season. Thereafter a section of the paper was going to be devoted to greyhound tips and greyhound results.

So, indeed, it came to pass. People who were expecting a piece denouncing the Bank of England and found instead a bit tipping Blazing Killarney Boy for the White City were disgusted, and wrote letters saying this could never have happened in the Old Days and the Tolpuddle Martyrs were rolling in their graves. Others were delighted, for, however shaky he may have been on Burma, as a dog-tipster he was the tops. In the raw financial blizzard which blew continuously through the office for months on end, he was a big comfort to the staff. Perhaps if the Moscow Gold other people wrote about had really existed one would not have bothered so much about what was going to happen at the tracks. Things being as they were, Blazing Killarney Boy was worth a whole lot of imaginary roubles.

The financial blizzard affected me less seriously than others because – although I had had to abandon *Time* and *Fortune* simply because I had no working hours left after dealing with *The Week* and the *Daily Worker* – *The Week* was now climbing steadily, and even making a profit.

It was also exerting a certain – quite undefinable but still perceptible – influence.

About the time when Hitler was marching into the Rhineland, in the spring of 1936, I was somewhat diffidently approached by Mr John Strachey, with a mysterious, if trivial, proposal. He desired me to furnish him with a potted autobiography. It must be done at once. It must be impressive. And I must not ask for what purpose it was wanted.

Mr Strachey was at that time very far indeed from being a member of the Government. On the contrary, he wrote for the *Daily Worker*, was generally, though mistakenly, believed to be a Communist, and spoke harshly of the leaders of the Labour Party. He was in touch with some of the Churchillian group of the Conservatives who were already alive, like him, to the Nazi menace. Also, as it turned out, he knew a man who knew a man who knew the King.

'But what *is* it wanted for?' I said once, twice and three times, and the third time Mr Strachey agreed to tell all, but not where walls might have ears. We hurried out and walked round and round Primrose Hill. 'It's simply,' said Mr Strachey

235

in a low murmur, 'that the King wants to know who you are.'

Mr Strachey, it seemed, was the friend of an intimate of Lord Louis Mountbatten, reputedly one of the closest and most influential advisers of King Edward VIII. And Lord Louis Mountbatten, said Mr Strachey, was a student of *The Week*.

Lord Louis was an early and, at that time, somewhat lonely anti-Nazi in high places. He was, Mr Strachey murmured to the discreet air of Primrose Hill, using *The Week* to convince King Edward that the real shape of things to come was very different from that foretold by Premier Baldwin and his colleagues. *The Week* had recently given a good deal of rather sensational advance information on Nazi moves which had proved correct. The King, it appeared, was impressed. 'But,' he had complained to Lord Louis with understandable petulance, 'you are asking me to prefer the information of an obscure political scandal-sheet, run by someone I never heard of, to that of all my Ministers.'

This was where the potted autobiography was to come in. It was to show His Majesty that the editor of the obscure scandal-sheet was one of the Right People, with ancestors, and an Oxford accent and a former connection with *The Times*. In the interests of this high-powered and beneficent project, I reached for a halo and rapidly presented Mr Strachey with a glowing testimonial to myself in about four hundred words. Later I received messages saying that things were going well. I gathered that *The Week* had become required reading at Fort Belvedere. I hoped His Majesty would not leave it lying about where an archbishop might see it. I also hoped we might soon see some practical political results.

I waited for months, and what I saw in the end was Mr Strachey, more serious than ever, suggesting that we take another open-air walk – this time, as I recall, in St James's Park.

We were in the middle of the Abdication Crisis. The newspapers were victims of a more than usually painful attack of discretional lock-jaw. They were determined to show responsibility, delicacy, restraint and the Best Possible Taste if it was the last thing they did before total paralysis gripped them. In the suffocating silence the trend was running strongly against the King.

In this situation, Mr Strachey murmured to a passing swan,

Lord Louis Mountbatten had conceived the idea that if certain 'inside information' of a particularly sensational character could be suddenly forced into the open, the trend might, just possibly, be reversed in the King's favour. There were facts which it was thought the regular newspapers and weeklies would be most unlikely to print. On the other hand, it had been noted that on several occasions in the past *The Week* had succeeded in securing wide publicity for matters thought 'not fit to print'. Things had, apparently, come to the paradoxical point where the 'obscure scandal-sheet' might be the most effective weapon available to save the King.

Lord Louis, I was informed, was of the opinion that if he could present the King with this concrete possibility, the King might agree to try it. The question therefore was: Would I, 'in principle', be prepared to publish certain facts if they reached me from Fort Belvedere? I was warned that they would immediately be denied by the Cabinet, that the resulting row would be certainly appalling and possibly catastrophic. His Majesty, I was told, as yet knew nothing of this project.

I was rather far from being a passionate champion of the monarchy, but the atmosphere of pompous discretion was almost unbreathable, and anyway it looked as though whatever happened we should have a lot of fun. Also, one got the impression that Lord Louis Mountbatten was a bonny fighter who ought to be encouraged. I accepted, of course.

Mr Strachey rushed to and fro with mysterious messages. I said that I would publish the story that was to save the King in a special edition of *The Week* – we could turn it off on the duplicator in a couple of hours. The police always showed a keen interest in the contents of *The Week*, and there was just a chance that it might be held up in the mails. I therefore arranged that there should be a score or so of my friends with cars and motor-cycles ready to rush a few hundred copies by hand to a selected list of influential subscribers in London and the home counties.

Late one Thursday afternoon I received word that the material would be in my hands within the next few hours, and should be published immediately. It would be brought by a despatch rider to *The Week's* office in the garret in Victoria Street.

I mobilised the necessary typists 'for special duty' and overhauled our rickety second-hand duplicator. The flying squad of distributors was alerted, and its members told to stand by their telephones.

At eight in the evening the main door of the office building was closed, and a sentry had to be posted there to meet the impending messenger and get the documents from him.

The two typists, the boy who turned the handle of the duplicator, the two friends who would stuff the finished product into the envelopes, and myself, sat eating sandwiches in the tiny office which would comfortably accommodate three people.

At eleven o'clock there was a telephone message to say that there had been a 'slight delay', but that the material would reach us before midnight.

By half an hour past midnight I was standing on a chair to lean out of the small, high window of the garret, listening to the profound silence of Victoria Street.

It was nearly one before I heard quite a long way off the loud noise of a big motor-cycle being ridden very fast.

I rushed down five flights of stairs and got to the street door at the same time as the despatch rider, who had shot past and had to turn. He handed me a small unaddressed envelope, and I knew from the size of it that it was going to be no good. I called to him to wait, there might be an answer. He said no, he had been told there was no answer. Inside the envelope was a single sheet of plain paper with this typewritten line.

It read: 'The situation has developed too fast.'

There was little time to attend thoroughly to the King business, because what we had now was the Spanish War.

A complacent ass who was, temporarily, Propaganda Minister of Catalonia, said to me: 'This is the most photogenic war anyone ever has seen.'

Considering that people were dying all around us – many of them having come to meet death with extreme heroism because they believed this to be the final battleground where, as in children's stories, the Good get to grips with the Bad – his remark was offensive. Indeed it indicated to any clear-sighted observer that the man thought we were probably going to lose, and was making jokes until he could make up his mind which way his cat would, or could, jump.

All the same, there was a streak of truth in what he so ineptly said.

238

That terrible war was also 'photogenic' in the widest sense of the word. Not just the press photographers turned up, everyone turned up who wanted to be in on the decisive thing of the century, the thing that was going to prove either that Democracy was going to stand up to the enemy there and then, or else that Democracy – it was the phrase people used at the time, and they believed in it – was going to take a terrible beating, and after that there would be a bigger and worse war.

The massacres and the battles and the subsequent massacres took place, too, in lovely surroundings.

I got there because I was a Red newspaper reporter and I had a job to do, but I do not share the sneers of those who, looking back, think disparagingly of a lot of people who really had no business to be in Spain at all, but who went there because – intellectually – the affair was so photogenic.

It is true that after the defeat – and it has often seemed to me that intellectuals somewhat tend to exaggerate both defeats and victories, as though taking it for granted that either of them might be final – a lot of European intellectuals left their souls dead on the soil of Spain and never again were able to face the continuing realities of life. (There were also some intellectuals who faced the Spanish realities with such sturdiness that they left their bodies on that soil too. These heroic men were the first proof to the nineteen-thirties that when some people talk about dying for a cause they mean it.)

But the others – although many of them never found out what it was all about, and, in their disillusionment ended up by being a nuisance – set a good example too. They proclaimed, however briefly, that a moment comes when your actions have to bear some kind of relation to your minds.

That is what is called the Moment of Truth.

Naturally, the rôle of the intellectuals, the troubles and dissensions and heroisms of the intellectuals, were in reality matters of insignificance compared to the troubles, dissensions and heroisms of the men who mainly fought the war – and they ranged from peasants out of Almanza, who walked all the way to Madrid to fight, to a steel-worker from Budapest who travelled all night hanging on to the undercarriage of the Orient Express so as to get to Paris and be sent on to fight, to men from Glasgow and Liverpool and Brooklyn and San Francisco who gave up everything they had to go out there and fight.

Nobody under the age of about thirty-five today has much notion of what the Spanish War meant to the people of that distant period in which it was fought, and nobody over that age will agree with any generalisation anyone makes about it. I personally disagree with about half the generalisations I made about it at the time. Rather than tussle with all that, it is better perhaps – for the moment at least – to remember some pictures.

When I got there, the man everyone went to see, if they could, was General Mangada – the only army general who had not joined General Franco's revolt and instead had remained loyal to the Republic. He was, I believe, a Cuban, or half a Cuban, and he looked strangely like some sort of cross between Gandhi and Gandhi's goat.

The other man who drove out with me to see him at his headquarters in the Sierra was a young man described as a 'Mexican', who, in reality, was one of the first of the Russian technical advisers sent to Spain. (This was at the early period when the Russians, who were rather naturally anxious to avoid doing anything that would give the Western Governments an excuse to turn the Germans loose on them in a war which would be described as having been 'provoked' by 'Red intervention' in Spain, were leaning over backwards being discreet, while Mussolini's bombers were already hovering above the supply routes of the Republican armies.)

General Mangada, after we had drunk a glass or two of sherry with him, asked if we would care to visit the front. We said Yes. We walked for a mile or so across lovely, deserted country – partly a sort of parkland, partly mountain foothills, with outcrops of rock baking in the sun.

We passed small detachments of troops sitting in what shade they could get, and then – after another mile or so during which we had seen nobody – we saw, perhaps six or seven hundred yards away, a line of riflemen in open order, moving about on the low ground ahead of us.

'Those, I suppose,' said the 'Mexican', 'are your advance patrols?'

'Not at all,' said General Mangada, surprised, 'those must be the advance patrols of the enemy.'

For the 'Mexican' and myself it was an ugly little moment. There we stood in no-man's-land, and there seemed a high possibility that within about ten minutes Spain's only Loyal General was going to be captured by the enemy, I was going to be shot as a Red Agent, and the 'Mexican' – unless his gullet was wide enough to swallow a lot of documents very fast – was going to be Exhibit Number One in a nasty international incident.

Awfully slowly, as it seemed to me, the General – who had the air of a man walking around his estate in Somerset on a Sunday afternoon – turned from his dreamy contemplation of the enemy patrols and we strolled back to his headquarters.

The 'Mexican' – a conscientious young man – said that perhaps he might be privileged to meet the General's Staff. General Mangada shook his head in his gentle manner. 'No Staff,' he said. 'In war Staff means betrayal.'

The 'Mexican' swallowed his astonishment with really creditable speed, and said, 'Well, I am afraid we do not have a great deal to offer, but we have made some remarkable progress recently in mapping, and it occurred to me that our experience in that department might possibly be of some assistance to. . . .'

Mangada interrupted him. 'No,' he said, 'no maps.' He put his chocolate-coloured hand on his left breast and tapped it gently. 'In war,' he said, 'the heart must be the map.'

In the vast requisitioned convent in northern Madrid where was being organised at nearly breakneck speed the Fifth Regiment, which was to become the model and nucleus of the New Army of the Republic, I talked one night with the Commandant and organiser-in-chief. At that time I knew this husky, bull-necked man, who combined almost superhuman driving power with an unbreakable gaiety, simply as Carlos, and all I knew of his past was that he had once been a steel-worker in Chicago. Later, he turned out to be an Italian called Videla, who was supposed to have organised the assassination, in Mexico, of Leon Trotsky.

He spoke of the problems of the New Army, and while he was talking one of them blew up right outside the room. From the former chapel of the convent we heard first the sound of shooting – volley after volley – and within minutes the barrack square was a scene of the wildest riot and turmoil. We rushed out, Carlos carrying a pistol in each hand – and he needed them because what we ran into when we got outside was a mob of armed militiamen milling about in the moonlight, looking for the Commandant and threatening to lynch him. By an extraordinary effort of domination and the help of the pistols, Carlos held them at bay long enough to get them sufficiently calmed down so that they allowed the man who seemed to be their leader, or one of them, to start to explain what it was all about.

The men were recruits – very poor peasants from some-where in the south, who had, of their own free will, marched half across Spain to join the New Army and fight for the Republic. They had reached Madrid and the convent late in the evening, and had been hastily bedded down for the night on the floor of the chapel. They had fallen into exhausted sleep, but a couple of hours later, when the moon rose, two or three of them had awakened, and what they saw was the moon shining upon the statues and images of saints which it had not occurred to anyone to remove. The men's reaction was one partly of terror, partly of rage – terror because these images could ill-wish them, could be far more dangerous warriors than the Franco troops they expected to meet on the battlefield, and rage because they believed that they had been lured into a trap; whoever was responsible for expos-ing them to these deadly powers must be an agent of the enemy.

The first men to wake up grabbed their old rifles or sport-ing guns and started firing at the images and statues, yelling to the others to wake up and help them fight their way out of this trap. Everyone started firing at the saints, and then rushed out to find the Commandant and kill him, too.

'You see,' Carlos said when things had quieted down under a powerful jet of oratory and exhortation from himself, 'our problems are not quite simple.'

They changed, but they got no simpler. When I, some weeks later, joined this same Fifth Army as a private and went to the Sierra Front with a company of barely trained peasants, the first time we went into action – our commander, a former captain in the Foreign Legion, soon deserted to the enemy, and in his capacity as military saboteur had ordered us to charge straight up a bare hillside against a fort full of Moorish machine-gunners – a lot of the men charged hold-ing their rifles high above their heads with one hand and giving the clenched fist salute with the other.

It emerged that they had taken the highly stylised and symbolical posters designed by the Madrid intellectuals, showing a Soldier of the Republic in this posture, as illustra-tions of correct military practice.

242

When they saw me dodging along, bent half-double and taking whatever cover there was, they thought the posture unworthy, despicable. A lot of them were killed or wounded before they got converted to the idea that, as instructional diagrams, there was something wrong with those posters.

For people who, like myself, have a claustrophobic distaste for organisation and discipline, this makeshift, ramshackle quality of the Spanish War, which could be terrifying because it kept reminding one of the odds against our sort of forces being victorious over the trained troops of the other side, was also a factor compensating the periods of terror and the periods of tedium which are, alternately, so large a part of any war.

Also the nature of my job kept me moving fairly briskly between Madrid, London, Paris, Geneva and Gibraltar – where I went to do a mixed job of propaganda and espionage, and escaped being assassinated only because a pro-Republican waiter in the hotel where I stayed warned me just in time to get out of town. I was afraid at the time I might be taking unnecessary precautions, but years later I met one of the organisers of the attempt who assured me the waiter's warning and my own fears had been perfectly well grounded.

I had been only a few weeks at the front, and had been promoted corporal after two of our sergeants followed the Foreign Legion captain across the lines to the enemy, when I was summoned abruptly to London to take a hand in the campaign to influence the policies of the Labour Party and Trades Union Congress against non-intervention. Despite my protests, I was billed as the star speaker at an enormous meeting in Shoreditch Town Hall – a grave mistake, because I am one of the worst public speakers who ever bored and exasperated an audience. I always had the feeling that no member of the audience at any of these meetings would ever read my written reports with much confidence again.

I was thankful when I was summoned to the Communist Party Headquarters by Mr Pollitt and ordered to write a book about the Spanish War instead. 'We need it,' said Mr Pollitt, 'in a hurry.' 'How much of a hurry?' 'Before the end of the week,' said Mr Pollitt, and I was locked into a bed-sitting-room in a nursing home run by a friend of mine, and told not to come out until the book was done. A nurse was in attendance to give me shots in the arm in case I fell asleep or dropped dead from exhaustion.

When I returned to Spain the atmosphere was a great deal more harsh, the aspect of the whole war more grim than it had seemed in the summer, but – although Franco was literally at the gates of Madrid – hardly anyone, I believe, even imagined that we could be defeated.

The food had become scarce and abominable, and the shells from the batteries outside the city kept falling in the Gran Via and around the Telefonica building, where the Correspondents had to go to transmit their messages. At breakfast one day in his room at the Florida Hotel, which more or less overlooked the nearest part of the front, Mr Ernest Hemingway was very comforting about the shelling. He had a big map laid out on the table, and he explained to an audience of generals, politicians and correspondents that, for some ballistic reason, the shells could not hit the Florida. He could talk in a very military way and make it all sound very convincing. Everyone present was convinced and happy. Then a shell whooshed through the room above Mr Hemingway's – the first actually to hit the Florida – and the ceiling fell down on the breakfast-table. To any lesser than Mr Hemingway the occurrence would have been humiliating. While we were all getting the plaster out of our hair, Mr Hemingway looked slowly round at us, one after the other. 'How do you like it now, gentlemen?' he said, and by some astonishing trick of manner conveyed the impression that this episode had actually, in an obscure way, confirmed instead of upsetting his theory – that his theory had been right when he expounded it and this only demonstrated that the time had come to have a new one.

Everyone was very happy to have Mr Hemingway there, partly because he was obviously a fine man to have around when there was war and trouble, and partly because to have so famous an author there, writing on behalf of the Republic, made people feel less alone in the world – in a sense, which was no fault of Mr Hemingway, it helped to foster the illusion that sooner or later the 'world conscience' would be aroused, 'the common people' in Britain and France would force their Governments to end non-intervention, and the war would be won.

The Russians, who lived in the Palace Hotel at the other end of the Gran Via, seemed to be the only people who could do without this illusion and still not become defeatist. Although they wrote as big words as anyone for publication, they could get along without them in private conversation.

They had an attitude which could be called cynical or just tough. They were refreshing because there were so many people about at the time – particularly the Visiting Firemen, VIPs of one kind or another from the United States and Britain – who seemed to have an irresistible need to use phrases as though they were facts, and if anyone punctured their phrases they became distressed and frightened about the future.

I spent a great deal of my time in the company of Mikhail Koltzov, who then was Foreign Editor of *Pravda* and, more importantly still, was at that period – he disappeared later in Russia, presumed shot – the confidant and mouthpiece and direct agent of Stalin himself. He was a stocky little Jew – from Odessa, I think – with a huge head and one of the most expressive faces of any man I ever met. What his face principally expressed was a kind of enthusiastically gleeful amusement – and a lively hope that you and everyone else would, however depressing the circumstances, do your best to make things more amusing still.

He had a savagely satirical tongue – and an attitude of entire ruthlessness towards people he thought either incompetent or even just pompous.

People who did not know him well – particularly non-Russians – thought his conversation, his sharply pointed Jewish jokes, his derisive comments on all kinds of Sacred Cows, unbearably cynical. And others, who had known them both, said that he reminded them of Karl Radek (an ominous comparison).

To myself it never seemed that anyone who had such a powerful enthusiasm for life – for the humour of life, for all manifestations of vigorous life from a tank battle to Elizabethan literature to a good circus – could possibly be described properly as 'cynical'. Realistic is perhaps the word – but that is not quite correct either, because it implies, or might imply, a dry practicality which was quite lacking from his nature. At any rate so far as his personal life and fate were concerned he unquestionably and positively enjoyed the sense of danger, and sometimes – by his political indiscretions, for instance, or his still more wildly indiscreet love affairs – deliberately created dangers which need not have existed.

As the Spanish War ground its way to its gruesome conclusion, and all over Europe people who had supported the Republic became truly cynical, despairing, without faith or enthusiasm for anything, I found myself looking forward

245

more and more eagerly to conversations with Koltzov, journeys in his company, estimates from him of the course of affairs. He was a man who could see the defeat for what it really was, could assume that half the big slogans were empty, and a lot of the big heroes stuffed, or charlatans, and yet not let that bother him at all, or sap his energy and enthusiasm.

For a good many months before the end of the Spanish War I had been working chiefly in London, Paris and Geneva, and occasionally in Prague. It was strenuous, stimulating work, because my function, as I saw it, was to develop on the one hand the 'circle' influenced by *The Week* – to mobilise, scare and prod into greater activity all those people who could be so prodded or assisted in what was now, evidently, a desperately critical phase. These 'friends of *The Week*' were, for the most part, very far from being Communists, and many of them were Conservatives, or their equivalents in the various capitals where *The Week* still circulated. To command even a little of their attention *The Week* needed the most sensational kind of 'inside news', but above all it needed to present the news in a particular style and pattern, so that even when there was really no available 'inside news' people felt that they were reading something new, getting a fresh and more exciting picture or story than they got from the newspapers, and getting it in, so to speak, a tone of voice such as they were accustomed to hear in their clubs. On the other hand, I regarded my work as Diplomatic Correspondent and reporter of the *Daily Worker* as equally – perhaps more – important in the business of bringing to bear against Nazism and the forces making for war such pressures as could be brought. But the effective style for the *Daily Worker* was entirely other than that required for *The Week*, so that it was necessary to develop, stylistically, a double personality. This, as I have said, is strenuous, because if you lose for a moment a vivid awareness of either of these two so different audiences, the story will fall to bits.

Also, I was working for a big illustrated publication in Chicago caled *Ken*. They required a different style, too; and on top of all this, towards the end of this period Koltzov had appointed me London Correspondent of *Pravda*. This position I held only for a short time because very soon came the news of his disappearance. As his personal appointee I had to be quietly dropped.

246

I do not know to this day what Koltzov had done or was supposed to have done in Moscow. His fall – and one presumes execution – came at the height of his power there, and a lot of people when they heard of it could not believe it. They spread stories that he had been sent to China as a top-secret agent under another name. A lot of his friends went on believing that for years, as a kind of wishful thinking to soften their grief. Others were thrown into total disarray by the news, became despairing and totally cynical.

For myself, though I missed him more than anyone I had known during that time, I cannot say I was surprised. And, oddly, I doubt if he was much surprised either. He had lived – and talked and joked – very dangerously, and he had absolutely no illusions so far as I know about the nature of the dangers. (Possibly his active taste for dangerous living had led him into some major conspiracy.) He would not, I thought, have been otherwise than satirically amused by some of the almost hysterically sentimental outcries which greeted his removal.

Curiously enough, he once – a few weeks before his fall – entertained me at lunch with a kind of fantastic burlesque based on the imaginary future trial of himself for counter-revolutionary activities, taking in turn the part of a grimly furious Public Prosecutor and of himself in the rôle of a clown who has been caught out and still cannot resist making fatal jokes.

This was in Prague at the height of the Munich crisis.

In those days it seemed as though half the international figures one had known in Madrid had assembled in Prague, and the sight of them seemed to be ominous. You felt that soon there would have to be shells cracking against the hotel to complete the picture. (It reminded one of the story of the famous Hearst reporter, specialist in political disasters, H. R. Knickerbocker, when he came to Vienna at some moment of crisis. 'Good God!' cried the hotel manager. '*You* here, Herr Knickerbocker? Is it then already so bad?') It looked like the end of an act, and it was.

I spent a lot of time with Koltzov at the Russian Legation, for that was the place where, if anything decisive were to happen, it would happen. And I knew that Koltzov was at least as important a figure on the stage as the Russian Minister, and perhaps much more important because of his double position at *Pravda* and at the Kremlin.

From this place of vantage I saw at very close quarters what

247

really was the last scene of the act – everything that happened after that was anti-climax.

It was the moment when there still seemed to be an outside chance that either the League of Nations, or at least Britain, France and the Soviet Union, would stand together on behalf of Czechoslovakia against Germany.

The Czechoslovak army was in position on the frontiers, and at the headquarters of the commander-in-chief in the field there was no doubt whatever that war was a matter of hours. In the same belief, the Soviet Union had despatched to Prague a force of fighter planes and bombers – an advance force which was to be massively reinforced at the moment of war. For obvious reasons this advance Soviet force was not officially there at all, and there were a good many people in the Czechoslovak Government who did not care for its presence – they thought Hitler would use it as a provocation.

As the tension grew almost intolerably, a message from President Beneš urgently summoned the Russian Minister to the Palace. The message said that the President wanted to put some urgent questions.

In the circumstances, it seemed likely that this meant that the forces in Czechoslovakia demanding resistance to Hitler (even if it meant that the Red Army would have to occupy Czechoslovakia in Czechoslovakia's defence) had won the day.

The Minister rushed off. When he got there, he told Koltzov afterwards, he found the President looking, as he said, 'like a photograph of himself.'

'If,' said Beneš, 'the League of Nations declares for resistance to Hitler's demands upon us, even at the cost of war, what would be the Soviet attitude?'

The Soviet Union, said the Minister, would in those circumstances certainly fight. He could hardly keep the impatience out of his voice as he answered so otiose a question.

'If,' said Beneš, 'the League does nothing, but Britain and France declare themselves ready to stand by us, even at the cost of war, what would then be the Soviet attitude?'

The Minister was impatient to get this question settled quickly, too. Of course, he said, the Soviet Union would fight.

He waited confidently for the next question – the third, the vital question. He wanted Beneš to ask what would happen if neither the League nor France and Britain acted, and if, nevertheless, Czechoslovakia resisted Hitler's demands at the cost of war. For he was authorised to state that in that case, too, the Soviet Union would fight.

There was a long pause. Neither of them moved. At last the Russian, disregarding diplomatic discretion, broke the silence. Was there not, he said, a third question which Beneš would care to put? A third potential situation?

Beneš sat absolutely still for several minutes.

'No,' he said wearily, at last, 'those are the only two questions I have to ask.'

Gloom and a sense of futility enveloped the Legation when the Minister returned with his report. It could only mean that after all there would be no resistance, because neither the League nor Britain and France would carry resistance to the point of war. Glumly orders were sent to the airfield to tell the Soviet flyers that their mission was over before it had begun. All they could do now was to go home. Even Koltzov at this moment seemed to have lost resilience. And then, it must have been a couple of hours later, came an abruptly urgent call from Beneš.

Would the Minister secure immediately from Moscow an exact, up-to-the-minute verification and reassurance of previous estimates of the pace and volume at which Soviet air power could get into action from Czechoslovak air bases? The Minister said he could get the required facts within an hour, and would rush with them to the Palace.

The Legation was wild with excitement, Koltzov dancing and kissing people and hurling his big beret repeatedly into the air. Counter-orders were rushed to the flyers at the airport. Two or three of them had just taken off, and one officer was so excited at the change in the news that he actually loosed off an anti-aircraft gun at them as the most emphatic possible signal.

And then – things were moving so fast now that policies were being made and unmade almost by the half-hour – the plot twisted again; someone, some force somewhere, intervened. The Minister dashed off to the Palace once again with the required information. And when he got there he was not even admitted to Beneš's presence.

'The Czechoslovak Government,' he was informed, 'is no longer interested in the reply to this request.'

With that, it was once again a certainty that Czechoslovakia would not act with Russia alone as her ally. The shape of the next act was certain. Hitler's next triumph was assured. It was the hour, too, in which the Russo-German Pact became inevitable.

Sadly, Koltzov reminded me of the story I had told him about M Claudel in Washington.

'Once again,' he said, 'the only thing to say is that in the little moment that remains to us between the crisis and the catastrophe, we may as well drink a glass of champagne.'